THE PARABLES AND SIMILES OF THE RABBIS

THE PARABLES AND SIMILES OF THE RABBIS

AGRICULTURAL AND PASTORAL

BY

RABBI Dr. A. FELDMAN, B.A., Ph.D.,

Dayan of the United Synagogue, London

CAMBRIDGE
AT THE UNIVERSITY PRESS
1927

CAMBRIDGE UNIVERSITY PRESS
Cambridge, New York, Melbourne, Madrid, Cape Town,
Singapore, São Paulo, Delhi, Tokyo, Mexico City

Cambridge University Press
The Edinburgh Building, Cambridge CB2 8RU, UK

Published in the United States of America by Cambridge University Press, New York

www.cambridge.org
Information on this title: www.cambridge.org/9781107640771

First edition 1924
Second edition 1927
First paperback edition 2011

A catalogue record for this publication is available from the British Library

ISBN 978-1-107-64077-1 Paperback

TO MY WIFE,
SON AND DAUGHTER

A man's wife is his home.
Yoma, 2 *a*

His children are his builders.
Berachoth, end

PREFACE

THIS book brings together and deals with Rabbinic Metaphors, Similes and Parables taken from Agricultural and Pastoral life. It is hoped to deal similarly on some future occasion with poetic figures gathered from other aspects of Nature and Life.

It is a field of study which has so far received inadequate attention, more especially from the Jewish point of view. And yet its utility must be readily recognised and generally admitted. For the subject has an interest and value from several different aspects; and this work, whilst constituting a useful compendium of Midrashic material, makes at the same time some attempt at considering the subject from those varied standpoints.

The selections from Rabbinic literature presented in this volume have all been culled from the original sources and translated anew. In the translation an endeavour has been made to preserve the distinctive characteristics of Talmudic style.

Having regard to the different points of view from which this subject may be treated, the collection has been made as comprehensive as possible. It comprises not only direct and obvious metaphors, similes and parables, but also many other figures of speech, which in a broader sense might be legitimately classed within the same category. The Allegory, which is only another form of Metaphor, has been noted. The Proverb (frequently introduced by the Rabbinic formula "as the people say") and the Aphorism have likewise been included, first, because in the Bible both these forms of expression come under the term *Mashal*, and secondly, because many of the Talmudic Proverbs are in their origin shortened anecdotes or parables. Thus *e.g.* the proverbial expression (*Sifré Num.* § 131, end) "the ass has upset the lamp," as applied to litigants outbidding each other in bribery, is reminiscent of a well-known story (related in *Shabbath*, 116 *a* and *b*) where the bribe of an ass made of gold given to the judge counteracted the lamp presented on the other side. Or again, the saying (*Sukkah*, 12 *a et cet. loc.*) "he swung an axe at it," meaning "he refuted the opinion," has reference to a well-known metaphorical dictum (*Kethuboth*, 10 *b*), "The eating of dates before bread is as injurious as the axe to the palm tree."

Some narrative and expository material which is akin to the parable has likewise been embodied. Even certain euphemisms have been incorporated, because they are in a sense bold metaphors. In short, all forms of speech which contain either implicitly or explicitly the germs of comparison have been gathered into this compendium, although even now the collection is very far from being exhaustive.

The extracts have been arranged according to the objects of Nature and Life which furnished the figures of comparison, analysed into their component parts and arranged in logical sequence.

The Midrashic quotations have been reproduced with their Biblical links and Scriptural references; the connection between the Biblical writers and their

Rabbinic followers is thus indicated. In Bible texts the current translation has in some cases been modified to accord with the Midrashic meaning assigned to them by the Rabbis. The exact or approximate periods during which the authors of the Rabbinic quotations lived are given in the text itself as well as in the Index. The many parallels in other literatures have not been cited (except in very few instances) in order to permit of the full quotation of as large a number of Rabbinic passages as possible. In the transliteration of Hebrew words and names an endeavour has been made to avoid as far as possible any form likely to be confusing to the general reader.

My thanks are due to many colleagues and friends for useful suggestions and helpful encouragement. I am especially grateful to the Rev. M. Rosenbaum, Dr. A. Marmorstein and Mr. Maurice Myers for invaluable assistance in the revision of the MS and the reading of the proof-sheets. My son helped me with the compilation of the general index.

A. FELDMAN.

May 1924

NOTE TO THE SECOND EDITION

I desire to acknowledge my indebtedness to the Rev. Dr. A. Cohen, M.A., Rabbi A. Mishcon, Mr. Philip Blackman, F.C.S., and Mr. J. H. Taylor, B.A., who have kindly re-read the book, and some of whose suggestions have been incorporated in this edition.

A. F.

March 1927

TABLE OF CONTENTS

INTRODUCTION

THE subject of Midrashic similes lends itself to treatment from several distinct points of view. It may be dealt with from the exegetical as well as from the poetic standpoint; moreover, it is of considerable importance in its social, economic, comparative and religious aspects.

The different aspects of the subject.

To the student of Biblical and post-Biblical exegesis the similes of the Talmud and the Midrashim present an additional illustration of the ability of the Rabbis in that direction, and supply a further insight into the main principles underlying their method of expounding the Scriptures.

Exegetical.

The student of the literary aspects of sacred Hebrew writings will see in this branch of the Midrash a reflection of the poetic and artistic bent which, contrary to a largely preconceived bias of many non-Jewish scholars, characterises even the so-called "legalists" of the Talmud. He will not fail to discover a kind of poetic kinship between them and the Prophets and Psalmists of the Bible, and will seek to estimate their relationship in the chain of sacred literature.

Poetical.

For the student of social history the figures of comparison, drawn as they all are from scenes of Nature and the movements of life, will throw numerous sidelights on the social and economic conditions of the period.

Social and Economic.

The student of comparative history and religion will discover in the form and substance of our Mid-

Comparative.

rashic similes ample material to elucidate his own particular sphere of research.

Religious. The student of religious thought will find in these popular expressions of the Rabbis the embodiment of many conceptions of the higher life, of the relationship between heaven and earth, the human and divine.

It is the purpose of this Introduction to crystallise a few of the general deductions which will occur to the student and strike even the ordinary reader, and they are here presented more or less tentatively.

The exegetical basis. The origin and basis of Midrashic Metaphors, Similes and Parables are to a large extent exegetical. This might well have been expected. For Midrash, as its root *darash* implies, means exposition. And one of the main objects of the Rabbis in the vast field of Talmudic and Midrashic literature was to expound the Law and to impress its true significance upon their immediate disciples and larger audiences.

This expository tendency was not confined to the legal or Halachic portions of the Bible, which resulted in what is known as the *Midrash Halachah*. It entered equally as much into its homiletic or Aggadic parts, which gave rise to what is called the *Midrash Aggadah*, and of this, metaphor, simile and parable form a prominent part[1].

[1] For a definition of *Halachah* and *Aggadah*, *vide* Mielziner, *Introduction to the Talmud*, pp. 56–7. *Halachah* includes "all expositions, discussions and reports which have the object of explaining, establishing and determining legal principles and provisions." *Aggadah* "comprises all historical records, all legends and parables, all doctrinal and ethical teachings and all free and unrestrained interpretations of Scripture." An aspect of the interrelation of the two is developed with great imaginative insight in a Hebrew brochure, *Halachah and Aggadah*, by Ch. N. Bialik, also translated into English and issued by the Bloch Publishing Co., N.Y. For the origin of the term *Aggadah*, *vide* Bacher in *J. Q. R.* vol. IV, pp. 406–429.

A very considerable number of Midrashic metaphors is obtained through an allegorical interpretation of the Bible Text. This method, which is so much in evidence in Jewish Alexandrine writers—*e.g.* Philo—goes back to an early period of the Rabbinic age. It is not altogether excluded from the field of Halachah[1]; but in the Aggadah it appears with far greater frequency. Already in the first century C.E. we find reference made to *Dorshé Ḥamuroth* and *Dorshê Reshumoth*[2], classes of Rabbinic teachers

Allegorical Metaphors.

[1] Thus, *e.g.* R. Ishmael (c. 130) explains allegorically the following three Halachic passages, (*a*) Ex. xxi. 19: If in a struggle between two persons the injured man "rise again and walk abroad *upon his staff*," *i.e.* "on his own support," *viz.* restored to his former health. (*b*) Ex. xxii. 2: In the case of a thief found breaking in: If "the sun be risen upon him," *i.e.* if it be known that the thief had peaceful intentions in regard to the owner's person (the sun being the symbol of peace), and yet the owner kills him, there shall be blood-guiltiness for him. (*c*) Deut. xxii. 17: "And they shall spread the garment before the elders of the city," *i.e.* they shall make the fact clear like a (white) garment, *vide Sifré Deut.* § 237, ed. Friedmann, p. 117 *b*; *Mechilta Mishpatim*, VI, Friedmann, p. 82 *b*. R. Akiba (50–132 C.E.) explains Lev. xix. 26, "Ye shall not eat with the blood," allegorically as implying a warning to Judges to abstain from food on the day they are considering a capital sentence, *vide Sifra Kedoshim, ad loc.* and *Synhedrin* 63 *a*.

[2] See Bacher, *Die aelteste Terminologie*, *s.v.*; Aruch, *s.v.* המר; Perles, *Etym. Studien*, p. 106; *R. E. J.* III, 109; cf. *R. E. J.* LX, 24–31; *J. Q. R.* (New Series) I, pp. 291 ff., and I, pp. 503 ff.; also *Miklat* I, 2, pp. 209 ff. According to Perles (*R. E. J.* III, pp. 109 ff.) the terms *Dorshé Ḥamuroth* and *Dorshé Reshumoth* as also the expressions דורש כמין חמר and כמין משל are one and the same and often interchangeable. They all signify "allegorists." He suggests that חמר equals המר, and denotes a "changed" or "figurative" meaning (רשם means "figurative") as contrasted with the "literal" sense. The term would thus correspond to the Greek ἀλληγορία (ἄλλος et ἀγορέω). Prof. Israel Lévi (*R. E. J.* LX, pp. 24 ff., where most of the Rabbinic instances of *Dorshé Reshumoth* are collated) adopts the view of Bacher as propounded in *Die aelteste Terminologie*, *s.v.*, and explains *Dorshé Reshumoth* in the sense of "symbolists," *i.e.* exegetes who give a full and edifying explanation to texts which are only "indicated" רשם in the Bible words. As most of the examples are preserved in the *Mechilta*, and moreover in the most ancient parts of it, Prof. Lévi concludes that

who interpreted the Law allegorically. Among the

these exegetes belong to a period anterior to the Schools of Shammai and Hillel. According to him there was in those early days a whole School of these Aggadists as opposed to literal exegetes. At the beginning of the second century, sayings of this School were still recorded with the heading of *Dorshé Reshumoth*, but later on this mark of identification disappeared. The *Dorshé Ḥamuroth*, though taken by some as synonymous with the *Dorshé Reshumoth*, are according to Lévi in so far distinguished that they reveal the symbolism of certain *laws* in the Pentateuch. In Talmud and Midrash the *Dorshé Reshumoth* are rarely quoted. This school of exegesis, he argues, declined, because of the danger attaching to the "allegorising" of the traditional laws, inasmuch as it might militate against the observance of these laws in concrete form, a danger which became real with the rise of the new religion. Prof. Lauterbach in *J. Q. R.* (N.S.) I, where the list of Rabbinic examples of *Ḥamuroth* and *Reshumoth* is given more completely, asserts that the *Dorshé Reshumoth* were Palestinian teachers, and that their method was a pure product of Palestinian exegesis. They interpreted Scripture words as *signs* and *symbols*, *i.e.* in a metaphorical or allegorical sense. This method found its way to Alexandria. The *Dorshé Ḥamuroth* on the other hand were not Palestinian in origin, but Alexandrian, an imitation of the Greek method, and from Alexandria this method found its way to Palestine. Lauterbach also asserts, like Lévi, that the *Dorshé Ḥamuroth* were the interpreters of the purpose of the Laws—who sought out the "weight points," the essence, the subject of an action or story. The objection to the *Ḥamuroth* interpretation was stronger, because of its foreign origin. The *Reshumoth* exposition, being home-bred, could not be so easily ousted. Examples of *Ḥamuroth* exegesis are preserved in the Babylonian Talmud only. In Palestine, in the atmosphere of controversy between Jews and neo-Christians, this form of exposition was discouraged and fell into disuse.

Dr Neumark in *Maybaum's Festschrift* (Berlin, 1914) inclines to the old interpretation of חֹמר as "pearl" or "gem," and of רשם as "marked" or "striking." According to him, *Dorshé Reshumoth* are not necessarily allegorists, whilst *Dorshé Ḥamuroth* are allegorists of a certain tendency, who try to find the philosophical maxims embodied in Scripture texts.

It may perhaps be suggested that the terms *Dorshé Reshumoth* and *Dorshé Ḥamuroth*, for allegorists or symbolists, rest upon the following etymological meaning of these expressions: חמורות is connected with חמר "plaster," that which "covers up" and "hides" what is underneath (cf. *Gittin*, 69 *a*, where חומרתא signifies a "receptacle," and similarly the expression חספא "clay" = חמר in association with מרגניתא, which may mean the "shell" that holds the pearl): רשומות is connected with רשם, which in Aramaic is a synonym for חתם "hide" or "seal" (cf. Heb. חתימת זקן and Aram. רשם דקן in Targ. Jonathan to Gen. xlii. 8).

sages of the Mishnah period (*Tannaim*) who explained Scriptural passages in this manner are R. Joḥanan b. Zakkai[1], his younger contemporary R. Gamaliel II[2], and R. Eleazar of Modiim[3].

R. Akiba occupies a prominent position in the field of allegorical interpretation. He was followed by his disciples R. Meïr, R. Judah b. Ilai, as well as by many other Rabbis of the Tannaitic times, including R. Judah I.

But the great age of Allegorism seems to have been reached in Palestine during the period of the *Amoraim*, who were as renowned for their homiletic teaching as for their Halachic exposition. Both as original authors and as repositories of older traditions they interpreted allegorically all parts of the Bible, the narrative and poetic, the historic and the legal, not excluding even the proper names of the Books of Chronicles[4]. Many of these allegories are highly poetic metaphors. To cull but a few examples,

[1] See *Tosefta* to *Baba Kama*, VII, 3; *Kiddushin*, 22 *b*.

[2] *Sotah*, 15 *a*.

[3] *Mechilta* to Ex. xvii. 8 f., *Beshallaḥ*, end.

[4] The allegorical and symbolic interpretation of proper names goes back to the Tannaitic age; cf. רבי מאיר הוה דייק בשמא, *Yoma*, 83 *b*, and רבי מאיר היה דורש שמות, ר׳ יהושע בן קרחה היה דורש שמות, *Gen. R.* 42, 5. R. Meïr was a pupil of R. Akiba who with three others entered the realms of metaphysical speculation נכנס לפרדס. The exposition of proper names דרישת שמות was a Greek characteristic of that time, *vide* Freudenthal, *Alex. Polyhistor*. p. 75. But in reality this characteristic of דרישת שמות is traceable already in the Bible. Not only was the name originally given to describe an event—and of this there are numerous examples—but the name was often taken as an indication of an event which happened subsequently; *e.g.* "Is he not rightly called Jacob? for he hath supplanted me these two times" (Gen. xxvii. 36); "Nabal is his name, and churlishness is with him" (1 Sam. xxv. 25), a forerunner of the Rabbinic phrase שמא גרים, cf. רות מאי רות אמר ר׳ יוחנן שזכתה ויצא ממנה דוד שריוהו להקב"ה בשירות ותשבחות, מנא לן דשמא גרים וכו׳ (*Berachoth*, 7 *b*).

we have such expressions as "the deep" representing the unfathomable power of Rome[1], "the night" or "the darkness" denoting "the exile[2]"; "the ram caught in the thicket" typifying "Israel the scattered," entangled among successive empires[3]; "the ladder set upon earth and the top of it reaching to heaven" symbolising Sinai[4], and "man's bosom friend" signifying his soul[5].

But whilst most of these expressions are original in their conception, quite a large number are in a sense *reflected* metaphors originating in, and suggested by, metaphors and similes already found in the Bible. Thus, when a Rabbi interprets the text "The spirit of God was hovering upon the face of the waters[6]" as meaning "The spirit of the divine was moved by human repentance" and thus makes "water" allegorical of "penitence," he is but harking back to the Biblical simile[7] "Pour out thine heart like water"; or when another Rabbi, expounding the texts "And they shall roll away the stone[8]," "The stone of darkness[9]," interprets the term "stone" as referring allegorically to the *Yeṣer Hara*, the evil inclination in the human heart, he is recalling a metaphor in Ezekiel[10]. Here the Prophet, speaking of the divine gift to Israel of a new heart and a new spirit, says "And I will take away the heart *of stone* out of your

[1] On Gen. i. 2; Simeon b. Lakish in *Gen. R.* 2, 4. [2] *Ibid.*

[3] On Gen. xxii. 13, *vide Jer. Taanith*, II, 65 *d* top, and *Gen. R.* 56, 9.

[4] On Gen. xxviii. 12, *vide Gen. R.* 68, 12; *Tanḥuma Vayeṣe*, 7, author R Simeon b. Joḥai.

[5] On Mic. vii. 5, *vide Taanith*, 11 *a*, author Ḥidka (2nd c.) a disciple of R. Akiba, *vide* Bacher, *Agada d. Tannaiten*, I, 447.

[6] Gen. i. 2, *vide Gen. R.* 2, 4, author R. Simeon b. Lakish.

[7] Lam. ii. 19. [8] Gen. xxix. 8. [9] Job xxviii. 3.

[10] xxxvi. 26.

flesh and I will give you a heart of flesh[1]." Again in the demand which Naḥash the Ammonite addressed to the men of Jabesh Gilead: "on this condition will I make a covenant with you that all your right eyes be put out[2]," the Rabbis allegorise "your right eyes" to denote "the Sanhedrin[3]." This is reminiscent of the metaphorical meaning of "eyes" in the Bible[4], where Moses entreats Jethro to accompany him on his journeyings through the wilderness that he may be to them as "eyes." It also recalls the plea of Job[5] for merciful consideration, because he had been "*eyes* to the blind and feet to the lame."

A comprehensive and annotated collection of allegorical interpretations of Scripture, arranged according to the sequence of the Hebrew text, would form an interesting poetic commentary upon the Bible, constitute an important chapter in the historic development of Biblical and Midrashic simile, and provide a valuable aid to the study of Jewish liturgic poetry with which Midrashic allegory is so profusely interwoven.

Metaphors expanded into similes.

A considerable number of Midrashic similes are formed by the expansion of compressed Biblical metaphors. The Psalmist, *e.g.*, speaks metaphorically of the vine brought out of Egypt, planted in a specially prepared place, where it took deep root and filled the land[6]. The Rabbis supply the very obvious comparison

[1] *Vide Tanḥuma* to *Mikeṣ*, I, author R. Simeon b. Lakish. See Bacher, *Pal. Am.* I, 354.

[2] 1 Sam. xi. 2.

[3] Buber, *Midr. Samuel*, XIV, 7, author Simon, 3rd and 4th c.; the real basis for this metaphor is probably Lev. iv. 13, "If the whole congregation of Israel shall err, the thing being hid from the *eyes* of the assembly"; cf. Num. xv. 24.

[4] Num. x. 31.

[5] xxix. 15.

[6] Ps. lxxx. 9 ff.

implied though not mentioned in the text. In this way a metaphor is transformed into a simile.

This exegetical process is by no means confined to the metaphorical expressions actually found in the Bible. It is applied also to many of the allegorical metaphors which have been read into the Bible by way of poetic exposition. That charming idyll—the Song of Songs—provides the example of an entire book of the Bible which Rabbinic interpreters have impressed with the stamp of religious allegory. By their poetic touch nearly every figure in the book has become an allegorical metaphor, and the source of fresh metaphorical expressions in Rabbinic and post-Talmudic literature. The following will serve as an example:

"Thy lips, O my bride (*Kallah*), drop as the honey[1]." By a probable association of ideas[2] this verse is interpreted as an allegorical metaphor referring to the *Talmid-Ḥacham*—the student-scholar. Upon this follow a number of expanded similes emphasising the functions of the student-teacher.

R. Joḥanan (3rd c.) said: "Whosoever preaches or expounds the words of the Torah in public without endeavouring to make his teaching acceptable to the audience and thus fails to become like a bride who is sweet and agreeable to her guests [Resh-Lakish reads: to her husband] on the wedding day—it were better that he did not preach or teach at all." R. Huna

[1] Cant. iv. 11.

[2] Since the same word *Kallah* is the technical term for the Assemblies of Babylonian students which were held in the months of Ellul and Adar. The use of נפת here and in connection with the Law in Ps. xix. "sweeter also than honey and the honey-comb" no doubt helped to suggest this simile.

said in the name of R. Simeon b. Lakish: "Just as the bride is modest and chaste, so should the student-scholar be." R. Ḥalafta said in the name of R. Simeon b. Lakish (3rd c.): "Even as the bride is seated in her litter and carried in procession, as if to say: 'behold I am chaste and this public display is evidence thereof,' so must the student-scholar be free from every kind of taint or reproach[1]."

The same method of metaphor-expansion has been applied by the Rabbis to the allegorical metaphors which have been read into all other parts of Scripture. In this way the metaphor-expanded similes of the Midrash have grown considerably in number and importance.

The expansion of Bible similes.

Many Midrashic similes are built up exegetically by the expansion of Biblical similes.

In the Hebrew Bible there are comparatively few fully worked-out similes[2]. The Biblical writers very often content themselves with a mere statement of the terms of comparison, leaving it to the imagination of the hearers to discover the points of similarity. The Rabbis of the Midrash have in most instances suggested these points and worked out the details. But this process of elaboration on their part was not always objective; the steps which they supplied for the comparison did not necessarily reflect the original intention of the author. The Rabbis frequently gave to the comparisons a new turn, a fresh point of view, and sometimes even a totally reverse meaning. These new expositions were often poetic and elevating, but sometimes also mechanical and dry. At times they

[1] *Cant. R. ad loc.*

[2] *Vide* C. G. Montefiore in *J. Q. R.* vol. III, p. 625.

coined a kind of composite simile by weaving together and expounding one or more Biblical similes.

The following instances will exemplify some of the aspects of this class of Midrashic simile. (*a*) "Thy children (shall be) like olive plants round about thy table" exclaims the Psalmist[1]. To which the Rabbis add: "Even as the olive plants are of pure growth, so shall there be no impurity amongst thy children[2]." This is an expanded simile which may or may not reflect the original idea of the author. (*b*) "For I have spread you abroad as the four winds of heaven, saith the Lord[3]." The Rabbis, in expounding this simile, declare: "Even as the world cannot exist without winds, so mankind cannot exist without Israel[4]." Here the original meaning of most distant dispersion and difficult reunion is entirely reversed in the process of elaboration; a new and favourable turn is given to this apparently untoward prophecy against Israel. (*c*) "The righteous one shall flourish like the palm tree (he shall grow like a cedar in Lebanon)[5]." In Midrashic poetry the terms of this Biblical comparison are widened and generalised. The righteous individual becomes the righteous people. "*Israel* is like unto the palm tree (and the cedar)," and the Aggadists proceed to work out the points of similarity which exist between the nature of this tree and the people of Israel. Like the palm Israel has a sound heart, all its members are of service, it cannot be attacked with impunity. (*d*) In the Bible Israel is compared to the dust and likewise to the stars[6]. Rabbinic poetry links together these

[1] Ps. cxxviii. 3. [2] *Shoḥer Tob*, *ad loc.* [3] Zech. ii. 10.
[4] *Taanith*, 3 *b*, author R. Joshua b. Levi. [5] Ps. xcii. 13.
[6] Gen. xxii. 17, Deut. i. 10, 1 Chr. xxvii. 23, Gen. xiii. 16, xxviii. 14.

two ideas and forms a new conception out of the combination of similes: When the children of Israel are brought low they are as low as dust, but once they are allowed to rise they rise even unto the stars[1].

Similes by suggestion and juxtaposition.

Quite a large number of Midrashic similes are the result of suggestion by word or juxtaposition of statement in the Bible. Such methods of exposition are well established in Halachah and Aggadah. Students of the Talmud are familiar with the methods which are known technically as *Gezerah Shavah* "analogy of expressions" (*i.e.* the analogy between two laws or two things which is based upon verbal congruities or common factors in the texts), *Hekkesh*, "close connection" (*i.e.* the "analogy" based on the connection of two subjects in one and the same passage); and *Semuchin*, "textual proximity" (an interpretation founded upon the proximity of two laws in Scripture)[2]. The application of these principles to the branch of metaphor and simile is therefore in strict conformity with the general method of Biblical exegesis as laid down by the Rabbis of the Talmud.

Let us take a few examples of this class of simile culled from different spheres and various periods of the Rabbinic age. First as to suggestion by word or phrase.

1 *Megillah*, 16 *a*.

2 For more detailed definitions of these rules of exposition and examples *vide* Mielziner, *Introd. to the Talmud*, pp. 143–155 and 177–8. For an application by R. Joḥanan of the principle of *Semuchin* for Aggadic purposes *vide Berachoth*, 10 *a*. David's outcry against the infidelity of Absalom in Ps. iii. follows immediately after his complaint against the rebellious attitude of "the kings of the earth and the rulers against the Lord and against his anointed" in Ps. ii. For should anyone be amazed at the rebelliousness of the servant against the Master, one could point to the still more unnatural rebelliousness of a son against his father. Both however have happened.

(*a*) "Neither is there any rock like our God[1]." The similarity of צור, the Hebrew word for "rock" in this text, to צַיָּר "the artist and designer" forms the basis of several similes in which the Rabbis of the first and second centuries compare and contrast the divine Designer of the Universe with the ordinary human artist[2].

(*b*) "O Lord the Hope of Israel[3]," "The Lord is the purifying source of Israel," says R. Eliezer ben Hyrcanus (2nd c.); "even as ritual ablution purifies the unclean, so does the Lord purify Israel." This simile is based upon the explanation of the word *Mikveh* (hope) in its technical Talmudic sense of "ritual fount of purification[4]."

(*c*) The Midrashic metaphor of the wheel of fortune[5] and the beautifully expanded simile wherein the world with the people's changing fortunes is likened unto a wheel-work or pumping-wheel by which the full buckets are drawn up to be emptied, and the empty ones are lowered to be filled[6], are deduced by the Rabbis of the first and second centuries from the use of the word בגלל in a text of Deuteronomy[7] which

[1] 1 Sam. ii. 2.

[2] See *Gen. R.* 1, 9, the argument advanced by a certain philosopher to R. Gamaliel "your God is a great artist, but He found good material which helped Him" etc. Also *Shoḥer Tob*, XVIII, 26, where a string of similes is taken from the artist's work; cp. also *Megillah*, 14 *a*, *Berach.* 10 *a*.

[3] מקוה ישראל ה׳ *Jer. xvii. 13, according to some the reference is to* Jer. xiv. 8.

[4] *Shoḥer Tob*, IV, 9, *Pesikta*, 157 *b*; in Mishnah *Yoma* end, given in name of R. Akiba. See Bacher, *Ag. Tan.* I, 111, note 2.

[5] גלגל שחוזר בעולם.

[6] דמי לגלגל אנטילייא דמלי מתרוקנן דמתרוקנן מתמלי. Cf. Shakespeare, 3 *Henry VI*, IV, 3.

[7] xv. 10, נתן תתן לו...כי בגלל הדבר הזה יברכך ה׳.

they translate as follows: "Thou shalt surely give him [*i.e.* the poor] and thine heart shall not be grieved when thou givest him; for *in the rolling* [of fortunes] shall this act of thine bring it to pass that the Lord thy God shall bless thee in all thy works and in all that thou puttest thine hand unto[1]."

(*d*) Palestine is called in the Bible "the goodly heritage[2]," "the glorious land[3]." The Hebrew word **צבי**, which in addition to "goodly" and "glorious" signifies also "a stag", suggested to R. Ḥanina b. Ḥama (3rd c.) the striking simile comparing the land of Palestine to the skin of the stag. For just as the latter can be stretched, similarly the former can be expanded and contracted according to the requirements of a varying population[4].

And now for examples of similes suggested by a likeness of words or textual proximity.

(*a*) The term "covenant" is used in connection with the salt of the Temple sacrifices[5]. The same term "covenant" is used also in the enumeration of the sorrows and sufferings consequent upon Israel's disobedience[6]. Just as salt, says R. Simeon b. Lakish, removes the impurities from the meat, and seasons it; even so do sufferings penetrate and purify the human body[7].

1 See *Shabbath*, 151 *b*, תני דבי ר' ישמעאל; *Exod. R.* 31, 14 and *Ruth R.* to II, 19, אמר ר"נ. *Vide* Bacher, *Ag. Tan.* II, 339, note 3, and *Am.* III, p. 147 (note).

2 נחלת צבי Jer. iii. 19.

3 ארץ הצבי Dan. xi. 41.

4 *Gittin*, 57 *a*, *Kethub.* 112 *a*, *Sifré* to Deut. xi. 40, § 37, Bacher, *Agada d. Palest. Amoräer*, I, 17–18, and note 1. See Delitzsch, *Jewish Artisan Life*, p. 7.

5 ולא תשבית מלח ברית Lev. ii. 13.

6 אלה דברי הברית Deut. xxviii. 69.

7 *Berachoth*, 5 *a*. This is in conformity with the Rabbinic theory of "chastisements of love."

(*b*) The words of the Law are like an asylum and refuge; they too offer shelter and protection. This simile is deduced by R. Joḥanan (3rd c.) from the sequence of the Biblical texts in Deuteronomy[1], where the words "And this is the Law which Moses set before the Children of Israel" follow immediately after the record of the setting up by Moses of three cities of refuge[2].

(*c*) God is the heart of Israel. This bold metaphor, which finds its companion figure in Jehudah Halevi's aphorism "Israel is the heart of the nations," is derived by R. Ḥiyya b. Abba (3rd and 4th c.) from the juxtaposition of the words צור לבבי "[God is] the strength [or rock] of my heart[3]," which are construed by this Rabbi as standing in apposition to each other, *viz.* צור "the rock," *i.e.* God, לבבי "is my heart[4]."

(*d*) Just as the sea is always open, and whosoever desires to wash therein can do so at all times, even so it is with Repentance; whenever a man wishes to repent, the Holy One, blessed be He, is ready to receive him. This simile is based by R. Samuel b. Naḥmani (3rd and 4th c.) upon the sequence of phrases in the Book of Psalms, which he expounds as "Who art an ever-open place of safety for them who come from all ends of the earth, in the same manner as the waters wide and deep[5]."

Illustrative parables.

The last group of Midrashic comparisons—exegetical in purpose—are the similes and parables

[1] Ch. iv. *vv.* 41–4.

[2] *Makkoth,* 10 *a*; see Bacher, *Pal. Am.* I, p. 234.

[3] Ps. lxxiii. 26.

[4] *Pesikta,* 46 *b*, *Pesikta R.* ch. xv, p. 70 *a*; *Cant. R.* 5, 2. *Tanḥuma* to *Toledoth* § 18, see Bacher, *Pal. Am.* II, 185; Cuzari ii, 36.

[5] Ps. lxv. 6, מבטח כל־קצוי־ארץ וים רחקים, *vide Shoḥer Tob, ad loc.* Cf. p. 6 *supra*.

which the Rabbis employ to explain a text, incident, or narrative in the Bible. These figures are very numerous; their form and characteristics are too familiar to need exemplification in this introductory chapter. They are of the nature of the *Mashal* and include all those examples which are generally covered by the term "Parable." These latter are introduced by many formulæ[1]. Their subject-matter ranges over a wide field and extends to all spheres of human life and activities. They are therefore of particular value and importance from the social and economic points of view, and offer a fruitful source of comparison with the *Mashal* or parable in kindred literatures.

The poetic point of view.

The preceding section dealt with the exegetical basis of Midrashic similes. But the question of their possible origin is not, as some critics maintain, destructive of either their freshness or poetic force. It is true that at times the figures of comparison as found in the Midrash are in many respects rather strained; occasionally they become precisely informative and prosaically detailed. This is due in a large measure to the strong exegetical bent of the Rabbis, to their innate tendency to exhaust the possibilities of interpretation. Comparison is stretched to its utmost limits. The principle of similarity is extended

[1] Amongst the most usual and most frequent introductory phrases are the following:
משל: משל לְ: משל אומר: מתלא אמר: משל הדיוט: היינו דאמרי אינשי: משל למה הוא דומה: משל דְ...למה הוא דומה: משל למה"ד: משלו משל למ"הד: אמשול לך משל למה"ד לְ: נמשלו...כְּ: לְ: למה; למה הדבר דומה ל: למה הוא דומה: למה הם [*or* היו] דומים [*or* דומין]: ...דומה לְ: כְּ: כזה שֶׁ: מה דרכה של...כך: כדרך שֶׁ...כך: כשם שֶׁ...כך: מנהגו של עולם: בנוהג שבעולם: עובדא הוה בְּ: מעשה: מעשה בְּ:

to the minutest details. It would not, however, be correct or just to underrate on that account the poetic value of Rabbinic similes. That the metaphors which are inventions of the Rabbis, that even the allegories which are grafted on to the Bible are imaginative and poetically suggestive, will be generally admitted. But even the developed similes, which bear a distinctly exegetical aspect, and at a certain stage degenerate into uninteresting exposition—these also display in many respects considerable beauty and charm. They are full of touches taken from all aspects and phenomena of Nature: the heavens, the earth, the land and the sea. They are drawn from the characteristic habits of animals, birds and fishes, such as the modesty, the gentleness, the chastity and the marital fidelity of the dove, the voracity of fishes, the cunning of the fox, the alertness of the stag, the pride of the lion, the paternal care of the eagle. They are taken from the nature of trees, plants and flowers. They reflect such natural phenomena as the beauty of the rising dawn, the grandeur of the seas, the majesty of the volcanic eruption of the earth[1]. All these comparisons throw a flood of light upon the deep and penetrating insight of the Rabbis into the life and movements of the world around them, and render the study of the subject from the poetic standpoint both fascinating and useful.

The social and economic points of view.

Midrashic similes likewise serve as a useful index of social and economic conditions. This is especially

[1] For some instances of such poetic figures, other than Agricultural and Pastoral (which are treated in this volume), *vide Cant. R.* to i. 15; iv. 8; vi. 10; viii. 14; *Exod. R.* 22, 1; 23, 14; *Mechilta*, ed. Friedmann, p. 62 *b*; *Abodah Zarah*, 3 *b*–4 *a*.

the case with the *Meshalim* or parables which are illustrative in character. For whilst some of the figures employed by the Rabbis are probably ideal or reminiscent, the majority constitute a reflection of realities and of sights actually beheld by the authors and understood by the audience. Even the vast number of expanded and expository similes, in spite of the exegetical tendency and moral motive which impelled their development, is full of objective natural touches. A Jewish scholar[1] has treated a large section of Midrashic similes as revealing their social and economic background. He has tried to show how Roman life and administration are reflected in the "royal" similes of the Rabbis during the Talmudic period.

Many other aspects in the life of the people will appear in our collection. We shall note the busy movements of town and village life. We shall meet with the builder, the potter, the dyer, and men of similar arts and crafts, the shopkeeper, the commercial traveller, the money-changer, the hawker, the spice-seller, the dealer in precious stones.

Contrasted with these we shall behold pictures of the calm and placid country life, both agricultural and pastoral, with its fields and orchards, its herds and flocks, the tenant-farmer, the field-labourer, the shepherd and the watchman. We shall catch a glimpse of the home-life of the people, their serious occupations, their lighter moments and their frivolous amusements, and gain an insight into their domestic arrangements, their mode of living, their ways of hospitality, their utensils, their food. In short, the

[1] Ziegler in *Die Königsgleichnisse des Midrasch* (Breslau, 1903).

numerous vivid touches of the Rabbinic similes will afford a valuable aid for the construction of a faithful picture of the social and economic life of the people.

The comparative aspect.

The comparative standpoint has now to be considered. Students of N.T. literature have recently begun to pay greater attention to the study of Rabbinic similes. They have rightly recognised that these figures of speech, forming as they do an important part in the development of sacred metaphor which stretches back to the Bible, possess both as regards form and substance a considerable value for the fuller knowledge of many of the images and parables of the New Testament.

A German scholar[1] has written an interesting comparative study on these lines. In his thesis he has brought together the Tannaitic similes contained in the *Mechilta* which fall within, or are close to, the period during which the N.T. similes had their birth; and he has indicated their bearing upon the parables of the N.T., belittling the value of Midrashic parables and regarding them as inferior to those of the N.T.

A more recent French writer[2] devotes a whole chapter to the consideration of the Tannaitic *Meshalim* and draws from them certain evidence to confirm his more conservative theories on the N.T. similes against the advanced position of the School of Jülicher[3].

But in view of the generally admitted fact that Rabbinic literature is a tradition, and that similes

[1] Paul Fiebig, *Altjüdische Gleichnisse und die Gleichnisse Jesu* (Tübingen, 1904).

[2] Le F. D. Buzy, in his *Introduction aux paraboles évangéliques* (Paris, 1912).

[3] *Vide* ch. IV, Buzy *op. cit.*

quoted by Rabbis of a later age may have had their origin and currency at a much earlier date (although not stated or clearly traceable as such), it is evident that for comparative purposes we may include all Rabbinic metaphors and similes—those of the Amoraic period, no less than those of the Tannaitic age. And whilst our material, part of which is presented in this volume, will corroborate some of the impressions which N.T. scholars have formed in regard to the exegetical character of the Rabbinic similes, it should at the same time help to remove many a prejudiced view which has crept into the researches of the scholars referred to. When, *e.g.*, the popular character of the N.T. parables and their powerful appeal to the masses is contrasted with the alleged heavy professorial nature of Rabbinic similes propounded to the students in the academies of learning, a most erroneous impression is evidently entertained of the whole object of Aggadic literature. These critics have failed to grasp the spirit which animated those Rabbi-preachers, the spiritual descendants of the Prophets and poets of the Bible, and have formed a wrong estimate of the composition of the audiences, the large masses of the rank and file of the people, who, as we know, and as the following story will confirm, flocked to hear them in the Synagogues and Houses of Learning. R. Abbahu and R. Ḥiyya b. Abba, relates the Talmud, met at one place. R. Ḥiyya b. Abba gave an Halachic exposition, and R. Abbahu delivered an Aggadic discourse. Whereupon all the people left R. Ḥiyya b. Abba and came to R. Abbahu. R. Ḥiyya b. Abba felt discouraged. R. Abbahu then said unto him: "I will tell thee a parable. To what may this be likened? To two men who once entered into the same town, the one offering for sale precious stones and pearls, the other tinsel. To whom do people crowd? Is it not to him who sells the tinsel [as being the more popular wares][1]?"

Again when it is alleged that from the point of view of doctrine the N.T. parables surpass the Rabbinic *Meshalim* in "all the grandeur of revelation and divinity[2]," a full and unbiassed study could not have been made of the subject-matter of the vast material comprised within the domain of Midrashic simile.

And this brings us to the last aspect of our subject, *viz.* the Religious Aspect.

The religious aspect.

It has already been stated that the Rabbis were the oral expounders of the written word of the Bible and the spiritual successors of the Hebrew Prophets and Psalmists. Being thus fully imbued with lofty ideas on Religion and Morality, these Rabbi-preachers conveyed them to the people in the course of their Midrashic addresses. This religious tendency is visible in many metaphors and similes expanded from the Bible. For, as has already been indicated, the Midrashic preachers do not in these cases supply merely the ideas implied by the Biblical authors, but in subjective manner introduce also fresh religious and moral conceptions for the elevation of the people. And the same tendency is noticeable in their general discourses, which, with a view to popularisation, are largely interspersed with poetic figures of speech,

[1] *Sotah*, 40 *a*.

[2] *Vide* Buzy, *op. cit.* p. 169, "Les παραβολαί surpassent les mechâlim... au point de vue de la doctrine, de toute la hauteur de la révélation et de la divinité."

such as metaphor and allegory, simile and parable. All these figures of comparison had a religious tendency. They spoke of God and man, of Israel and the world, of Torah—the Law—and practice, the future life and Resurrection. They reflected principles and doctrines which the Rabbis sought to impress upon the people in the ordinary course of preaching and teaching, but very often also in dialogue and controversy, in order to meet and refute insidious attacks that were being made upon Jewish ideas by the heathen philosophers and the *Minim* (sectarians) of the age[1]. It was but natural that there should be a certain unevenness in the plane of elevation of these Rabbinic *Meshalim*, extending, as they do, over a period of several centuries, and containing the religious teachings of a host of different preachers. But there are certainly very large numbers of these *Meshalim* which, no less than the parables in kindred literatures, are also distinguished by "all the grandeur of revelation" and are likewise touched by "the spirit of the divine." "If thou desirest to recognise and to know God, and to cleave to His ways, study the Aggadah," say the Rabbis[2]. And the Midrashic similes are an important part of the Aggadah.

This ethical and moral spirit which characterises Midrashic similes and parables will appear with sufficient clearness on reading the selections presented in the subsequent chapters.

[1] *E.g.* R. Joḥanan b. Zakkai in *Yalk.* I, § 397. *Tosefta*, pp. 357–8; also R. Gamaliel II, R. Joshua b. Ḥananiah, R. Akiba and others.

[2] *Sifré Ekeb* to XI, 22. Lauterbach (in *J. Q. R.* N.S. I, p. 305) explains this to mean "learn Haggadah," *i.e.* the right method of interpreting Scripture הגדת הכתוב, so as to be able to gather the full meaning of the Scriptural word and what it seeks to tell us.

Here attention will be drawn to a few instances only by way of illustration:

(1) The religious duty, according to the true Jewish conception, of maintaining a healthy body as well as a pure soul, the Rabbinic insistence on the great part played by the body in religion, were taught by the great Hillel in the following parable: Behold the royal statues placed in theatres and circuses; see how carefully they are looked after, washed and cleaned by those appointed to have charge over them. And why so? Because these statues reflect the likeness of the king. How much more scrupulously then should we take care of our bodies, seeing that they bear the reflection and contain the image of the King of kings[1]?

(2) The divine guardianship of, and association with, Israel is taught by R. Simeon b. Lakish in the following parable: To the key of a precious jewel-box in his possession the king fastened a chain so that it might not easily be mislaid or lost. Even so did God attach His name "*El*" אל to Isra*el* ישראל to guard against their being lost among the nations of the world[2].

(3) And the converse conception—the beautifully mystic idea of man clinging to God, which plays such an important part in Rabbinic and ethical Jewish literature—is emphasised by a Rabbi in another simile: When a passenger on deck falls into the sea, the captain of the boat throws out to him the line, saying, "Grasp it firmly and slacken not thine hold upon it at the peril of thy life." Even so,

[1] *Lev. R.* 34, 3.

[2] *Jer. Taanith*, II, 6, p. 65 *d*.

amidst the troubled seas of his earthly voyage, should man cling to the precepts and thereby remain attached to God in order that he may live[1].

(4) The great social doctrine of the interdependence of mankind is impressed upon his hearers by a Rabbi-preacher in the well-known parable of the passenger who was found boring a hole in his cabin and who, when taken to task for so dangerous an occupation, advanced the obviously fallacious argument that this personal action of his was no concern of his fellow-passengers[2].

(5) Rabbi Akiba, in rejoinder to the Roman conception of man's justifiable hard-heartedness towards the poor, whom, as the heathens alleged, God desired to punish and afflict, spoke in parable: When a king in a momentary outburst of anger against his son orders him to be put in prison and deprived of food and drink, he is yet grateful to the man who shows this son of his all kindness and consideration, and provides him with the necessaries of life. Even so is it with the poor and afflicted on earth who are none the less the children of the King of kings[3].

(6) The broken Tables of Stone no less than the whole ones had a place in the Ark of the Covenant[4] says a Rabbi, speaking in poetic simile; meaning thereby that the aged and saintly scholar, whose physical powers are broken, is entitled to honour and respect, equally with the young and vigorous one.

(7) The effect of Divine Revelation upon each individual is taught by a Rabbi in the following artistic simile: Even as a statue, when viewed by a

[1] *Tanḥuma Shelaḥ, ad fin.*
[2] *Lev. R.* 4, 6.
[3] *Baba Bathra,* 10 *a.*
[4] *Ibid.* 14 *b*

thousand people at one and the same time appears to gaze upon them all, so did every one at Sinai feel God's words directed upon him[1].

(8) The conception of the Immanence of God is reflected in the following parable: When the sea is stormy and overflows the land, the cave by the sea-shore is filled with water, whilst the sea loses nothing of its contents. Even so was the Tabernacle filled with the glory of the Divine Presence, whilst neither heaven nor earth became emptied thereof[2].

(9) The soothing doctrine of יסורין של אהבה "chastisements of love," so beautifully developed in Talmudic literature, runs through many a Rabbinic simile. The Potter, says one Rabbi, in testing the work of the kiln, examines it by striking the well-wrought vessels only; he does not try thus the more fragile ones, which but one blow suffices to break. Even so God afflicts only those who in a spirit of piety and resignation can bear the test of sorrow and suffering[3].

(10) Man's exit from the world, as compared and contrasted with his entry into it, is portrayed by a Rabbi in the following figure: Of two boats sailing on the high seas the one that has come into port is in the eyes of the wise much more an object of joy than the boat that is only just leaving the harbour. Even thus should we contemplate man's departure from the world without sorrow or fear, seeing that at death he has already entered the harbour—the haven of rest in the world to come[4].

[1] *Pesikta*, 110 *a*; R. Levi, 3rd and 4th c.
[2] *Pesikta R. K.* 2 *b*.
[3] *Gen. R.* 55, 2.
[4] *Exod. R.* 48, 1.

(11) The doctrine of the Immortality of the Soul, and life after death, is reflected in many Midrashic parables: If a glass vessel, says one Rabbi, which is fashioned by the breath of man, can be restored again, after it is broken, how much more so can the soul of man be restored seeing that it has been produced by the breath of God[1]?

Who, on reading such examples of Midrashic similes and parables—and it must be remembered that many similes of the Midrash are in reality undeveloped parables and may for purposes of comparison as regards subject-matter be legitimately included in our consideration—will deny them at least an equal measure of the "grandeur of revelation" and "the spirit of the divine" with which Christian scholars have credited the parables of other literatures?

These poetic figures of expression, as part of the literature of the Midrash, were equally intended to elevate and inspire the masses. In fact the term "Aggadah" is explained to mean, being able to "draw" and attract the heart of man[2]. And that this object was fully and successfully achieved is clearly evinced by the powerful influence which this great literature has exercised directly and indirectly throughout all the ages upon the life and the outlook of the Jewish people.

[1] *Synhedrin*, 91 *a*, a Rabbi of the School of R. Ishmael.

[2] האגדות שמושכות לב אדם. *Sifré* to Deut. xxxii. 14, § 317.

I

THE FIELD, ITS CULTIVATION AND PRODUCTS

Agricultural Imagery.

AGRICULTURE is an aspect of Nature closely interwoven with the poetry of the Bible, since it concerned and touched the actual life and movements of the people.

The eyes, ears and hearts of the people of Israel to whom the Prophets spoke and the Psalmists sang were attuned to the music breathed from the green fields and the open meadows, the garden and the orchard, the trees and the flowers; and the divinely-inspired messengers, who often spoke in parable and simile, utilised these well-known objects of Nature for the purpose of impressing great truths and important messages. The Rabbis—the spiritual successors of these Biblical writers—voicing the message of the Bible and with a deep sense of the poetic, likewise paid due regard to the agricultural figures of speech. They elaborated them by exposition, and extended them by special methods of their own.

Field-work in the Bible.

While the field in its general aspect is left untouched by the Bible as a subject of poetic comparison, its cultivation and the ingathering of its products are used by it as images of deep spiritual significance. Thus: "ploughing" not only stands as the symbol of individual oppression—"The plowers plowed upon my back[1]"—and of national distress—"Judah shall plow, and Jacob shall break his clod[2]"—but it also

[1] Ps. cxxix. 3. [2] Hos. x. 11.

typifies the preparation of man's spiritual constitution for the conduct of an evil life—"You have plowed wickedness[1]." It likewise symbolises the fashioning of the heart for the reception of the nobler impulses —"Break up your fallow ground[2]."

In similar manner the metaphor of "sowing," as a companion figure to "ploughing," is made to express the practice of vice or virtue, whilst "reaping" and "gleaning" denote their results: "He that soweth iniquity shall reap vanity[3]"; "Sow to yourselves according to righteousness, reap according to mercy[4]." In the bolder imagery of the prophet, reaping the harvest symbolises also the destructive process of death. "Put ye in the sickle, for the harvest is ripe[5]."

The field in Midrashic poetry.

To the authors of Midrashic literature the field as such, and not merely its cultivation and the ingathering of its increase, suggested several figurative ideas.

To the mind of one Rabbi of the second century (R. Judah b. Ilai) the "field," possibly as an emblem of openness and complete freedom from obstacle, is an allegorical representation of the Mishnah, the style of which, when compared with the Talmud, is clear, open and unobscured by dialectics[6]. Commenting upon the text "The king is served by the field[7],"

[1] Hos. x. 13; cf. Job iv. 8.
[2] Hos. x. 12 *b*.
[3] Prov. xxii. 8.
[4] Hos. x. 12 *a*.
[5] Joel iv. 13, cf. Job v. 26; cf. Longfellow:

"There is a reaper whose name is death,
And, with his sickle keen,
He reaps the bearded grain at a breath."

[6] *Lev. R.* 22, 1; Bacher, *Ag. Tan.* II, 265–6. R. Judah b. Ezekiel (3rd and 4th c.) in the name of Rab (3rd c.) actually speaks of the reasons of the laws being *open* and *revealed*, *like the field*. שכל טעמי תורה מגולין להם כשדה (*Synhedrin*, 102 *a*).

[7] Eccl. v. 8.

Rabbi Judah says: the "king," *i.e.* the student of the Talmud, "is subservient to the 'field,'" *i.e.* the student of the Mishnah, who is the repository of ordered Halachah.

Another contemporary Rabbi (R. Neḥemiah) takes quite a different view. He regards the "field" as typical of the larger and more extensive sphere of the Talmud, and assigns this allegorical interpretation to the text in Ecclesiastes quoted above. To him the labour and toil spent upon the cultivation of the field probably suggest the efforts involved in the production of this branch of literature[1].

But the "field," like the "garden," in Biblical as well as Talmudic poetry[2], is used by the Rabbis already in the Mishnaic period as a metaphor for "woman." "Whilst in thy possession, and under thy control, thy field has been flooded[3]," is the metaphorical plea which, in Talmudic Law, may be advanced by a newly-married wife against whom the husband has laid charges of wantonness[4]. This alle-

[1] Cf. Raba's exposition of the text (Cant. vii. 12) "Come, my beloved, let us go forth *into the field*"—"come and I will show thee the *disciples of the wise, who toil in the study of the Torah amidst pressure and need*" (*Erubin*, 21 *a*). For a general discussion as to the respective values of the study of Mishnah and Talmud *vide Baba Meṣia*, 33 *a*, *b*. That R. Judah however regarded Talmud study also as of very high importance is evident from his utterance, *ibid.*, where he assigns to the Talmud student alone the title of *Talmid-Ḥacham*. This is in keeping with the tradition that he was the author of the *Sifra*, a work which derives the *Halachoth* from the Biblical text by Talmudic methods. Cf. also *Kidd.* 49 *a*, where R. Judah (as against R. Meïr) sees even in the term "Mishnah" a collection of Halachoth on the lines of the *Sifra* (*vide* Rashi *ad loc.*).

[2] Cf. Cant. iv. 12 "a garden shut up is my sister," and *Pirke di R. Eliezer*, ch. 21, אין גן אלא האשה, the expression "garden" (Gen. iii. 3) signifies woman.

[3] נסתחפה שדך.

[4] Deut. xxii. 17; *vide Kethuboth*, 12 *b*. Cf. the Exposition of R. Zadok,

gorical conception of "field[1]" was a natural one in view of the fact that זרע in the Bible denotes also human seed, and the same meaning was continued in Midrashic literature[2]. It was probably this combination of ideas which gave rise to the further series of euphemistic metaphors which in the Midrash have become associated with the cultivation of the field. Thus, *e.g.*, most of the Rabbinic ploughing metaphors are euphemistic in their nature[3]. "Whoever takes unto himself a wife that is unsuitable is regarded by Scripture as if he had ploughed the whole world and sown it over with salt," says Rabbah bar Bar Ḥanah (3rd c.)[4].

But the image of ploughing is used by the Rabbis also for other purposes. Thus, a Rabbi refers to the use of parallelism in Biblical literature in the following manner: "Even a common man will not plough a ridge within a ridge, but the Prophets do plough a ridge within a ridge. [The Psalmist says][5] 'Touch not mine anointed ones and do my prophets no

who, commenting on the text Gen. iv. 8, "And it came to pass when they were in the field," says "field" signifies "woman" who is compared to the field. Great hatred entered into the heart of Cain, not only on account of his rejected offering, but because the twin sister of Abel was beautiful among women, and he loved her in his heart (*Gen. R.* 22, 7, *Yalkut Gen.* § 38, esp. *Pirke di R. Eliezer* ch. 21).

1 Cf. *Synhedrin*, 74 *b*, אסתר קרקע עולם היתה, Esther was like natural ground (that is being ploughed), *i.e.* a mere passive agent in her relations with the King.

2 *Vide Kohel. R.* ch. 11, § 6, on the text בבקר זרע את זרעך, "In the morning sow thy seed and in the evening withhold not thy hand."

3 *Vide Jer. Yebamoth* 1, *init.* 2 *b*. Of José b. Ḥalafta (2nd c.), who married his deceased brother's wife, it is said חמש חרישות חרש וחמש נטיעות נטע; cf. *Gen. R.* 85, 5, also 98, 4, the saying of R. Aḥa (4th c.), כל החרישות שחרשתי באמך לא ברחל הייתי ראוי לחרשן

4 *Kiddushin*, 70 *a*.

5 Ps. cv. 15.

harm'" (repeating the same idea in the two parts of the same verse[1]).

The yoke. The yoke used in ploughing is employed figuratively already in the Bible, where it typifies either slavery and oppression[2], or a burden of iniquity[3]. In Lamentations "yoke" has the meaning of religious discipline: "It is good for a man that he bear the yoke in his youth[4]."

In Midrashic literature this metaphorical conception of yoke as a religious discipline is not infrequent. R. Neḥunia b. Hakkanah[5] (Tanna, 1st and 2nd c.) speaks of the "yoke of the Torah," as typifying the discipline of Faith and Deeds, the loving burden of Religious Ethics and Morality, which counteracts the "yoke of earthly dominion," and "the yoke of worldly cares."

Other Rabbis allude in similar manner to the "yoke" of the kingdom of heaven as the divine discipline, which ennobles and uplifts, in contrast to the yoke imposed by an earthly power, which humiliates and crushes[6]. This idea is used with great effect in the following parable: "The Lord trieth the righteous; but the wicked and him that loveth violence his soul hateth[7]." Rabbi Eleazar (b. Pedath, 3rd c.) said: This might be compared to a husbandman possessing two cows, one of which is strong and the other weak. Upon which does he place the yoke? Is it not upon her which is strong? Even so does the Holy One,

[1] *Gen. R.* 67, 9, *vide* Dukes, *Blumenlese*, p. 35.

[2] 1 Kings xii. 4, Is. ix. 3.

[3] Lam. i. 14.

[4] Lam. iii. 27.

[5] *Aboth* 3, 6, *vide* Taylor, *Pirqe Aboth*, "Sayings of the Jewish Fathers," *ad loc.* note 14.

[6] *Vide* Schechter, *Aspects of Rabbinic Theology*, "The Kingdom of God, esp. pp. 70–1; cf. Matt. xi. 29–30.

[7] Ps. xi. 5.

blessed be He, try the righteous, as it is said: "The Lord trieth the righteous[1]."

The yoke is also used in Rabbinic literature in the sense of desire, ambition and greed. Commenting upon the text "And he shall put a yoke of iron upon thy neck[2]," R. Eleazar b. Pedath (3rd c.) said: That means avarice and cupidity[3].

The goad

Another object connected with ploughing and employed in the Bible in a metaphorical sense is the goad. It is used by Ecclesiastes[4], who compares it with the words of the wise.

The Midrashic figures associated with this implement of field-work are confined mainly to an expansion of this one Biblical simile. A few characteristic touches, however, are added by the Rabbis, which serve to bring out the intention of the Biblical preacher, as the following examples will show:

He too (*sc.* R. Eleazar b. Azariah, 1st and 2nd c.) interpreted the text: "The words of the wise are as goads[5]." Why are the words of the Torah compared to goads? Just as the goad directs the cow to the furrows and thus helps to bring life to the world, even so do the words of the Torah turn the students away from the ways of death and direct them in the paths of life[6].

Just as the goad guides the cow to plough in its furrow, even so do the words of the wise guide man into the ways of the Holy One, blessed be He[7].

[1] *Gen. R.* 55, § 2, cf. Parable of the Potter trying only the stronger vessels, Introd. p. 24.

[2] Deut. xxviii. 48.

[3] רעיון, cf. Hos. xii. 2, רעה רוח; *Jer. Shabbath*, 14 *c*, Bacher, *Pal. Am.* II, 41.

[4] *Ibid.* XII, 12.

[5] Eccl. xii. 11.

[6] *Ḥagigah*, 3 *b*, see Bacher, *Ag. Tan.* I, 233 and references.

[7] *Num. R.* 14, 4; *Pesikta R.*, Friedmann, p. 7. In *Tanḥuma Behaal.*

Just as the goad induces understanding in the cow, even so do the words of the wise make understanding abide with men, imbuing them with knowledge and teaching them the ways of the Holy One, blessed be He[1].

"I am the Lord thy God, who teacheth thee for thy profit[2]." Who trains thee (through sufferings), adds the Rabbinic interpreter, even as the goad traineth the cow[3].

Sowing and reaping.

By an extension of the Biblical metaphor, the term "sowing" is made in the Midrash to signify "begetting," whilst "reaping" typifies "burial."

R. Simeon B. Joḥai (2nd c.) once said unto his son: These are men of worth[4]. Go unto them that they may bless thee. He went unto them and found them engaged in reconciling apparently contradictory verses of the Bible. He told them the purpose of his visit, whereupon they said unto him: May it be His will that thou sow and reap not, that thou bring in and send not out, send out and bring not in, that thy house be vacant and thine abode inhabited, that thy table be disturbed and that thou behold not a new year. Returning home he related to his father that they had cursed him instead of blessing him. But the father on being told the words of the message rightly construed them as full of good omen. "That thou sow and reap not" means: Mayest thou beget

the reading is "even so do the words of the wise direct the students to pronounce their opinion upon what is permitted and what is forbidden."

1 *Pesikta R.*, Friedmann, p. 8, דרבן is explained as a kind of *Notarikon* for שמ'ד'יר ב'ינה בפרה, "it causes understanding to dwell in the cow."

2 Is. xlviii. 17, מלמדך להועיל.

3 *Pesikṭa Baḥodesh*, p. 153 *a*, מלמדך suggesting מלמד הבקר Judg. iii. 31.

4 אנשים של צורה.

children and not lose them. "That thou bring in and send not out"—Mayest thou receive thy daughter-in-law into thy house and not be compelled to send her away owing to thy son's death. "That thou send out and bring not in"—Mayest thou give thy daughter in marriage and have no cause through her husband's demise to take her into thy house again. "That thy house be vacant, and thine abode inhabited"—May thy grave [thy more permanent resting-place] remain empty and thy abode [thy temporary dwelling-place on earth] be occupied. "May thy table [*i.e.* thy meals] be disturbed [by the noise of thy children]," and "Mayest thou not witness another new year"—by having to remarry and thus enjoy a new year of freedom[1].

The following is a further instance: "What is it that caused them [*sc.* the generation of Noah] to rebel against me? Is it not that they were sowing and not reaping [*i.e.* begetting children and not burying them]? Henceforth there shall be both seed-time and harvest, they shall beget and bury," says R. Aḥa (4th c.)[2].

Reaping in due season.

Israel's redemption at the appointed time is portrayed under images which include the harvest, the vintage and sweet-smelling spices.

It is likened unto the harvest: When a field is reaped out of its proper season, even the straw is not good, but when reaped in due season, it is good. Wherefore Scripture says[3] "Put forth the scythe, for the harvest is ripe."

[1] *Moed Katon*, 9 *a*, *b*. The newly-married husband was absolved from military service and other duties (Deut. xxiv. 5).

[2] *Gen. R.* 34, 11; *vide* Bacher, *Pal. Am.* III, 130.

[3] Joel iv. 13.

It is likened unto the vintage: When a vineyard is gathered out of its proper season, even its vinegar is not good, but when it is gathered in due season, it is good. Hence the text[1] "When the vineyard has ripened into red wine sing unto it."

It is likened unto spices: When the spices are gathered tender and moist, their odour does not spread, but when they are gathered dry, the scent doth spread. [Hence the verse[2]: "upon the mountains of spices[3]."]

Sowing without reaping.

"Sowing seed in vain" as an indication of useless effort is found already in the Bible[4]. It is similarly and more clearly applied in Rabbinic literature.

R. Joshua b. Korḥah (T., 2nd c.) said: Whosoever studies the Law and does not repeat it is like unto a man who sows but does not reap[5].

One other Rabbinic simile taken from the scattering of the seed may here be mentioned. It is based upon a Biblical conception, but has a certain freshness and originality of application, and acquires a special interest from the historic and religious point of view. R. Eleazar (*sc.* b. Pedath, 3rd c.) said: The Holy One, blessed be He, exiled Israel among the nations in order that proselytes might be added unto them, even as it is said: "And I will sow her for Me throughout the earth[6]." When a man sows a *Seah* of seed, is it not in order that he may gather in several *Khors*[7]?

But much more numerous are the Rabbinic meta-

[1] Is. xxvii. 2. [2] Cant. viii. 14.
[3] *Cant. R. ad fin.*, cf. *Yalkut* Ps. § 639. [4] Lev. xxvi. 16.
[5] *Synhedrin*, 99 *a*, Bacher, *Ag. Tan.* II, 312. [6] Hos. ii. 25.
[7] *Pesaḥim*, 87 *b*; cf. *Lev. R.* 27, 1: "Even as the mountains are adapted for sowing and they produce fruit, so do the righteous produce fruit to benefit themselves and others."

phors and similes which relate to other aspects of the field and its work.

The fence.

The wall and fence idea is used already in the Bible in a figurative sense. God speaks of His own work of restoration in Judah under the image of closing up or walling in the breaches[1], and in a similar manner He designates the rebuilders of Israel as the "repairers of the breach[2]." He describes the man of action as the one "that should make up the hedge and stand in the breach[3]."

This conception of the fence, erected round the field to shield and protect it against inroads and spoliation (for in the figurative language of the Midrash "a breach invites the thief[4]"), supplies the Rabbis with interesting metaphors in the sphere of Religion. It has been made to characterise the new regulations introduced from time to time by Israel's spiritual guardians, the men of the Great Synagogue, the Sanhedrin[5] and the sages of a later age. These

[1] Amos ix. 11. [2] Is. lviii. 12.

[3] Ezek. xxii. 30; xiii. 5.

[4] *Sukkah*, 26 *a*, פרצה קוראה לגנב; cf. the Proverb לאו עכברא גנב אלא חורא גנב, *Gitt.* 45 *a*. For examples of פרצה "breach" in a metaphorical sense, *vide Yalkut Ps.* § 888, פרצה של פורענות. The inroad of divine visitation (*i.e.* pestilence) פרצה של מגפה *Ruth R.* Introd. § 6. In the sense of demoralisation, *vide Gen. R.* 26, 5, the saying of R. Simeon b. Joḥai כל פרצה שאינה מן הגדולים אינה פרצה demoralisation which does not proceed from the leaders is a demoralisation which need not give grave concern.

[5] "The inhabitants of Gedarah" (1 Chr. iv. 23) or the dwellers among the hedges—these are the Sanhedrin, who sat and made hedges or fences around the words of the Torah. (*Sifré* to Num. x. 29.) In *Baba Bathra*, 91 *b*, the reading is as follows: These are the Sanhedrin who healed the breaches of Israel. Cf. *Lev. R.* 1, 3, the exposition by R. Huna *nom.* Aḥa (*vide* Bacher, *Pal. Am.* III, 127 note) of *Avi-gdor*, 1 Chr. iv. 4, Israel had many fence-makers (guardians against sin), Moses was the father of them all.

"fences" were intended as a precautionary measure against the possible violation of the Torah generally: "Make a fence for the Law" was already a guiding principle with the men of the Great Synagogue and a leading characteristic of their contribution to the evolution of Jewish religious life[1]. The "fences" were meant also to preserve some particular aspect of Law, such as the precepts relating to family purity, and thereby reached down to the very roots of Jewish life[2].

Fences were further raised by Rabbinic authorities to restore the breaches in the Law already made; "Rab (3rd c.) found an unguarded field and fenced it in[3]" [*i.e.* he found people transgressing the Law in ignorance and instituted preventive regulations]. Moreover, these "fences" aimed at preserving throughout the generations the social order of the world[4]. But the actual fences erected round the gardens and fields were not too heavily constructed, so that in case they fell they should not crush and destroy the vegetables and plants. This fact was

[1] ועשו סייג לתורה *Aboth*, I, 1, *vide* Taylor, *Pirqe Aboth*, *ad loc.* note 1 and additional note 2.

[2] For the "fence of chastity," cp. the saying of R. Joshua b. Levi, *Jer. Berachoth*, III, 6 *c*: "A custom which fences in Israel and guards him from sin"; also *Gen. R.* 70, 12 "the people of the East fenced themselves in against unchastity"; *Synh.* 21 *a* (in the name of R. Joshua b. Korḥah) "Tamar erected a tall fence," *et cet. loc.* For the metaphor of "fence" as a check against any other failing, cf. the exposition by R. Huna in the name of R. Aḥa of Gen. xviii. 23 האף תספה (with a play upon האף) "Thou fencest in [controllest] anger, but the anger does not fence Thee in [control Thee]." *Gen. R.* 49, 8.

[3] *Ḥullin*, 110 *a*; cf. the saying of R. Z'era (4th c.). If thy nation is decaying (*sc.* in faith) stand up and fence her in, *Jer. Berachoth*, IX, *ad fin.* 13 *c*.

[4] שגדרו חכמים מפני תקון העולם *vide Mechilta* to *Mishpatim*, Friedmann, p. 100.

used in Midrashic simile to urge the need of moderation in the construction of religious "fences." In connection with the text "Ye shall not eat of it, neither shall ye touch it[1]," R. Ḥiyya (3rd and 4th c.) taught as follows: Thou shalt not make the fence of more consequence than the field itself, lest it fall down and destroy the tender plants. When the Holy One, blessed be He, said: "For in the day that thou eatest thereof thou shalt surely die[2]," Eve did not convey it [the command] in this wise, but thus: "God said, Ye shall not eat of it, *neither shall ye touch it, lest ye die*[3]." And this additional stringency brought about the violation of the divine injunction.

The serpent, says R. Samuel b. Naḥman (3rd c.), was usually found between the fences because he had broken the "fence" of the world, thereby opening the way to lawlessness and disturbing the ideal state of the Universe[4].

"A fence fenced around," and "a breach broken into[5]" are metaphorical comments of the Rabbis upon the two Bible texts: "He will keep the feet of his saints[6]"; "Surely he scorneth the scorners[7]."

"May the Lord fence in thy breach[8]" [*i.e.* may

[1] Gen. iii. 3. [2] *Ibid.* ii. 17. [3] *Gen. R.* 19, 3.

[4] Referring to the story of the Serpent in Genesis; see *Lev. R.* 26, 2. In its sense of poetic justice this saying is reminiscent of Eccl. x. 8: "And whoso breaketh an hedge, a serpent shall bite him."

[5] *Jer. Shebuoth*, II end, 33 *c*, סייגין סייגה ותרעין תרעה. In reference to the Biblical verses which state that God protects the pious (against sin) and brings the evil-doers to destruction, a Rabbi asked: Was this in conformity with divine justice? would one fence round further a fenced place, and completely break through a broken fence? And the reply of the same Rabbi was: The text tells us that if a man guards himself against sin two or three times, God continues to guard him against it.

[6] 1 Sam. ii. 9. [7] Prov. iii. 34.

[8] *Jer. Moed Katon*, III, 83 *c*, יסוג תורעתך, R. Ḥanina b. Papa's message

He guard thee from further trouble] was a Rabbi's message of comfort to a colleague in mourning.

Removing the landmark.

Reference may be made here to the extended metaphorical conception assigned by the Rabbis to the concrete Biblical command[1]: "Thou shalt not remove thy neighbour's landmark, which they of old time have set." The extension of meaning assigned to this term is to be found already in the Wisdom literature of the Bible: "Remove not the ancient landmark, which thy fathers have set[2]."

But in Rabbinic literature the prohibition of many questionable dealings in the moral and social life of Israel has been made to hinge round this land precept, and, like the companion figure of "breaking the fence," the term "removing the boundary[3] or landmark" has assumed a particular significance in the ethical vocabulary of Rabbinic literature.

Unfair competition with our fellow-men or undue interference with their source of livelihood, outmanœuvring them in a pending transaction, forcing oneself upon the notice of a vendor whilst he is in negotiation with another, attempting to undersell or overbid, offering bribes to little children in order to divert the parents' shopping from a neighbouring place to one's own, interference with another's rights and privileges, even if it be only to outwit a poor man who is roaming round a stack of corn (waiting

to R. Tanḥum b. Ḥiyya. This metaphorical expression was part of the recognised mourner's lament, *vide Berachoth*, 19 *a*, "He [*sc.* the mourner] justifies the divine decree, saying: 'Lord of the Universe, I have often sinned before Thee and Thou hast not exacted punishment from me for one in a thousand. May it be Thy will, O Lord our God, to fence in our breaches and the breaches of all Thy people, the house of Israel, in mercy.'"

[1] Deut. xix. 14. [2] Prov. xxii. 28. [3] יַהסגת גבול

for its removal by the owner and the chance of taking up eventually a forgotten sheaf which is his right), or forbidding him to glean in one's field, or placing a basket under the vine so as to preserve the windfalls for one's own use—all these offences, including even those of plagiarism and infringement of copyright, are comprised by the Rabbis within the compass of the prohibition against "removing a neighbour's boundary[1]."

The cultivation of the field was frequently carried out not by the owner himself but through a tenant-farmer, who either worked as an *Aris*, tilling the owner's ground for a fixed proportion of the produce, or as a *Ḥoker*, paying the landlord a certain rent in kind, irrespective of the yield of the crops.

The cultivation of the field.

The *Aris*—the tenant-farmer—enters to quite a considerable extent into the metaphorical imagery of the Midrash.

The *Aris* often acted selfishly and without consideration towards his landlord. Explaining the text "And Cain brought of the fruit of the ground[2]," the Rabbis add—"from the inferior kind." This might be compared to a bad *Aris* who himself ate the first fruits and presented the late (stunted) fruits to the king[3].

The bad *Aris*.

"For whose sake was it that the Holy One, blessed be He, revealed himself in Egypt? It was for the sake of Moses [whose message in God's name Pharaoh had disregarded]."

Disregarding the owner's wishes.

R. Nissim said: This might be compared to a priest

[1] *Vide Kiddushin*, 59*a*; *Baba Bathra*, 21*b*. *Peah*, chs. 5, 7, and *Ḥoshen Mishpat*, chs. 156, 237, *et cet. loc.*

[2] Gen. iv. 3.

[3] *Gen. R.* 22, 5; *Yalkut Gen.* § 35.

who had a garden of figs with a place therein which was declared to be ritually unclean[1]. Being desirous of eating some figs, he said unto someone, Go, and tell the *Aris* that the owner of the garden has ordered thee to bring him two figs. He went and told him thus. Whereupon the *Aris* replied: "What care I for the owner of the garden? Get thee to thy work." Then said the priest unto him: "I shall go myself into the garden." "But thou wilt be going into an unclean place," they objected. And he replied: "Even though there be 100 grades of uncleanliness, yet I shall go thither, so that my messenger shall not be put to shame[2]."

The *Aris*, wise and not wise.

Among the *Arisim* there were some who dealt wisely, and therefore with profit to themselves, whilst others acted unwisely, and therefore to their own disadvantage. This is illustrated in the following parable: Rabbi Ḥanina (*sc.* b. Ḥama, 3rd c.) said: There is one *Aris* who acts wisely in making his request, and there is another who does not act wisely. The wise one, seeing that he is sinking (going back) in his tenancy, summons up courage; he combs his hair, dons a clean garb, assumes a pleasant air, takes his stick in his hand, puts the ring on his finger, and makes his way to the master of the estate. "Enter thou in peace, my good tenant," is the latter's greeting. "How farest thou?" "Well," replies the tenant. "And how fares the land?" he enquires. "Thou shalt have the privilege to enjoy fully of its produce," is the answer. "And the oxen?" "Thou shalt, with God's

[1] A garden with a *beth-p'ras* (a field declared unclean on account of crushed bones carried over it from a ploughed grave).

[2] *Exod. R.* 15, 19.

grace, have the fill of their fat." "And the goats?" "Thou shalt live to see their young." "And what is it thou requirest?" asks the master. "If perchance thou hast 10 Denarii to give me?" replies the tenant. "Take 20, if thou have need of them," suggests the master.

But he who is not wise in his requests wends his way to the master of the estate, leaving his hair unkempt, his raiment soiled; and with gloomy visage thus makes his request. "How fares the land?" enquires the owner. "Would it might yield at least what has been planted therein," is the reply. "And how fare the oxen?" "They are feeble." "And what is it thou needest?" asks the master. "Perhaps thou hast 10 Denarii to give me," answers the tenant. "Thou hadst better return unto me what thou already hast of mine," remarks the master.

The goodly tenant.

R. Ḥoni says: David was the goodly tenant. At first he broke forth into a song of praise, exclaiming "The heavens declare the glory of God[1]." "By the heavens," said God, "perhaps forsooth thou hast need of something?" "And the firmament sheweth His handiwork," proceeded David. "Perhaps thou requirest aught?" he was further asked. But David continued with the enumeration of the divine praises. "Day unto day uttereth speech," etc. Whereupon the Holy One, blessed be He, said: "What is it thou wishest?" And he replied: "Who can understand his errors"—"errors I have committed in Thy presence." "These are remitted and forgiven thee," came the answer. "Cleanse Thou me from secret faults"—"from the hidden transgression." "From these too thou

[1] Ps. xix. 1.

art absolved." "Keep back Thy servant also from presumptuous sins," meaning by these the premeditated conscious sins. "Let them not have dominion over me, then shall I be upright"—*sc.* "belong to the class of those who conquer sin." "And I shall be innocent from great transgression." "Master of the Universe," continued David before the Holy One, blessed be He, "Thou art a great God, and as for me, my transgressions are great: it befits a great God to remit great sins." And this is the sense of the text[1]: "For Thy name's sake, O Lord, pardon mine iniquity, for it is great[2]."

The Landowner's relations with the *Aris.*

The relations between the Landowner and the *Aris* were generally of a friendly character. In illustration of the text: "And I will set My tabernacle among you...and I will walk among you[3]," the Rabbis adduce a parable: Unto what may this matter be likened? Unto a king who went forth in order to roam in the *Pardes* with his tenant-farmer, but the tenant was hiding himself. Whereupon the king said unto the *Aris,* "Why dost thou hide before me? Behold I am thine equal." Even so will the Holy One, blessed be He, in the world to come, range with the righteous in the Garden of Eden, but they, beholding Him, will tremble in His presence. Whereupon the Holy One, blessed be He, will say unto the righteous: "Why tremble ye before me? Behold

[1] Ps. xxv. 11.

[2] *Lev. R.* 5, 8, in *Synhedrin,* 107 *a,* the second part alone is given in contracted form, beginning: R. Dostai of Beri (in Galilee) said: Unto what may David be likened? Unto a Cuthean merchant, etc. Contrast this parable with the relationship between the landowner and husbandman in Matthew xxi. 33 f.

[3] Lev. xxvi. 11–12.

I am like unto you. But peradventure you might think that ye need no longer pay me due reverence; therefore [the text continues]: 'And I will be your God, and ye shall be My people[1].'"

The liberal landowner.

The landowner even showed himself liberal in his dealings with his tenant-farmer, as the following example indicates. On the text "Let the house of Aaron say[2]," the Rabbis adduce a parable: Unto what may this be likened? Unto a landowner who acted liberally with his tenant-farmers. At the time of reckoning he dealt with them in no niggardly manner. In the harvesting season he left them the remnants of the threshing-floor and in the time of gleaning he left them the remainders of the press. Yet we know not of his dealings within his own household. And who is it then that does know these? Surely his retainers and the inmates of his palace. And the servants of the Holy One, blessed be He, are the house of Aaron. It was they who offered the sacrifices before Him at all times. Therefore it is written: "Let the house of Aaron now say"—let them say what I did unto all who rose up against them. Korah rebelled against them, and the earth swallowed him and his followers. Uzziah in rebellion sought to offer incense, and leprosy broke forth on his forehead[3]. And wherefore did I pay him [Aaron] this reward? Because he walked before me in uprightness and studied my Law, even as it is said[4]: "The law of truth was in his mouth[5]."

[1] *Sifra* to Lev. xxvi. 12 and *Yalkut ad loc.*, where the order of the Hebrew is more correctly indicated.

[2] Ps. cxviii. 3.

[3] 2 Chr. xxvi. 19.

[4] Mal. ii. 6.

[5] *Shoḥer Tob*, *ad loc.*

Paying the owner his respects.

And yet the landowner often treated his *Aris* in an off-hand manner, as would appear from the following: R. Phineas (4th c.) said: This might be compared unto a king whose tenant-farmers and stewards came to pay him their respects. When one of them arrived to do him honour, the king enquired who he was. "It is thine *Aris*," he was told. "Then take what he has brought as his tribute," was the royal command. Another came and paid his respects. "Who is that one?" enquired the king. "It is thy steward," he was informed. "Then take his tribute," again he ordered. Then entered another. "And who is this one?" he asked. "He is neither thine *Aris* nor thy steward, but nevertheless he came to do thee honour." "Give him a stool whereon to seat himself," ordained the king. Even thus [is it with the offerings]. The sin-offering is brought to atone for a transgression [and is due to God in accordance with prescribed law], and likewise the guilt-offering, but the thank-offering is not brought as an atonement for sin [it is a free-will gift to God][1].

The field-labourer.

Many parables are drawn by the Rabbis from the sphere of the field-labourers, who worked either for the *Aris* or for the landowner himself, sometimes under the landlord's own direction, but more often under the direction of a steward or manager of the estate. The following extracts from the Midrash bear upon the field-labourer, his work and his wages and the consideration which he generally received from his employer:

The labourer—Nature's physician.

R. Ishmael and R. Akiba happened to walk through the streets of Jerusalem in the company of another

[1] *Lev. R.* 9, 4.

man, when an ailing person met them. "My Masters," said he, "wherewith can I be healed?" "Do thus and thus until thou art healed," they replied. Whereupon their companion said unto them, "And who is it that has so afflicted him?" And they replied: "It is the Holy One, blessed be He." "What, did you meddle in a matter which does not concern you?" he asked; "do you prescribe a cure when He smote!" "And what is *thy* occupation?" they rejoined. "I am a field-labourer," he replied, "behold the scythe in my hand." "Who created the vineyard?" they enquired. "The Holy One, blessed be He," he replied. "What, dost thou interfere in a matter which does not belong to thee? Seeing that He created it wilt thou cut its fruit?" And he said unto them: "See ye not the scythe I hold; if I did not go out to plough, hoe, manure and weed it, it would produce nothing." Whereupon they said: "Thou foolish one, hast thou not heard what Scripture says[1]? 'As for man, his days are as grass.' The tree could not spring up if the ground were not manured, weeded and ploughed, and even if it did spring up but were not watered, it would not live but fade into decay; even so the tree is the body, the manure is the drug, the labourer is the physician[2]."

The labourer and his wages.

R. Samuel b. Naḥmani (3rd c.) came up from Babylon to ask three questions. He found R. Jonathan Ish ha-Birah, and said unto him: What is the meaning of the text[3] "The inhabitants of the villages ceased, they ceased in Israel..."? He further enquired of him: Why does Scripture say "To the Lord our God belong mercies and forgivenesses, *for* we have

[1] Ps. ciii. 15. [2] *Midrash Sam.* Buber p. 54. [3] Judg. v. 7.

rebelled against Him[1]"? Rather should it have said: "for we have kept His Law." Whereupon Jonathan replied: Well does Scripture say thus. For, according to the common custom, when a labourer works faithfully with his master, and the latter gives him his wages, under what obligation is the workman to his employer? But when is it that the labourer is filled with gratitude? At a time when he does not work with him faithfully and yet the master does in no way withhold his wages. Therefore it is written: "To the Lord our God belong mercies and forgivenesses—*although* we have rebelled against Him[2]."

The intensity of the labourer's toil.

"And he loved Rachel more than Leah, and served with him yet seven other years[3]"

R. Judah bar Simon (4th c.) said: It is the common custom that a labourer works faithfully with his master for two or three hours and in the end he relaxes his labours. But not so was it in this case. Even as the first years were full ones, so were the last ones; and as the first were years of faithful service, so were the last also years of faithful service[4].

The labourer's hire.

"And he gave them the lands of the heathen[5]." R. Ḥanina asked of R. Ḥiyya bar Abba (3rd and 4th c.) as follows: Scripture says "And He gave them the lands of the heathen." And why? "That they might observe His statutes, and keep His laws. Praise ye the Lord." When a labourer has worked with a landowner, and when the latter with whom he toiled gives him his wages, has the workman any

[1] Dan. ix. 9, מרדנו בו ׳.

[2] *Shoḥer Tob*, 3, 3; the Hebrew word כִּי can mean either "for" or "although."

[3] Gen. xxix. 30.

[4] *Gen. R.* 70, 20.

[5] Ps. cv. 44.

cause to feel grateful? And R. Ḥiyya replied: If the labourer has worked faithfully with his master and the latter gives him his wages, the workman has no special cause to be beholden unto him. And how is it with us? God gave us the lands of the heathen, although we had not yet studied the Law, for it is said: "In order that they might observe His statutes and keep His Law." We did not yet keep the Law, and still He gave us the lands. Should we not feel grateful unto Him for having given us the lands of the heathen? And what is it that we must do? Sing before Him a song of praise, even as it is written: "Praise ye the Lord[1]."

The single coin as wages.

It is the common usage, when a labourer works with his master, ploughing, sowing, weeding and hoeing on his estate, that the master gives him but one coin and he departs. But not so is it with the Holy One, blessed be He. A man longs for children and He gives them unto him, even as it is said: "Lo, children are an heritage of the Lord[2]." He desires wisdom, and He gives it unto him, as it is said: "For the Lord giveth wisdom[3]." He wishes for worldly possessions, and He gives them unto him, as it is said: "Both riches and honour come of Thee[4]."

And so said Solomon before the Holy One, blessed be He: "Master of the Universe, when a king hires good labourers, who do their work well and he gives them their wages, what wondrous merit hath the king shown? But when is he praiseworthy? When he hires labourers who are indolent and he yet gives them their wages in full." Even so said Solomon: "Our

[1] *Shoḥer Tob*, 105, 13. [2] Ps. cxxvii. 3. [3] Prov. ii. 6.
[4] 1 Chron. xxix. 12; *Mechilta Beshallaḥ*, Friedmann, p. 41 *b*.

fathers toiled and received goodly reward, what merit is it that they had toiled and received payment? We are slothful labourers, give us a goodly wage, and this will be an act of great goodness." Hence Scripture says: "The Lord our God be with us, as He was with our fathers[1]."

The delayed reward.

And unto what was David like? Unto a labourer who all his life was working with the king who had not yet given him his wages. And the labourer was sorely grieved, saying: "Peradventure I shall receive nought." The king hired another labourer. He had only worked with him one day and the king gave him to eat and to drink and his wages in full. Then said the labourer who had worked with him all his lifetime: "If this be done unto him who has worked with the royal master one day only, how much more will be done unto me who have worked with him all the days of my life?" The casual worker departed, and he who had toiled with the master all his life began to rejoice at heart. Even so said David: "Thou hast put gladness in my heart from the time that their corn and their wine increased." When did joy enter my heart? When I beheld what Thou hadst done unto the wicked: "From the time that *their* corn and *their* wine increased[2]."

Intensive work recognised.

When R. Abun the son of R. Ḥiyya (4th c.) died, R. Z'era came and delivered the funeral address from the following text[3]: "Sweet is the sleep of the labourer." Unto what might the case of R. Abun the son of R. Ḥiyya be likened? Unto a king who possessed a vineyard and hired many labourers to

[1] 1 Kings viii. 57; *Shoḥer Tob*, 26, 4.
[2] Ps. iv. 7; *Shoḥer Tob*, 37, 3.
[3] Eccl. v. 11.

tend it. Among these was one labourer who greatly excelled all the rest. What did the king do? He took him by the hand and ranged throughout the length and breadth of the vineyard. At eventide the labourers came to receive their wages and that workman too came with them. The king paid him his wages in full. Whereupon the labourers began to feel aggrieved, saying: We have toiled throughout the whole day and that one toiled but two hours, and yet the king gave him his reward in full. Then said the king unto them: Wherefore are ye grieved? This man hath completed by his diligence within the two hours what you in your toil had not accomplished throughout the whole of the day. Even so did R. Abun the son of Ḥiyya accomplish in the sphere of study at the age of 28 what a veteran disciple could not have mastered in a hundred years[1].

The long-service labourer.

"And I will have respect unto you[2]." The Rabbis spake in parable. Unto what may this matter be likened? Unto a king who had many labourers and among them was one who had done work for him for many days. When the labourers came in to receive their wages, that workman came in with them. Whereupon the king said unto that workman: My son, I will have respect unto thee and deal with thee at my leisure. These others, though greater in numbers have done but little work for me, and unto them I have to give but small wages; but as for thee, I have large reckoning to make with thee. Even so did Israel in this world claim their reward from God, and the

[1] *Kohel. R.* 5, 11.

[2] Lev. xxvi. 9. The Hebrew term ופניתי, "and I shall turn," is taken as containing a reference to פנאי, "leisure."

other nations also sought to obtain their guerdon. Whereupon God said unto Israel, My children, I shall have respect unto you and deal with you in my leisure. The other nations did but little work for me, and I have small reward for them, but with you I have a long reckoning to make. Therefore it is said: "And I shall turn to you in my leisure[1]."

General field improvements.

As to the more general field improvements, some of them were of the ordinary kind, and others of a more specific character, such as the digging of wells for the purpose of irrigation and the levelling of the surface-soil by the removal of unnecessary mounds and the filling up of useless trenches. These field operations supplied the Rabbis with effective similes.

The following may serve as an example of a simile taken from ordinary field improvement:

Rabbi Simeon b. Joḥai (Tanna, 2nd c.) said: Israel will never behold *Gehinnom*. Unto what may this be likened? Unto a king who had a field of poor quality. Some people came and hired it for ten *khor* of wheat per year. They manured it, dug it up, watered it and cleared it, but could only make it produce one *khor* in the year. How is that? enquired the king. And they said unto him: "Our Royal Master, thou hast knowledge of the field which thou gavest us; formerly thou couldst not make it yield anything, but now that we have manured it and cleared it and watered it, we could just make it yield one *khor* of wheat only. Even so will the children of Israel say before the Holy One, blessed be He, Master of the Universe, Thou knowest how the

[1] *Sifra* to Lev. xxvi. 9.

Yeṣer Hara, the Evil Inclination, enticeth us, as it is written[1]: "For he knoweth our *Yeṣer*[2]."

The opening of wells by the purchaser of a field of no great intrinsic value, and the planting therein of gardens and parks, thus increasing the worth of his possessions, provided a Rabbi of the second century with an illustrative parable, portraying the deep chagrin felt by the Egyptians when they began to realise the true value attaching to Israel whom they had hurriedly sent out of their land.

Irrigation.

"And the heart of Pharaoh was turned[3]." R. José the Galilean said: To what might this be compared? To a man who inherited a farm requiring a *khor* of seed, and he sold it for a small price. The purchaser opened some wells in it, and planted gardens and parks. Thereupon the seller began to feel sore[4] because he had disposed of his inheritance for a trifle. Even so was it with the Egyptians, who sent Israel out of their land and did not realise the treasure they were thereby losing. It is of them that the text speaks[5]: "Thy shoots [*i.e.* they whom thou didst send forth][6] are an orchard of pomegranates[7]."

But irrigation in Palestine was carried out not only by artificial means through wells, aqueducts and ditches[8], but also in a natural way through the regular

[1] Ps. ciii. 14. [2] *Aboth di R. Nathan*, ch. xv. [3] Ex. xiv. 5.

[4] התחיל ליחנק, *lit.* like choking. [5] Cant. iv. 13.

[6] שְׁלָחַיִךְ pointing to שלח.

[7] *Mechilta, ad loc.* p. 26 f.; *Pesikta*, 84 *a*, *vide* Bacher, *Tan.* I, 370. Practically the same in *Cant. R.* to iv. 12 in the name of R. Jonathan (3rd c.); R. Simeon b. Johai (T., 2nd c.) uses the figure of an inherited *palace*, in which the purchaser discovered hidden treasures; *vide* Bacher, *Ag. Tan.* II, 142. R. Levi (3rd c.) (*Exod. R.* 20, 5) uses the parable of a field converted by the buyer into a beautiful and well laid-out vineyard.

[8] A field so irrigated through נחלים and שלוליות was known as שדה בית השלחין.

rain supply[1]. The Rabbis made use of these facts connected with irrigation in a Midrashic parable in order to express the favoured position of Palestine in this respect as compared with Egypt and Babylon.

This might be compared unto a king walking by the roadside. Seeing a certain man of noble descent engaged in work, he assigned him a servant to wait upon him. When he saw yet another man of noble descent and delicately nurtured engaged in hard toil, since he knew him and his ancestors, he said unto him: I feel compelled to undertake to help thee with mine own hand and supply thee with food.

Even so did God assign agencies to serve the other lands; Egypt derives its water supply from the Nile, and Babylon from the rivers. But not so is it the case with the land of Israel[2]: "It drinketh water as the rain of heaven cometh down[3]."

Clearing a mound.

Again the clearing of a mound of earth from a field—a rigorous task demanding exceptional perseverance on the part of the labourer—was used by another Rabbi as an encouragement to the would-be toiler in the uneven field of the Torah.

"His head is as the most fine gold, his locks are bushy[4]," says Scripture. R. Joḥanan of Sepphoris (3rd c.), playing upon the resemblance of *Taltalim* "bushy" or "wavy" to *Tel, Tillim* "heaps" or "mounds," interpreted this verse as a parable taken

[1] A field watered in this natural manner was known as שדה בית הבעל, an expression which was primarily connected with the heathen idea of the Baal god and afterwards assumed a metaphorical meaning; *vide* Krauss, *Talmudische Archaeologie*, II, pp. 163–4, and notes, also Robertson Smith, *Religion of the Semites*, p. 102.

[2] *Vide* Deut. xi. 10–11.

[3] *Sifré Ekeb* to Deut. xi. 10–11.

[4] Cant. v. 11, קוצותיו תלתלים.

from a mound of earth (which was to be levelled and cleared). The foolish one, what does he say? "Who is able to level this [mound]?" But the wise man says, "I will carry off two loads by day and two loads by night and to-morrow I shall do likewise, till I shall have levelled the whole of it." Even so, the foolish one says, "Who can master the whole of the Law?" [*Nezikin*, 30 chapters, *Kelim*, 30 chapters, and so forth.] But the wise man says, "I shall learn two laws to-day, and two to-morrow, until I have mastered it all[1]."

The mound and the trench.

Ahasuerus, says R. Abba b. Kahana (3rd and 4th c.), was delighted with Haman's offer to remove Israel from the country without any labour or cost. Just as the owner of a field, with an awkward mound in it, gladly accepts the offer of a neighbour who, in order to refill a ditch in his own estate, is willing to remove free of charge the mound in his neighbour's plot.

"And the king said unto Haman, The silver is given to thee, the people also, to do with them as it seemeth good to thee[2]." R. Abba (3rd c.) said: To what may this be likened? To two men, of whom the one had a mound in his field and the other a trench. The owner of the trench said, "Would that I might obtain this mound for money!" The pro-

[1] *Cant. R. ad loc.*; *Midrash Sam.* ed. Buber, p. 58. In *Lev. R.* 19, 2 the expressions used for removing the mound are לְקַצּוֹת...קוֹצֵץ, in *Yalkut Cant.* § 989 לְפַנּוֹת...קוֹדֵחַ. R. Jannai (3rd c.) uses the simile of a loaf of bread suspended in the air (לככר נקוב שתלוי באויר) and where an effort is needed to reach it. R. Levi (3rd and 4th c.) employs the figure of a perforated basket which is ordered to be filled with water: לְקַרְסְטָל נקוב ששכרו בעליו פועלים למלאתו מים, *vide* Buber's notes *ad loc.*

[2] Esther iii. 11.

prietor of the mound said: "O that I might procure that trench for money!" After a time the two met. "Sell me thy mound," said the owner of the trench. "Take it for nothing," replied the other, "only take it[1]!"

Sowing and sprouting of grain.

Even more numerous similes are suggested by the actual products of the field. Some similes in illustration of important principles of Jewish belief are taken by the Rabbis from the sowing and the springing up of the grain and similar products; this phenomenon was used by R. Meïr (2nd c.) in explaining to a distinguished heathen enquirer his views upon the doctrine of the Resurrection—an eschatological problem which occupied and troubled the popular mind in the early centuries of the Common Era.

Queen Cleopatra asked of R. Meïr as follows: "We know," said she, "that the dead will live again, for it is written, 'And they of the city shall flourish like the grass of the earth[2].' But when they rise, will they rise up naked or clothed?" And he said unto her, "We can deduce the answer by argument [*sc. Kal Vaḥomer—a minore ad majus*] from the growth of wheat-grain. If the wheat-grain, though put into the ground naked, comes forth arrayed in many garments, how much more so [may we expect] will the righteous, who are buried in their garments [*sc.* rise up again clothed[3]]?"

[1] והלואי, *Megillah*, 14 *a* top. *Vide* Bacher, *Pal. Am.* II, 509.

[2] Ps. lxxii. 16.

[3] *Synhedrin*, 90 *b*; in *Kethuboth*, 111 *b*, the tradent is R. Ḥiyya ben Joseph, *vide* Bacher, *Tan.* II, 69 (note); cf. 1 Cor. xv. 35–8 and John xii. 24. The sowing of wheat bare was the more general custom, although even wheat was *sometimes*, as *e.g.* barley and lintels were *always*, sown with the husks on, *vide Ḥullin*, 117 *b*, 119 *b*,

תני דבי ר׳ ישמעאל (ויקרא יא׳) על כל זרע זרוע כדרך שבני אדם מוציאין לזריעה חטה בקליפתה ושעורין בקליפתן ועדשים בקליפתן:

A somewhat similar illustration by R. Jonathan in the name of R. Jonathan of Beth-Gubrin (3rd c.) affords a most interesting indication of the great value attached by the Rabbis to Nature similes for explanatory purposes. In reply to a question by a Cuthean[1]: "How will they [*i.e.* the dead] rise [*sc.* on the day of Resurrection]?" he [R. Jonathan] answered that they would arise clothed in their garments. "How can you prove it to me?" he asked. And he said: "I shall answer thee neither from the Scriptures nor from the Mishnah, but by an example taken from the domain of Nature. Hast thou ever sown beans?" "Yes," he replied. "How didst thou sow them, undressed or dressed?" "Undressed," he replied. "And how did they come up, dressed or undressed?" "Dressed." "Thine ear doth not hear what thy mouth speaks," retorted the questioner. "If the beans, though sown undressed, spring up dressed, the dead who left this world clothed, how much more so will they come to life again clothed[2]!"

Of beans.

A Rabbi of the 3rd century also used the simile of the kernel under the clod, which grows fast once it has sprouted forth, to typify the student of Rabbinic lore whose reputation once it has risen, begins to spread far and wide[3].

The kernel under the clod.

To possess one large field which might conveniently accommodate different kinds of produce, including vegetables, was generally regarded, on account of its time- and labour-saving advantages, as a source

Intensive *v.* extensive culture.

1 "Cuthean" is a member of the sect of Samaritans, but here, as in many other places, it is probably equivalent to "Min" a Jewish infidel, or a Jew-Christian. The change in appellation was due to the censor's influence.

2 *Kohel. R.* to v, 10.

3 *Taanith*, 4 *a*, האי צורבא מרבנן דמי לפרצידא דתותי קלא דכיון דנבט נבט

of wealth and blessing to the owner, whilst to have the same amount of produce spread over a number of fields, involving, as it necessarily must have done, a waste of effort, was from the owner's point of view a source of weakness. This agricultural fact supplied R. Meïr with an illustrative simile for enforcing his own particular view as to the extreme usefulness of receiving one's general instruction from one Master only:

R. Meïr (2nd c.) used to say: "Whosoever learns Torah from one teacher, to what is he like? To a man possessing one field, part of which he sowed with wheat, part with barley, part with olive trees, and part with other trees. He is found to be full of wealth and blessing. But when one receives instruction from two or three teachers, he is like unto him who possesses many fields. He sows one field with wheat and one with barley. In one he plants olive trees, and in another trees of other kinds. This man has scattered himself over many lands, reaping no profit and gaining no blessing[1]."

The different species of vegetation.

But Rabbinic metaphor and simile associated with the field clustered also very largely around the different species of vegetation, and were based chiefly upon their peculiarities of form, appearance and taste.

[1] *Aboth di R. Nathan*, ch. viii. p. 18 *b*; *vide* Bacher, *Ag. Tan.* II, 20. Cf. *Gen. R.* 82, 8, the reply given by two pupils of R. Joshua during the period of religious persecution בשעת השמד to a Roman officer *στρατιώτης* סרדיוט אחד who asked for an explanation of the text Prov. xxviii. 19: "He that tilleth his ground shall have plenty of bread. But he that followeth after vain things shall have poverty enough." And they said unto him: "He is better off who rents as Ḥoker one field, manures and hoes it, than he who rents as Ḥoker many fields and lets them lie fallow." אמרו לו טוב מי שהוא חוכר שדה אחת ומזבלה ומעדרה ממי שהוא חוכר שדות הרבה ומובירן

The grass of the field has in Midrashic literature the usual symbolic significance which it suggested to the Prophets and Psalmists of the Bible. It typifies the transitoriness of human life. "The sons of men are like unto the grass of the field; some blossom and others fade," said Rab (2nd and 3rd c.) to R. Hamnuna (3rd c.)[1]. But this same object supplied the Rabbis also with another kind of simile, conveying a slightly modified conception. Commenting upon the text: "And they two were alone in the field[2]" Rabbi Judah (3rd c.) said, in the name of Rab: In the estimation of King Jeroboam and Ahijah the Shilonite, all scholars were as worthless as the grass of the field[3]. The grass.

And the similes of the Midrash extend to other products of the field:

When Ben Azzai (2nd c.) desired to characterise the insignificance which, in his opinion, marked all Jewish scholars with the sole exception of the bald-headed Akiba, he said that they all appeared to him "as the husk of a garlic[4]." Garlic.

Again, in order to convey the idea that the scholar of the future may be recognised by his utterances during childhood, a thought expressed somewhat more generally in the Book of Proverbs[5], a Rabbi employed an apparently well-known proverb[6] about the growth of the pumpkin in the field. "A young pumpkin is known by its stalk," said Rabbah to The pumpkin

[1] *Erubin*, 54 *a*. [2] 1 Kings xi. 29.

[3] *Synhedrin*, 102 *a*. There is an interesting simile in Apocryphal Literature (*Adam and Eve*, x. 1), "But Eve heard and believed and went out of the water of the river, and her flesh was (trembling) like grass, from the chill of the water."

[4] *Bechoroth*, 58 *a*. [5] Prov. xx. 11. [6] היינו דאמרי אינשי.

Abbaye and Raba, when, pleased with their clever reply as to the place where God dwelt[1], he foretold their future greatness in Rabbinic lore[2].

Turnip.

The metaphorical expression "the Turnip," *Halifton*, was used in Rabbinic writings to designate the priest whose head was of abnormal shape, wide above and narrow below, resembling the upper slice of a turnip[3].

The cabbage.

The ruin of the righteous in the devastation which overtakes the sinful is conveyed in Midrashic metaphor by the agricultural dictum "With the shrub the cabbage is smitten[4]." The same vegetable supplies a simile illustrating Israel's relation to his adversaries: To the verse, "My children are desolate, because the enemy hath prevailed[5]," R. Aibo (4th c.) said: It is like a cabbage stem, the larger the cabbage grows, the smaller becomes the stem[6].

Bitter herbs.

The subtle nature of Israel's gradual enslavement in the land of Egypt is expressed by a simile taken

1 Raba pointed to the top of the roof. Abbaye went outside and pointed heavenwards.

2 *Berachoth*, 48 *a*, בוצין בוצין מקיניה ידיע, the reading of *Aruch* and *Rashi*. In Babylonian dialect בוצין is a young pumpkin in contrast to קרא, the full-grown one. Cf. the proverb, *Megillah*, 12 *a*, איהו בקרי ואתתיה בבוציני, "He (*sc.* the husband) occupies himself with the old pumpkins and his wife with the young ones," *i.e.* the wife follows the husband's example and bent: a faithless husband makes a faithless wife. The editions have מקטפיה, "by the sap which oozes out of it." בוצינא מקטפיה ידע, *vide* Rabbinovicz, *Dikduke Sopherim*, *Variae lectiones*, *et cet.*, *ad loc.* "What oozes out" would perhaps be a better simile for the "utterances" of the young scholars.

3 גרגלידא דליפתא, *Bechoroth*, 43 *b*, cf. *Synhedrin*, 19 *b* below: "And he (*sc.* Boaz) was startled" וילפת (Ruth iii. 8). Rab (3rd c.) said: His body became soft like (boiled) turnip heads כראשי לפתות.

4 בהדי הוצא לקי כרבא, *Baba Kama*, 92 *a*.

5 Lam. i. 16.

6 *Lament. R. ad loc.*

from the characteristics of the bitter herb, technically called "*maror*," and used for ritual purposes during Passover. "And they made their lives bitter with hard service[1]." R. Samuel b. Naḥmani (3rd c.) said in the name of R. Jonathan[2] (3rd c.): "Why are the Egyptians likened unto the bitter herb (*maror*)? To tell thee that just as the *maror* has a mild taste when first eaten, and grows more pungent towards the end, even so were the Egyptians kindly in the beginning, but grew harder in the end[3]."

The lentil.

The lentil too provides an interesting series of similes, which moreover have an additional value for the sidelight they throw upon early Jewish mourning customs. "And Esau came from the field and behold he was weary[4]." The Rabbis say: This was the day on which Abraham died, and Jacob our ancestor prepared a dish of lentils to comfort Isaac his father. And why of lentils? In the West [*i.e.* Palestine] it was said in the name of Raba bar Mari (3rd c.): Just as the lentil has no mouth [*i.e.* slit] even so has the mourner no mouth [*i.e.* in his anguish he is struck dumb]. A variant explanation is the following: Just

1 Ex. i. 14 וימררו, they made it like מרור the bitter herbs.

2 R. Jonathan b. Eleazar.

3 *Pesaḥim*, 39 *a*, *vide* Bacher, *Pal. Am.* I, 79; in *Jer. Pesaḥim*, II, 5 (where the author is R. Ḥiyya, in the name of R. Hoshaya, and where the term used is חזרת, which according to these Rabbis is the real species required for the performance of the rite), it proceeds to explain: the Egyptians were considerate at first, as it is said (Gen. xlvii. 6) "In the best of the land make thy father and thy brethren to dwell." Cf. the Rabbinic interpretation of the preceding verse (Ex. i. 13) "And the Egyptians made the children of Israel to serve בפרך *with rigour*" by enticing them בפה רך "with soft speech": cf. the proverb מריר עיסקך כי חסא, thy ware is as bitter (*i.e.* thy goods are disliked) as lettuce, *Berachoth* 56 *a*.

4 Gen. xxv. 29.

as the lentil is round and rolls along, so does mourning roll on and go the round of the inhabitants of the world[1].

Poppy plants.

There is a simile in the style of the Book of Proverbs taken from the poppy plants. Rab Ḥisda (3rd c.) said: Faithlessness in the house is like a worm in the poppy plant. Anger in the house is like a worm in the poppy plant[2].

Pepper.

Pepper, either by itself, or mixed with salt and spice, is used in simile or composite comparison, to symbolise either a certain part of the Jewish law, or a certain type of Talmudic scholar.

Why is the Torah compared to salt, the Mishnah to pepper and the Talmud to spices? The world cannot exist without salt, or without pepper or without spices, and the rich man provides himself with the

[1] *Baba Bathra*, 16 *b*. There are different versions of the simile, see also *Yalkut Gen.* 110; cf. the following: Just as the lentil is spherical in shape, even so is the world made like a sphere. Even as the lentil has no aperture, so is the mourner (according to Jewish law) forbidden to open his mouth in speech (*Gen. R.* 63, 14). Concerning lentils as food for mourners, *vide J. Q. R.* vol. VI, p. 227, the reference in Jerome to this custom of the Palestinian Jews of his time; *vide* also *Jer. Berachoth*, III, 1, כד דמך ר׳ שמואל בר רבי יצחק קביל רבי זעירא אבילוי ואייכלון טלופחין מימר כמה דהוא מנהגא, which the commentaries explain to mean "when R. Samuel died, R. Z'era kept mourning for him, and they ate lentils according to custom." But see the explanation of the passage by Bacher, in *Hagoren*, I, p. 64, who translates it: "R. Z'era received the mourners and gave them lentils to eat [prob. in the סעודת הבראה] according to custom." *Pirké di R. Eliezer*, ch. XXXV. ר׳ אליעזר אומר העדשים מאכל צרה ואבל הם; *Pseudo-Jonathan Targ.* Gen. XXV. 29. Lentils were used also on festive occasions, *vide Beṣa*, 14 *b*, *Tanḥuma* to Gen. XXV. 29, שמקדם היו מכניסין אל האבל עדשים ולבית המשתה עדשים and *Gen. R.* 63, 14, but no indication is given of the symbolic reason (if any) for such use.

[2] *Sotah*, 3 *b*:

זנותא בביתא כי קריא לשומשמי: תוקפא בביתא כי קריא לשומשמי

three. Even so the world cannot exist without the Scriptures, without the Mishnah, or without the Talmud. (Man therefore should become possessed of them all[1].)

The flax, as a common product of the field, has given rise to some Midrashic similes. The appearance of the flax-stalks after they are soaked, beaten and baked, was ironically employed to describe a woman's hair. R. Ishmael bar José (Tanna, 2nd c.) in trying to discover some redeeming feature in an otherwise not too prepossessing woman, in order to regain for her the regard of her husband, who had referred her to him for his opinion, enquired with a touch of humour if her hair were beautiful. The reply was that it resembled flax-stalks[2]. Flax.

But the following example of a flax simile is more replete with poetic beauty and lofty religious thought, and forms a better index of the use made of this agricultural produce for the purpose of comparison. "The Lord trieth the righteous[3]. R. José b. Ḥanina (3rd c.) said: When the flax worker knows that his flax is good, he keeps on beating it, and it grows better; he continues to flog it and it improves (it acquires more body). But when he knows that his flax is bad he scarcely beats it at all, and then it

[1] *Soferim*, 15, 8. Cf. and contrast the following: Salt is cheap, pepper is dear; the world can exist without pepper, but not without salt. (?R. Samuel b. Naḥman of the 3rd c.) *Jer. Horayoth*, 3, *ad fin.* 48 *c* top; Rabina (3rd and 4th c.) said: Hence the popular proverb "One grain of pepper is worth more than a basketful of pumpkins," היינו דאמרי אינשי טבא חדא פלפלתא חריפתא ממלי צנא קרי, *i.e.* a sharp, reasoning mind is worth more than acquired learning, *Megillah*, 7 *a*. Cp. the use of פלפלן for the keen dialectician as contrasted with סודרן the systematic collector of traditions.

[2] *Nedarim*, 66 *b*.

[3] Ps. xi. 5.

bursts. Even so does the Holy One, blessed be He, not try the wicked, but only the righteous[1]."

The farmers' disappointments.

The vegetable field did not always realise the hopes placed on it by the anxious farmer. Very frequently this disappointment was due to natural causes such as the failure of the crop, but often it was the result of trespass committed by field-plunderers, an occurrence not infrequent in those early days, if one may judge by the number of similes drawn from this practice. The disappointments incidental to agricultural life were used by the Rabbis for illustrative and comparative purposes.

A vegetable field faded.

Israel disappointed the fond hopes which God had placed in them, by making a golden calf soon after the Revelation. R. Ḥama, the son of R. Ḥanina (3rd c.), said: "This might be compared to one who had a bed full of vegetables, but rising up early in the morning, he found they had withered[2]."

Gone into seed.

"And in the morning thou makest thy seed to blossom[3]." Rabbi Ḥama and R. Ḥanina and R. Samuel b. Naḥman (3rd c.) expounded this verse as

[1] *Gen. R.* 32, 3; *vide* Bacher, *Pal. Am.* I, 439; in a more concise and clearer form in *Cant. R.* to הרועה בשושנים, II, 16, where there are analogous parables by Jonathan (instead of Joḥanan as given in the text) who takes his simile from the potter exhibiting his wares and Eleazar, who uses the simile of the two cows of different strength; *vide* Bacher, *Pal. Am.* I, 439 note. In *Cant. R.* to II, 16, the parable is as follows: R. José b. Ḥanina (3rd c.) said: When the flax is hard, the flax worker does not beat it too much, but when his flax is good, the more he beats it the better it becomes. Even so does the Lord not try the wicked, but only the righteous (Ps. xi. 5).

[2] *Lev. R.* 18, 3, *vide* Bacher, *Pal. Am.* I, 532, based on Is. xvii. 10–11; R. Samuel b. Naḥman (3rd c.) said: This might be compared to one who had a bed full of flax. He rose up early in the morning and found it had bolled, ומצאה גבעולין (and therefore it was no longer good for linen).

[3] Is. xvii. 11, ובבקר זרעך תפריחי.

follows: One of them said: To what might this be compared? To a king who had a garden full of excellent fruit. He entered at twilight, looked at it and exclaimed: "How goodly is all this! On the morrow I shall sell it to the merchants, and fill my purse with gold coins." On the morrow he went to gaze at the garden, and found that its products had become over-ripe and seedy[1]. "May a blight fall upon thee[2]," he said; "in the evening thou wast fair and praiseworthy, and in the morning behold thou art undone." Even so did God say unto Israel: "And in the morning thou makest thy seed to flower[3]."

Despoliation of the garden

Garden spoliation is thus employed by the Rabbis for Biblical illustration: "Where is Abel thy brother?" asked God. And Cain replied: "I know not. Wherefore seekest thou him from me? It is I who seek him from thee." Whereupon the Holy One, blessed be He, said unto him: "O thou wicked one, the voice of thy brother's blood cries unto me from the earth." This might be likened unto one who entered a garden, gathered some cabbages and ate them up. The owner of the garden ran after him, saying: "What hast thou in thy hand?" "I have nothing," the latter replied. "But," remonstrated the owner, "are not thy hands soiled[4]?"

and the field.

Again, commenting upon the text: "And ye perish quickly from off the good land which the Lord giveth you[5]," the Rabbis say: This will be brought about through exile following upon exile. Both the ten tribes and the tribes of Judah and Benjamin were

[1] שהפריגה = שהפריחה. [2] תיפח רוחך.

[3] *Num. R.* 7, 4; *vide* Bacher, *Pal. Am.* I, 461.

[4] *Vide Gen. R.* 22, 9. [5] Deut. xi. 17.

exiled many times. R. Joshua b. Korḥah (2nd c.) said: This might be compared to a robber, who entered the farmer's field and cut down the standing corn. The owner took no heed. He cut the ears of corn, and yet the owner cared not, until the robber had filled his basket and gone out. Even so it is said[1]: "Shall there be no more gloom to her that was in anguish? Now the former hath lightly afflicted the land of Zebulun and the land of Naphtali, but the latter hath dealt a more grievous blow by the way of the sea beyond the Jordan, in the district of the nations[2]."

The grain in Midrashic poetry.

We now come to the more important part played by the field in supplying material for comparison, *viz.* the field as the source from which the staff of life is obtained. There is a whole series of Midrashic similes, some reminiscent of Biblical images, and others purely Rabbinic in conception, which are drawn from the produce of the grain in its varied stages of development, beginning with the ears of corn, and ending with their conversion into bread.

Since a large number of these similes is based upon a figurative expression in the Song of Songs[3], a book which Rabbinic authority explained as an allegory referring to Israel, it was but natural that many of the Midrashic metaphors and similes taken from the corn-field should be employed in praise of Israel.

"Israel is the grain of the world[4]," is an expressive metaphor in Midrashic poetry. And just as wheat is

[1] Is. viii. 23.
[2] *Sifré Ekeb*, § 43 *ad fin.*, *vide* Bacher, *Ag. Tan.* II, 317.
[3] vii. 3.
[4] *Pesikta Rabb.* x, p. 36 *a*.

an absolute necessity, and forms the mainstay of life, so Israel is the world's mainstay and its life-power.

Wheat a necessity of life.

Commenting upon the allegorical interpretation of the text in the Song of Songs already referred to as an allusion to Israel, R. Huna (4th c.) said in the name of R. Iddi (Bab. Am., 4th c.): Is not a heap of kernels of the stone pine (fruit of the cedar), or a heap of pepper better than a store of wheat; and as the Holy One, blessed be He, loves Israel, ought He not rather to call them a heap of pepper? But, continued the Rabbi, the world can exist without the fruit of the cedar and without pepper; it cannot exist without wheat. If the world were short of the fruit of the cedar or of pepper, what would it matter? But, if wheat should be lacking, then could there be no life even for an hour[1].

Its importance.

The superiority of the small ear of corn over the tall and haughty stalk on which it grows, the value attached to it by the owner, when bringing the produce into the storehouse and measuring it out at sowing and harvest time, the inclusion of the offal of the wheat with the grain when put up for sale are all employed by Midrashic preachers to illustrate the theory of Israel's superiority over the other nations, notwithstanding the latter's boastful claims to higher recognition. The same simile is also used to account

[1] *Pesikta Rabb.* ch. x, p. 35 *a*; in *Cant. R.* it is quoted anonymously; in *Tanḥuma ki Tissa* the author is given as R. Iddi; *Yalkut Cant.* in the name of R. Jacob bar Iddi; in *Midrash Tehillim* to ii. 12 the simile reads thus: "As the world cannot exist without wheat, so it cannot do without Israel"; and the expressive phrase is used שהם חיותם של עולם. "Moisture-absorbing wheat" is a figure used by R. José b. Ḥanina (3rd c.) in explanation of Is. lxi. 6; *vide Cant. R.* to vii. 3 and Bacher, *Pal. Am.* I, 431.

for the repeated divinely-ordained numberings of the Jewish people in their early career, as well as for the inclusion, amongst those numbered, of the different classes constituting the people of the Lord.

The growing grain.

In exposition of the wheat simile from the Song of Songs[1] the Rabbis say: This might be compared to a grain of wheat. The grain of wheat rises straight up like a stick[2], its stalk is long, its leaves are long and wide, and the grain is on the top of the stalk. "For me the field is sown," says the stalk boastfully. "No, for our sake is the field sown," retort the leaves. "To-morrow," replies the grain, "harvesting will come[3], and then will all be convinced for whose sake it is that the field has been sown." The field yielded a goodly crop. And when harvest came, the straw went into the fire, the stubble to the wind, the thorns were thrown to the flames, but the ears were gathered for storage, and whoever took them up kissed them[4].

Even so do the nations say, "It is for our sake that the world has been created." But in the time to come, when the Day of Judgment draws nigh, they will be dragged down to *Gehinnom*, as it is said[5], "And the people shall be as the burnings of the lime, as thorns cut down, that are burned in the fire"; and as it is further said, "Put ye in the sickle, for the harvest is ripe[6]." But Israel alone will remain, as it is said, "The Lord will lead him alone[7]."

[1] Cant. vii. 3. [2] מִתַּמֵּר ועולה כמקל. [3] הגרן יבוא

[4] Ref. to נשקו בר Ps. ii. 12, "kiss or huddle the corn."

[5] Is. xxxiii. 12. [6] Joel iii. 13.

[7] Deut. xxxii. 12, ה' בדד ינחנו, perhaps "will let him remain" or "give him rest," *vide Shoḥer Tob* to ii. 12.

Bringing the grain into the store-house.

R. Ḥanina (3rd c.) basing his discourse on the same text from the Song of Songs[1] said, in reference to the explanation of R. Simeon b. Lakish (3rd c.): Why is Israel compared to wheat? To tell thee that it is with him as with the farmer who has in his house a steward[2]; when he comes to reckon with him, he does not say, "How many baskets[3] of straw, or how many bundles of stubble dost thou bring into the store-house?" He gives him the thorns for fuel, and casts the straw to the wind. What then is it that he does say? "Set thy mind on how many *Khor* of wheat thou bringest into the store, because that alone is the source of life to the world."

The farmer is the Holy One, blessed be He, to whom the whole world belongs, as it is said: "The earth is the Lord's, and the fulness thereof[4]." The steward is Moses...What said the Holy One, blessed be He, unto him? "Regard not the heathens, for they are like straw," as it is said: "It consumeth them [*sc.* the heathen Egyptians][5] as the stubble." And what fate awaits the straw? It is cast out to float upon the water, even as Scripture says: "Pharaoh's chariots and his host hath He cast into the sea[6]." And the nations are further likened unto thorns. But Israel is compared to wheat; and therefore "The Lord spoke unto Moses, saying: When thou takest the sum of the children of Israel[7]."

1 Cant. vii. 3. In *Cant. R. ad loc.* given as the saying of R. Nehemiah *nom.* R. Abin; these passages have reference to the controversies between the different Christian sects, *vide* Bacher, *Pal. Am.* III, 412.

2 בן בית.

3 מְשַׁפְּלוֹת, wicker-baskets carried on a pole over the shoulder.

4 Ps. xxiv. 1. 5 Ex. xv. 7. 6 Ex. xv. 4.

7 Ex. xxx. 11 f.; *Shoḥer Tob* to ii. 12.

Measuring the grain at sowing and harvest.

R. Simeon b. Lakish (3rd c.) expounding the simile from the Song of Songs said: Just as wheat, when taken to be sown, goes out by measure, and when gathered[1] is brought in by measure; even so the Israelites, going down to Egypt, came thither by number, and returning, went out by number[2].

The different kinds of grain.

The Holy One, blessed be He, said unto Moses: The idolaters are worthless grain[3], as it is said: "And the people shall be as the burnings of lime; as thorns cut down[4]." Therefore have no care for their number. But the Israelites are righteous, all of them are as wheat for storage[5], as it is said: "Thy people also shall be all righteous[6]," and as it is further said: "Thou art all fair, my love[7]." Therefore be thou heedful of the number of the Israelites. Moses acted thus. He counted them in order to find how many *Khor* they contained, even as it is said: "Take ye the sum of all the congregation of the children of Israel[8]."

Measuring the grain for sale.

R. Simeon b. Lakish (3rd c.) commenting upon the text from the Song of Songs said: As with the wheat, where the gleanings are included in the measure, so is it with Israel [*sc. all* are reckoned in] "from the hewer of thy wood unto the drawer of thy water[9]."

[1] *Cant. R.* and *Pesikta* add "unto the threshing floor."

[2] *Shoḥer Tob* to Ps. ii. 13. In *Num. R.* 1, 4 it is given anonymously: As the wheat goes into the store by number, so did the Holy One, blessed be He, say that the Israelites should be numbered every hour, therefore is it written (Cant. vii. 3): "Thy belly is like a heap of wheat." In *Cant. R. ad loc.* and in *Pesikta R.* ch. x, p. 36 *b*, the author is R. Isaac (3rd and 4th c.), see Bacher, *Pal. Am.* II, 272.

[3] טינופות.

[4] Is. xxxiii. 12.

[5] Instead of חטים אגודיהם read חטים אֲגורין הם, *i.e.* wheat fit for storage, of superior quality.

[6] Is. lx. 21.

[7] Cant. iv. 7.

[8] Num. i. 2; *Num. R.* ch. 4 *init.*

[9] Deut. xxix. 11; *Cant. R.* to vii. 3, *vide* Bacher, *Pal. Am.* I, 402.

The importance of proper storehouses to the owner of agricultural products is used as a simile to convey a lofty religious conception and impart fresh meaning to a Bible text. Store-houses.

"The fear of the Lord is pure, enduring for ever[1]": Thou mightest come across a man pursuing the study of Midrash, *Halachoth* and *Aggadoth*, yet if he has not the fear of sin, he is possessed of nothing. This may be likened to one who says unto his friend: "I have a thousand measures of grain, a thousand of oil and a thousand of wine." Whereupon the friend replies: "Hast thou storehouses into which to put these? If thou hast, then everything is thine. But if thou hast them not, thou art possessed of nothing."

Even so when a man has learned all things, it may be said unto him: If thou hast the fear of sin, everything is thine, as it is written[2]: "And the stability of thy times shall be abundance of salvation—wisdom and knowledge; the fear of the Lord is its storehouse[3]."

Special care had to be exercised in the storing of the field's produce, and in order to prevent the possibility of rottenness and decay, certain preserva- Care in storing.

1 Ps. xix. 8. 2 Is. xxxiii. 6.

3 *Exod. R.* 30, 14. Cf. *Shabbath*, 31 *a*. Point is given to this parable by the explanation of R. Simeon b. Lakish of the verse in question as alluding to the main "*Sedarim*," orders or sections of the Mishnah, which comprise the essence of Jewish lore, *viz.* "stability" refers to *seder* "*Zeraim*," dealing with land productions; "times" refers to "*Moed*," the *seder* treating of Sabbaths and Festivals; "strength" (translated here "abundance") alludes to *seder* "*Nashim*," which deals with marriage and divorce (family life is the strength of a nation); "salvation" has reference to *seder* "*Nezikin*," which embraces a great part of the civil and criminal law (justice brings salvation); "wisdom" refers to "*Kodoshim*," which treats of the sacrificial law; and "knowledge" alludes to "*Toharoth*," which treats of the laws concerning the clean and unclean: all this knowledge must be accompanied by the fear of the Lord.

tives were used. This fact suggested to the authors of the Midrash a simile of deep religious significance.

"The fear of the Lord is his treasure[1]." Raba (Bab. Am., 279–352 C.E.) said: When man is brought up for judgment, he is asked: "Didst thou (while on earth) deal honestly, fix hours for the study of the Torah, help in the propagation of the human species and hope for salvation; didst thou search after wisdom and by argument deduce one thing from another?" And then, if the fear of the Lord was his treasure, all will be well, but if not, all will not be well with him.

This might be compared to a man who said unto his messenger: "Didst thou mix with it a *Kab* of *Humton*[2] powder?" "No," replied he. "In that case," said the man, "it were better hadst thou not taken the wheat up at all[3]."

The following storing simile may here be added:

R. Akiba is a well-filled treasury of knowledge.

Unto what was R. Akiba like? Unto a labourer who took his basket and went out into the field. When he found wheat he put it into the basket, and repeated the process when he found barley, spelt or beans. On reaching home he picked out the wheat and set it apart, and did the same to the barley, the spelt, the beans and the lentils. Even so did R. Akiba: He classified the Laws according to their respective impresses[4].

The selling of the grain in the wheat market also supplies the Rabbis with the following illustrative parable:

[1] Is. xxxiii. 6.

[2] A sandy soil containing a salty substance and used for the preservation of wheat.

[3] *Shabbath* 31 *a*.

[4] *Aboth di R. N.* ch. XVIII.

Shouldst thou desire to know what crowds there were in Jerusalem, thou couldst tell it from the number of priests.

In the wheat market.

R. Joshua of Sichnin (4th c.) said in the name of Rabbi Joshua b. Levi (3rd c.): This might be compared unto a heap of grain standing in the wheat market. All came to estimate its contents but could not do so. Among them was a clever man who said: "Do you wish to estimate its contents, you can adduce it from the amount of *Terumah*[1]."

The heap of corn.

And here we may refer to the Rabbinic expansion of another Biblical simile, taken from the world of agriculture, and used for the purpose of expressing the selection of Israel and his superior worth over the nations. In this simile, however, the conception is taken not from any of the physical aspects of land-work, but from the ritual observance connected with the agricultural life of the Jew.

"Israel is the Lord's hallowed portion, His firstfruits of the increase[2]." As the stack stands ready for the priest to come and take from it his *Terumah*, even so has the Holy One, blessed be He, made the world stand ready as a stack, and lifted Israel [or our ancestors] out therefrom as His *Terumah*[3]."

The carting of corn.

Israel has shown himself equal to the responsibilities thus thrown upon him. With patience and fortitude has he borne the loving burden of religious duties imposed upon him, whilst the other nations resented even the smaller tasks assigned to them. This idea is conveyed by a Rabbi in an agricultural simile taken from the carting of the corn:

[1] Portion of the crops and produce set aside; *lit.* "lifted off" or separated as the priest's due. *Lament. R. s.v.* העיר, 1, § 2.

[2] Jer. ii. 3.

[3] *Exod. R.* 31, 9.

R. Simeon b. Joḥai (2nd c.) said: This might be compared to a man who went out to the barn, taking his dog and his ass along with him. He loaded the ass with five *Seah*[1] and the dog with two. The ass walked with patience, but the dog panted. The master took off one load from the dog and put it on the back of the ass. The dog still panted. Then said the master: "When burdened thou pantest, and when unburdened thou pantest still." Even so, when the descendants of Noah could not endure the seven precepts which they had received[2] God took them away and put them on Israel's shoulders[3].

Master of the wheat.

But the teaching of the grain similes is not confined to the subject of the selection of Israel. Some of the similes drawn from the field with its produce are applied also to the domain of the Torah and religious belief. With a possible continuation of the Rabbinic conception, which, as we noted above, sees in the "field" an allegorical representation of Talmudic study, the authors of Midrashic poetry refer to the erudite scholar as "the Master of the wheat." The Rabbis have taught: The man rich in property—the openly and popularly rich—by this is meant the master of *Aggadoth*. The man rich in coins—the man of hidden or uncertain riches—that is the master of Dialectics. The man rich in measured corn or oil

[1] *Seah* is a measure of capacity about 13,184 cubic centimetres.

[2] The "descendants of Noah" denotes the human race, and the seven laws given to them are the "universal laws" obligatory upon all mankind, in contradistinction to such as bind Israelites alone. Cf. *Tosefta Abodah Zarah*, VIII, 4, the Gentiles have been given seven laws, *viz.*: concerning justice, idolatry, blasphemy, immorality, murder, robbery, the eating of a part cut off from a living animal.

[3] *Lev. R.* 13 *init.* § 2, *vide* Bacher, *Ag. Tan.* II, 103; anonymous in *Sifré* to Deut. xxxiii. 3, § 343, and in *Yalkut Hab.* § 563.

—the rich man of the store-room or cellar—that is the master of Traditions. All however are dependent upon the master of the wheat[1].

Such a scholar, the Rabbis advise, should possess some modicum of pride. But it must be natural and becoming.

The ear of the grain.

R. Ḥiyya bar Ashe (3rd c.) said in the name of Rab: A scholar should be possessed of the fraction of one-eighth of an eighth of pride[2]. Rabbi Huna (4th c.), the son of R. Joshua, said: And such fraction of pride adorns [or protects] man just as the awn of grain adorns [or protects] the ear[3].

Wheaten bread.

This association of wheat with knowledge has an early origin, for when R. Meïr (2nd c.) in expounding the text "And the tree of knowledge of good and evil[4]" asserted that the plant of which the first man

1 *Horayoth*, 14 *a*, *Baba Bathra*, 145 *b*,
תנו רבנן עתיר נכסין עתיר פומבי זה הוא בעל הגדות עתיר סלעין עתיר תקוע זהו בעל פלפול עתיר משח עתיר כמס זהו בעל שמועות הכל צריכין למרי חטיא
The whole saying is somewhat difficult in interpretation; *vide* Commentaries *ad loc.* and Friedmann, *Mebo* to *Mechilta*, p. xli. The owner of the wheat is acc. to *B.B.* "the master of *Gemara*," and acc. to *Hor.* "the master of *Mishnah* and *Baraitha*." It is remarkable that there should have been this difference of opinion as to the exact significance of a well-known popular proverb.

2 אחד משמנה בשמינית; the term שמינית stands, according to Rashi *ad loc.*, for a well-known small measure of capacity (also a weight) called *Ukhla*, which was one-eighth of a fourth of a *Kab* אחד משמנה ברובע; the quantity here mentioned therefore is an eighth of an *Ukhla*, called here שמינית. But ordinary haughtiness was condemned; R. Avira discoursed as follows: Any man who is possessed of haughtiness of spirit will in the end grow small, as Scripture says (Job xxiv. 24), "They are exalted for a little while, and they are gone." And what means the text (*ibid.*), "And like the tops of the ears of corn they shall be cut off"? It was taught thus in the school of R. Ishmael. This might be likened unto a man entering his field [to reap]; he keeps on gathering in the high stalks (*Sotah*, 5 *a*).

3 *Sotah*, 5 *a*, ומעטרא ליה כי סאסא לשבולתא.

4 Gen. ii. 9.

ate was the wheat, he quoted in support of his theory the popular saying current in his days, and which spoke of the man devoid of knowledge as one who had never eaten wheaten bread in his life[1].

And there is possibly also a subtle allusion to these metaphorical conceptions in the description which the Talmud gives of the sittings of the Sanhedrin:

The granary.

"The Sanhedrin were [seated] in circular form like the half of a [circular] granary so that they might see one another[2]."

Wheat symbolic of sin.

By a process of word-suggestion, a frequent source of simile-building in Midrashic literature, the wheat in Rabbinic imagery also represents "sin[3]."

Samuel (3rd c.) said: The evil inclination is like a kind of wheat[4], it crouches at the entrance [*i.e.* valves] of the heart, as it is said: "Sin croucheth at the door[5]."

[1] *Yalkut Gen.* § 21, see *Gen. R.* 15, 7. Similarly in *Berachoth*, 40 *a*, in the name of R. Judah: It was the wheat, for an infant does not know how to call father and mother until it has tasted food of grain; *vide* Bacher, *Ag. Tan.* II, 18. For the metaphor of "bread," as signifying "Torah," *vide Gen. R.* 70, 5 and *Num. R.* 8, 9, where Aquilas the proselyte is consoled by R. Joshua, who explained the text "loving the גר stranger (or proselyte) by giving him *bread* and *raiment*" as meaning by teaching him Torah; for bread typifies Torah even as it is said (Prov. ix. 5), "Come, eat ye my bread"; *vide* also *Ḥagigah*, 14 *a*, where the removal from Jerusalem of "the stay of bread" (Is. iii. 1) is symbolically explained as referring to the "Masters of the Scriptures."

[2] *Synhedrin*, 36 *b*, היתה כחצי גרן עגולה. עגולה is prob. adjectival to סנהדרין, *viz.* היתה עגולה כחצי גֹרן. That גרן was circular in form and served as a figure for "roundness" *vide Cant. R.* where אגן הסהר is translated by אדרא דאזהרה, and אדרא = גֹרן. Cf. *Pesikta R. ki Tissa*, Section 10, p. 34 *b*.

[3] חִטָּה suggesting חַטָּאת.

[4] כמין חִטָּה.

[5] לפתח חטאת רֹבץ Gen. iv. 7, *Yalkut Gen.* § 37, *Berachoth*, 61 *a*. On the other hand the חטה סדוקה the wheat grain which is split and therefore distinct from all other grain is made to typify Israel who are distinguished from the other nations by virtue of the covenant of Abraham. R. Iddi (Bab. Am., 4th c.) thus explains the comparison in Cant. vii. 3, *vide Shoḥer Tob* to Ps. ii. 13, נשקו בר; cf. *Cant. R.* to vii. 3.

There are several other similes drawn from the domain of agricultural life and used to emphasise the importance of religious belief and religious practice. The offal of the wheat—the stubble and the straw—is used already in the Bible to typify the sinful. But Midrashic literature, in illustration of the effects of sin, supplies one or two rather strange parables having an indirect association with the work of the threshing floor, and with the separation of the chaff and the straw from the grain, as the following examples will show:

The offal in the threshing floor.

R. Levi (3rd c.) said: This might be compared to two men, one curly-headed[1] and the other bald-headed, who both stood near a threshing floor. The chaff fell upon the curly-headed man and remained fast in his hair. When it touched the bald-headed man, he removed it easily with his hand. Even so does the wicked Esau defile himself with sin all the days of the year, without the means for removing it and making atonement. But when Jacob becomes defiled with sin throughout the year, he has the means of removing it when the Day of Atonement comes[2].

A house full of straw.

R. Eleazar (b. Pedath, 3rd c.) said: There was counsel of heresy (infidelity) among them [*sc.* Doeg and Ahithophel who conspired against David]. To what were they like? To a house full of straw, in which were holes allowing the straw to pass. After a time the straw which lodged in these holes began to drop out, and then everyone knew [what apparently

[1] קָוּוֹץ or קְוּוּץ.

[2] *Gen. R.* 65, 15; *vide* Bacher, *Pal. Am.* II, 421. There is a subtle allusion here to the physical nature of the two men; for Esau was a "hairy" man and Jacob was a "smooth" man (Gen. xxvii. 11).

they had not suspected before] that that house had been full of straw. Even so was it with Doeg and Ahithophel. They at first practised no precept; and although they became in later time students of the Law, they yet remained as heretofore. Hence (does Scripture say) "For wickedness is in their dwelling, in the midst of them[1]."

R. Samuel b. Naḥman (3rd c.) said: The epicurean [the sceptic, heretic] is like unto a house which is full of straw; even if thou wert to remove the straw, thou wouldst find the chaff remaining therein and undermining the walls[2].

Burning straw and stubble.

And here may be mentioned a parable from the burning of straw and stubble, which is interesting for the religious idea it conveys:

"And his eyes became dim, so that he could not see[3]." R. Eleazar b. Azariah (Tanna, 1st and 2nd c.) explained this to mean that they were made dim so as not to see the evildoing of that wicked man [*i.e.* Esau]. The Holy One, blessed be He, said: Isaac will be going out into the market-place, and the people will say: Here is the father of that wicked man! Therefore shall I make his eyes dim, so that he remain in his home.

This is like unto a great man who had a beautiful and much praised palace. The neighbours kept burning stubble and straw and made the smoke enter into

[1] Ps. lv. 15, *Num. R.* 18, 17. The Rabbis explain the whole of Ps. lv. as having reference to the relations between Ahithophel and King David. *Vide Shoḥer Tob* and *Yalkut*, *ad loc.*

[2] *Jer. Synhedrin*, 27 *d* below; *vide* Bacher, *Pal. Am.* I, 499; R. Eleazar (3rd c.) uses the image of an arch in which a stone is loosened and which is thereby threatened with destruction.

[3] Gen. xxvii. 1.

it through the window; whereupon the owner went and stopped up the window.

Even so when the wives of Esau were worshipping the idols and Isaac was sorely grieved at the sight, his eyes immediately grew dim[1].

A simile from the winnowing of barley is used in Midrashic poetry for the further elucidation of Biblical texts. Winnowing.

"And I will scatter you among the heathens[2]." This, say the Rabbis, is a severe measure for Israel, for when the inhabitants of a province go into exile and settle in one and the same place, they come into contact with each other and are comforted. But concerning Israel, Scripture says, I will scatter you among the nations, so that none of you shall be near unto his neighbours, as it is written: "And I will scatter thee among the heathens and disperse thee in the countries[3]," and as it is further written: "And I will fan them with a fan in the gates of the land[4]." This is like unto a man fanning barley with a winnowing fan, so that not one grain touches the other[5].

And there is the following parable connected with the preparation of the corn for the threshing floor: Turning over the grain.

Commenting upon the text "And Isaac intreated (וַיֶּעְתַּר) the Lord for his wife[6]," R. Eleazar (3rd c.) said: Why may the prayer of the righteous be likened to [*i.e.* symbolised by] a shovel[7]? As the shovel turns the grain in the granary from place to place, so does the prayer of the righteous turn the

[1] *Gen. R.* 65, 10; and *Yalkut Gen.* § 114, quoted from *Midrash Abkir*.
[2] Lev. xxvi. 33. [3] Ez. xxii. 15. [4] Jer. xv. 7.
[5] *Yalkut Lev.* § 675. [6] Gen. xxv. 21.
[7] The root עתר being used for prayer, and the word signifying also a shovel or pitchfork.

dispensations of the Holy One, blessed be He, from anger to mercy and lovingkindness[1].

Milling.

The processes of grinding the wheat and of milling the flour likewise supply a number of similes in Midrashic literature, many of which, carrying on the previous idea, stand as figurative expressions for the study of the Law, which played such an important part in the life of the Jew.

The ever-grinding millstone.

Commenting upon the text "And the grinders cease[2]," R. Samuel bar Naḥman (3rd c.) said: Israel is compared to the grinders [millstones]; even as the millstones never cease their grinding, so does Israel never cease from the study of the Law either by day or by night[3]."

And a similar metaphorical interpretation is given to the text: "The sound of the grinding is low[4]." This, explain the Rabbis, is because Israel ceased from studying the Law. R. Samuel b. Naḥman (3rd c.) said: The study of the Law is allegorically

[1] *Sukkah*, 14 *a*; *vide* Bacher, *Pal. Am.* II, 14. In *Yebamoth*, 64 *a*, the author is R. Isaac. In *Num. R.* 10, 5, it is given in the name of R. Simeon b. Lakish (3rd c.). But Bacher, in note (5), proves that R. Eleazar b. Pedath is the original author. There is also a winnowing simile from the threshing floor based upon word-suggestion, and having reference to the Rabbinical theory of a biological fact. R. Ḥanina bar Papa discoursed as follows: What is the meaning of the text (Ps. cxxxix. 3) "Thou measurest (זרית) my going about and my lying down and art acquainted with all my ways"? This is to tell us that man was created by a process of selection. Thus it was taught in the school of R. Ishmael: It was like a man winnowing (שׁוֹזרה) in the threshing floors. He takes away the nutritive part and leaves the offal (*Niddah*, 31 *a*). See Bacher, *Ag. Tan.* II, 342, under the school of Ishmael; in *Lev. R.* 14, 6, the simile is given in the name of Resh Lakish.

[2] Eccl. xii. 3.

[3] *Lament. R.* Introduction, § 23, *Kohel. R.* to xii. 4; *vide* Bacher, *Pal. Am.* I, 490, note.

[4] Eccl. xii. 4.

spoken of as a mill; for just as the mill does not stop grinding either by day or by night, so of the words of the Law it is said: "And thou shalt meditate therein day and night[1]."

And in continuation of the same idea, "the grinders[2]" are taken to signify the great Mishnah collections, *e.g.* the Mishnah of R. Akiba, the Mishnah of R. Ḥiyya, the Mishnah of R. Hoshayah, and the Mishnah of bar Kappara[3].

And if the grinding of the corn typifies study, the flour obtained by this process of grinding, as well as by the subsequent act of sifting it, symbolises the results secured by a special devotion to the study of the Law.

Grinding and sifting the flour.

Issi b. Judah[4] in his enumeration of the characteristics of the scholars remarked that the teaching

[1] Josh. i. 8; *Kohel. R. ad loc.*; *vide* Bacher, *Pal. Am.* I, 490; *vide* also Bacher, *Am.* II, 396 f., *s.v.* Levi, where he draws attention to the use of גרם in similar figures: גרם denotes the rough crushing or grinding, cf. גרש כרמל Lev. ii. 14, גריסין *Maasroth*, v, 8, ריחיים של גרוסות *Menaḥoth*, x, 14, הגרוסות *Moed Katon*, II, 5, the mill of the grist grinders; hence גרם means study, which does not imply acumen such as committing to memory Halachoth and traditions. טחן like דייק, which means finer grinding, stands for deeper and more profound investigation (cf. עוקר הרים וטוחנן זו בזו בסברא), such as discovering reasons for Halachoth, cf. the sayings דייק ולא גרים, גרם ולא דייק. It says in Ps. cxix. 20 גרסה נפשי my soul "heaps" up, and not טחנה "grinds," "learns" but not "analyses." Levy and Jastrow take the same view, *vide* their Dictionaries, *s.v.*

[2] Eccl. xii. 3.

[3] *Lament. R.* Introduction, § 23; and *Kohel. R.* to xii. 7; and *Cant. R.* to viii. 2; the whole section is headed אמר ר׳ יהושע דסכנין (4th c.). Portions of "the Mishnah of R. Akiba" are embodied in our Mishnah. The Halachic Midrashim, *e.g. Mechilta* of R. Simeon b. Joḥai, *Sifra*, *Sifré*, are ascribed to the disciples of R. Akiba, who followed his method, *vide Synhedrin*,* 86 *b*. The other terms refer to the *Tosefta* and to similar Halachic collections.

[4] A Tanna of the post-Hadrian epoch.

(Mishnah) of R. Eliezer b. Jacob (1st c.) is only a *Kab* [*i.e.* little in quantity], but a well-sifted one[1]. R. Simeon b. Joḥai (2nd c.) grinds much and loses little[2], and that which he does lose is only bran.

Sifting. R. Simeon b. Joḥai (2nd c.)[3] said: "The full soul loatheth a honeycomb[4]"; this speaks of a disciple who has not started his learning from first beginnings. "But to the hungry soul every bitter thing is sweet[5]"; this signifies a disciple who has studied from the first elements. The text has been otherwise explained thus: The full soul presses like the action of a sieve[6]. Just as the sieve presses out the flour, the bran and the coarse meal independently of each other, even so does the disciple of the wise sit down, and, after rigid examination, sift and analyse the words of the Torah. He argues inwardly thus: Such and such an authority prohibits, and another authority permits; one declares a thing unclean, and the other rules it as clean[7].

R. Eleazar b. Simon (2nd c.) said: When one expounds to the people words of Torah which are not pleasant to the hearers, like the fine flour which has

[1] *Kab*, a measure of capacity, is one-sixth of a *Seah* and equal to 2197 cubic centimetres. See *Yebamoth*, 49 *b*; wherefore subsequent generations generally adopted Eliezer's views as Law (*Yebamoth*, 60 *a*).

[2] A *Baraitha* explains the expression here used, ומוציא קמעא, as meaning: He forgets little, *Gittin*, 67 *a*. Part of the whole passage is expanded in *Aboth di R. N.* ch. XVIII, *vide* Bacher, *Tan.* II, 71, note. Compare the following: Whosoever meets you with this objection, cares not sufficiently what kind of flour he grinds (*i.e.* is not particular as to the kind of argument he offers), *Pesaḥim*, 84 *a*; Raba (B.A., 279–352) said: Who is it that does not care what flour he grinds (*i.e.* does not concern himself about his teaching)? *Yoma*, 46 *a*.

[3] In *Yalkut R.* Simeon b. Menasia.

[4] תבוס נפת Prov. xxvii. 7 *a*.

[5] *Ibid.* 7 *b*.

[6] תבוס = presses; נפת = נפה = sieve.

[7] *Sifré* to Deut. xi. 22, § 48.

passed through the sieve[1], it were better he had left them unsaid[2].

The sinner repents through suffering.

R. Levi (3rd c.) says: If thy sieve be stopped up knock against it [and the holes will open out][3].

Euphemism of grinding

But the grinding metaphor in Midrashic literature, as do the other features of agricultural life already alluded to, also relates to the realm of marriage, and is used in a euphemistic sense[4].

One or two further metaphors and similes associated with the mill and its work deserve mention. The burden of matrimony is expressed metaphorically by a millstone round the neck.

The millstone round the neck.

R. Judah (b. Ezekiel, Bab. Am., 220–299 C.E.) in the name of Samuel (Bab. Am., 175–254 C.E.) said: The Law is that a man should first marry and then

[1] כסלת זו שצפה על גבי נפה. This expression has presented difficulties. Some (*e.g.* Jastrow in Dict.) have explained it as "fine flour which adheres to the sides, על גבי, of the sieve." This seems contrary to the sense of the Hebrew and the meaning of the comparison. על גבי can well mean here as everywhere else "on the surface," cf. על גבי נהר, and צפה indicates the movement; שצפה על גבי הנפה would mean "which had moved upon the surface of the sieve," *i.e.* been through the process of sifting and resulted in סלת, fine flour.

[2] *Cant. R.* to iv. 11, "Thy lips, O my bride, drop as the honey-comb." נפת תטפנה שפתותיך, cf. *Mechilta* to Ex. xvi. 31, רבי אליעזר אומר כסלת זו שצפה על גבי נפה ונלושה בדבש וחמאה. For סלת שצפה בנפה, cf. *Tanḥ. Ekeb*, § 2, and Buber's notes, *ad loc.*, *Jer. Sotah*, IX, 14 (p. 24 *b*), ונפת צופים אמר רבי אלעזר דבש הבא בצפייה: אמר ר׳ יוסי ברבי חנינא סלת צפה על גבי נפה לושה בדבש וחמאה.

[3] *Gen. R.* 81, 3, מהולתך חרשה אקיש עלה.

[4] The text "And my lord is old" (Gen. xviii. 12) is explained by the Rabbis by the phrase טוחן ולא פולט, *Gen. R.* 48, 17; cf. Judg. xvi. 21, ויהי טוחן בבית האסורים, and the saying of R. Joḥanan, *Sotah*, 10 *a*, אין טחינה אלא לשון עברה; cf. also Lament. v. 13, בחורים טחון נשאו, and the Rabbinic interpretation *Lament. R. ad hoc*, לשון נקיה הוא. Hence the verse in the Dirge for the 9th of Ab: בחורים טחון נשאו . כי בבית זונה נמצאו, a suggestion of מדה כנגד מדה, "measure for measure."

study the Torah. But R. Joḥanan (3rd c.) controverted this view: He has a millstone round his neck [*i.e.* a wife and children to support] and shall he occupy himself with the Law[1]?

The moving millstone.

Again, to give a popular explanation of an astronomical phenomenon—the course of the planets in the celestial sphere—the Rabbis describe it as being like the movement of the block of the mill[2].

Grinding ground flour.

To grind flour already once ground is a metaphor used in Midrashic poetry for the useless expenditure of energy and effort.

A *Bath-Kol*[3] went forth and said unto him [*i.e.* Nebuzaradan], "Thou didst slay a people already slain, thou didst burn a Temple already burnt. Thou didst grind flour already ground" [*i.e.* you conquered a doomed people][4].

The scattering of flour is used as a simile for the dispersion of Israel, the rôle foretold for him by the prophets.

Scattered like flour.

Because of the sins of idolatry the Israelites be-

[1] ריחיים על צוארו ויעסוק בתורה, *Kiddushin*, 29 *b*; *vide* Bacher, *Pal. Am.* I, 235. The varying opinions are due to the difference in the economic conditions prevailing in Palestine and in Babylon in the 3rd c. The Babylonians married first and then studied. For the metaphor of "the millstone hanged about his neck," cf. Matthew xviii. 6, Luke xvii. 2.

[2] כסדנא דריחיא, *Pesahim*, 94 *b*, R. Aḥa bar Jacob (3rd c.); the סדנא is the millstone; the בוצינא is the pivot remaining stationary; בוצינא דריחיא is the reading of רבינו גרשם; the *Aruch nom.* R. Ḥananel reads כסדנא דריחיא.

[3] *Lit.* daughter of a voice: A heavenly voice proclaiming a divine message.

[4] *Synhedrin*, 96 *b*. In *Cant. R.* to iii. 4, with play upon Is. xlvii. 2 וטחני קמח, the reading is as follows: Thus said Jerusalem to the daughter of Babylon, "Ground flour didst thou grind, a slain lion didst thou slay, a burning pyre didst thou set aflame." Another metaphorical expression for unnecessary effort is "to carry straw to Afarayim" (*vide Menaḥoth*, 85 *a*; *Gen. R.* 86, 5).

came like unto flour, as Scripture says: "Take the millstones and grind meal[1]"; and the Holy One, blessed be He, scattered them among the nations, even as it is written: "But I will scatter them with a whirlwind among all the nations whom they have not known[2]."

Fine flour on the other hand is used as a figurative expression to denote purity of descent.

Pure sifted flour.

R. Eleazar (b. Pedath, 3rd c.) said: Ezra did not leave Babylon until he had made her [*i.e.* in regard to the Jews dwelling there] like sifted flour of the purest sort [*i.e.* established the purity of descent of their families by careful investigation][3].

And finally there is the cumulative metaphorical passage which refers to all the processes of labour resulting in the production of the loaf.

From the field to the bake-house.

R. Ḥaggai (4th c.) said in the name of R. Samuel b. Naḥman (3rd cent.): Those before us have ploughed, sown, weeded, reaped, ground, sifted (through the sieve), kneaded, formed the dough, smoothed its surface and baked, and yet we have no mouth wherewith to eat it [*i.e.* in spite of all efforts of earlier generations in the elucidation of the Law, we have not yet acquired the capacity to enjoy it][4].

[1] Is. xlvii. 2.

[2] Zech. vii. 14, *Num. R.* 9, 45.

[3] *Kiddushin*, 69 *b*, 71 *b*. Cf. the following: And I took twelve men of you (Deut. i. 23) out of the chosen ones ברורים, out of the select ones מסולתים among you (*Sifré*, *Deut.* § 21); cf. also *Yalkut* to Cant. i. 1, § 980, "of all the wisdom of Solomon the Song of Songs alone was fine and well sifted מכל חכמתו של שלמה לא סֹלֶת אלא שה״ש לישראל. The contrasting metaphorical expression to "pure sifted flour" is *Isah*, עיסה, "dough"—a mixed family, a family suspected of containing an alien admixture. *Eretz Yisrael* was regarded as "*isah* to Babylon." *Kiddushin*, 69 *b*.

[4] *Jer. Shekalim*, v *init.* p. 48 *c*.

II

THE GARDEN

In Biblical imagery.

IN the literature of the Bible we have several similes drawn from the garden in its special aspects. "The fading garden that hath no water" represents idolatrous Jerusalem suffering under divine judgment[1], and the "watered garden" or "the garden by the river side" is employed as a figure of comparison for the parched soul refreshed and satisfied[2]. In the Parables of Balaam[3] the goodly tents of Jacob are compared among other things to the garden by the river side, without any indication as to the exact point of the comparison. The garden which causes the plants to spring forth is made to symbolise the ultimate breaking forth of righteousness and praise before all the nations[4]. And in the Song of Songs[5], "the garden enclosed and barred" is used as a simile for the chaste virgin bride. This expression, however, refers more to the *Gan*—the vegetable garden. The *Pardes*—the park, the orchard—hardly enters into the imagery of the Bible. The only comparison drawn from it is contained in the Song of Songs[6].

The garden in Midrashic poetry.

In Talmudic literature we find an interesting expansion of one of the Biblical garden similes, which, while showing the acquaintance of the Rabbis with garden cultivation, reveals their insight into human psychology.

[1] Is. i. 30. [2] Is. lviii. 10–11; Jer. xxxi. 11. [3] Num. xxiv. 6.
[4] Is. lxi. 11. [5] iv. 12. [6] iv. 13.

R. José (4th c.) said, in comment upon the text "Like gardens by the river side[1]": Balaam compared Israel to "gardens." What is the nature of gardens? If the weeds are not removed from the vegetables and if the refuse is not thrown away, they rot and decay [implying that Israel had long fallen into decay on account of their sins]. But the Holy One, blessed be He, said unto him: [They are like gardens] "by the river side." Even as the river carries off the refuse, so does the Day of Atonement wipe away their sins, as it is written[2], "For on that day shall he make atonement for you, to cleanse you, that ye may be clean from all your sins before the Lord."

The same Biblical simile of "the gardens by the river side" is explained by the Rabbis as typifying the "teachers of little children" who bring forth from their hearts wisdom and understanding, knowledge and discernment[3].

The *Pardes.*

But it is principally the *Pardes* (the cultivated orchard or park) which forms the subject of the Midrashic similes. This is due no doubt to the fact that in the Rabbinic period, when the Jews were under Roman influence, the *Pardes* played an important part in the social, no less than in the industrial life of the people. This highly cultivated object of Nature under its many aspects has supplied

[1] Num. xxiv. 6.

[2] Lev. xvi. 30.

[3] *Yalkut Num. ad loc.* § 771. We have likewise a garden simile with a euphemistic tendency which is reminiscent of the Song of Songs. אמר ר׳ אבין משל לגנת ירק שהמעין לתוכה כ״ז שהמעין לתוכה היא עושה בריכין כך כל מי שהולך אצל אשתו נדה עושה בנים מצורעים. *Lev. R.* 15, 5; Bacher, *Pal. Am.* III, 429; in *Yalk. Lev.* § 554 the reading is היא עשויה ביצין.

a series of *Meshalim*, conveying a number of lofty Jewish teachings.

Thus the *Pardes* is variously made to illustrate the Holy Land, the World, and the realm of metaphysical speculation; and many figures of comparison are taken from the tenant-farmer, the workers and the watchmen of the *Pardes*.

A precious possession.

The garden, or park, as the most prized gift from the king to his dearest child, is made by a Rabbi of the 3rd and 4th c. to symbolise the gift of that divine justice which came from God to Israel, the most beloved of His children:

"Judges and officers shalt thou make thee in all thy gates[1]." R. Levi said: To what may this be likened? To a king who had many sons, but loved the youngest best of all. He also possessed a *Pardes* which he cherished above all his possessions. And so he said: The *Pardes* which I prize above everything I shall give unto my youngest son, the most beloved of my children. Even thus did the Holy One, blessed be He, say: Of all the nations that I have created it is Israel that I love best, even as it is written: "When Israel was a child, then I loved him[2]." And of all things which I have created, it is justice that I love most, as it is said: "For I, the Lord, love justice[3]." I will give the thing that I love best unto the people whom I love best; hence "Judges and officers shalt thou make thee[4]."

[1] Deut. xvi. 18.

[2] Hos. xi. 1.

[3] Is. lxi. 8.

[4] *Deut. R.* 5, 7; *Yalkut*, I, § 907. In the same ch. in Is. (v. 11) we have the simile of the "garden causing the things that are sown in it to spring forth," typifying the breaking forth of צדקה, righteousness. Was this the underlying idea that suggested the comparison in the text?

A rich source of supply.

The *Pardes* was further regarded by its royal owner as a fitting gift for his favourite son, because of its extreme usefulness as a bountiful supply of household provisions. It was under this figure that a Rabbi expressed the motive of the divine King of kings in assigning the Holy Land to Israel. "But I said, How shall I put thee among the children and give thee a pleasant land, the goodliest heritage of nations? And I thought thou wouldst call me, My father, and wouldst not turn away from me[1]." This might be likened unto a king who had some concubines and many sons. He had also one son born to him from a Matrona[2], and for him the king cherished a special affection. He gave fields and vineyards to all the children of the concubines, but to his son (by the Matrona) he presented a *Pardes*, out of which came all his provisions. Thereupon the son went and enquired of his father: "Thou gavest to the sons of the concubines fields and vineyards, but to me thou hast presented one *Pardes* only." To which the king replied: "By thy life, it is from the *Pardes* that all my stores and provisions have come, and just because I love thee more than thy brothers have I given it unto thee."

Even so is it with the Holy One, blessed be He. He is the Creator of all the nations of the world. "There are threescore queens and fourscore concubines[3]," says Scripture; these denote the nations. "My dove, my undefiled is but one[4]"; this denotes the congregation of Israel. To the nations of the world the Holy One, blessed be He, apportioned fields

[1] Jer. iii. 19.
[2] A Roman lady of quality.
[3] Cant. vi. 8.
[4] *Ibid.* v. 9.

and vineyards, as it is said: "When the Most High gave to the nations their inheritance[1]," but to Israel He gave the land of Israel, the storehouse of the Lord[2]. From it came the sacrifices, the shewbread, the first ripe fruits, the measure of barley—all the good things of the world. And why all this? In order to make a distinction between the son of the Matrona and the sons of the concubines, even as it is said in our text (above)[3].

The *Pardes* and its plants.

The intrinsic value of the *Pardes* naturally depends upon the fruitfulness and utility of its trees. The owner would therefore periodically improve his estate by the addition of specially selected plants. This idea also was employed by R. Simeon b. Lakish (3rd c.) for the purpose of a *Mashal*.

When R. Ḥiyya b. Adda (first half of 3rd c.) the nephew of bar Kappara died, R. Simeon b. Lakish, his teacher, made lament for him and delivered a funeral oration as follows: The matter may be likened unto a king who had a son that was very dear to him. What did the king? He planted for him a *Pardes*, and whenever the son carried out his father's will, the king searched the whole world to find a goodly plant to place in his *Pardes*. But when the son provoked him to anger, the royal father cut down all the plants.

Even so is it with Israel. When Israel performs the divine will, then does the Holy One, blessed be He, search the world in order to discover among the nations some one who is righteous, and He brings him in and joins him unto Israel, as He did with Jethro

[1] Deut. xxxii. 8. [2] קילרין של הקב"ה=cellarium, κελλαριον.
[3] Jer. iii. 19; *Tanḥuma Lev.* p. 78; *Yalkut*, § 615.

and Rahab. But when Israel provokes God to anger He removes the righteous from their midst[1].

Its fruit-bearing and fruitless trees.

Although the fruit-bearing trees formed the paramount attraction in the *Pardes,* nevertheless the fruitless trees too had a utility of their own. This value of the fruitless trees suggested to R. Levi (3rd c.) a beautiful simile in which was expounded the well-known and oft-repeated Rabbinic theory that in the eyes of God the seemingly worthless among His creatures have their place in the world and their own sphere of usefulness:

R. Levi said: This might be compared to a king who had a garden in which he planted both fruitless and fruit-bearing trees. His servants enquired of him: What profit hast thou from those fruitless trees? And he said unto them: Just as I have need of the fruit-bearing trees, even so do I want the fruitless ones, for were it not for these how could I heat my baths and furnaces? Such is the meaning of the text "And He gave them charge concerning the children of Israel and concerning Pharaoh[2]." In the same way as the praise of the Holy One, blessed be He, ascends unto Him from the Garden of Eden, out of the mouth of the righteous, even so does it rise from *Gehinnom* out of the lips of the wicked[3].

Watering and hoeing the *Pardes.*

But whilst the owner's general care was bestowed upon *all* the trees of the *Pardes*, his attention was directed in particular to those plants which possessed

[1] *Jer. Berachoth*, 5 *c*; *Cant. R.* 6, 2. The idea that the righteous are taken away for the sins of their contemporaries is an oft-repeated theological doctrine, cf. *Shabbath*, 33 *b*, בזמן שהצדיקים בדור צדיקים נתפסים על הדור; the basis for this doctrine is Ezek. ix. 4–6, "Go ye after him through the city and smite...and begin at my sanctuary"; *vide* Rashi, *ad loc.* and on *Kethuboth*, 8 *b*.

[2] Ex. vi. 13.

[3] *Exod. R.* 7, 4.

a special value. R. Eleazar (3rd c.) asked[1]: It is written, "The Lord is good to *all*[2]," and again it is said, "The Lord is good unto *them that wait for Him*[3]." This might be likened unto a king who had a *Pardes*; in watering it he watered it all, but in hoeing it he hoed only the best[4].

The health-giving and poisonous trees.

"And Abraham gave all that he possessed unto Isaac[5]." R. Ḥana (3rd and 4th c.) said: He did not bestow any blessing even upon him [Isaac] but only material gifts. This might be compared unto a king, who had a *Pardes*, which he leased to a tenant-farmer. It had two trees intertwined. The one produced a health-giving medicine, the other a noxious poison. Then said the tenant-farmer, "If I water the health-giving tree, then will the poisonous one be watered with it; and if I do not water the poisonous tree, how can the other thrive?" "But," continued he, "I am an *Aris*, I will carry out my contract [*sc.* in what concerns the garden], and [*sc.* as for these two trees] let the master of the *Pardes* do whatsoever seemeth good unto him."

Even so thought Abraham: "If I bless Isaac now, then will the sons of Ishmael and Keturah be included in the blessing; if I do not bless the sons of Ishmael and the sons of Keturah, how can I bless Isaac? But," continued he, "I am but mortal; to-day I am here, to-morrow I shall be in the grave. I have now

[1] רמי, *lit.* raised an objection; called attention to an apparent contradiction between two texts.

[2] Ps. cxlv. 9.

[3] Lam. iii. 25.

[4] *Synhedrin*, 39 *b*; in *Lekaḥ Tob*, Gen. p. 1 *init.*, the second verse quoted is Ps. lxxiii. 1: "Truly God is good to Israel, even to such as are of clean heart."

[5] Gen. xxv. 5.

done my duty [*sc.* and brought all my children into the world]. Henceforth let the Holy One, blessed be He, do for His world whatsoever it pleaseth Him to do[1]."

Weeding out the thorns.

The *Pardes* required frequent pruning and clearing, more especially as regards the weeding out of thorns. Even so was it with God's garden, the Universe.

R. Levi (3rd c.), as many a Rabbi before and after him, embodied this conception in an illustrative *Mashal* which, as he himself rightly indicates, is of Biblical origin, thus pursuing an idea which has an important bearing on certain aspects of ethics.

"I am thy shield[2]." R. Levi said: Abraham our father was in fear. "Perhaps," thought he, "among those levies of troops that I have slain there was one righteous and God-fearing man." This might be likened unto one who was passing in front of the royal *Pardes.* He saw a bundle of thorns and turned aside to remove it. When the king observed him, he began to hide. Why dost thou hide? enquired the king; how many workmen would I have needed to gather them; now that thou hast done it, come and receive thy reward :—"Thy reward shall be exceeding great."

Even so did the Holy One, blessed be He, say unto Abraham: The hosts which thou hast slain were but cut thorns. Even as Scripture says[3]: "And the people shall be as the burnings of lime, as thorns cut down that are burned in the fire[4]."

1 *Gen. R.* 61, 6; in *Shoḥer Tob*, p. 6, the reading is: "And why did he not bless him?" משל etc.

2 Gen. xv. 1.

3 Is. xxxiii. 12.

4 *Gen. R.* 44, 4.

The thorns and the lily.

But just as one precious plant often saves the whole of a neglected *Pardes* from merited destruction, so in human society one worthy person may prove the salvation of the multitude.

R. Azariah said in the name of R. Judah ben R. Simeon (4th c.): This might be compared unto a king, who possessed a *Pardes* in which were planted rows of fig trees, vines, pomegranates and apples. He entrusted it to a tenant-farmer and went away. After a time the king returned, and looking into the *Pardes* to know what had been done, found it full of thorns and thistles. He thereupon brought in some woodcutters to clear away the overgrowth. But on looking among the thorns he beheld a lily. He took it in his hand, smelt it and felt refreshed. Then said the king: Because of this single lily, shall the whole *Pardes* be saved. Even so was the whole world created solely for the sake of the Torah. After twenty-six generations the Holy One, blessed be He, looked into His Universe to know what had been done there, and He found it all in deluge and devastation—the generation of Enosh, the generation of the Flood, and the generation of the "Confusion of Languages." He brought in the destroyers, to wipe them out, as it is said: "The Lord sat as king at the flood[1]." Thereupon He espied amongst them a solitary lily [*i.e.* Israel]. He took it up, made proof of its fragrance at the hour when he gave the Ten Words, and His soul was refreshed, when they replied, "We will do and obey[2]." Then said the Holy One, blessed be He: "Through the merit of this lily shall the *Pardes* be spared;

[1] Ps. xxix. 10. [2] Ex. xxiv. 7.

through the merit of the Law and of Israel shall the world be saved[1]."

The *Pardes* and the tenant-farmer (the *Aris*)

The work carried out in the *Pardes* provided a number of *Meshalim* portraying the activities of mankind, especially of Israel, in promoting the spiritual welfare of the world. And whilst as labourers in the divine *Pardes* they received the promise of a due recompense, the actual nature of this reward was not divulged by the Owner, in order that the whole of their task might be performed with uniform zeal and devotion.

Simeon b. Ḥalafta (2nd c.) said: Whosoever has studied the Law and fails to fulfil it is liable to a severer punishment than he who never studied at all. Unto what may this be likened? Unto a king who had a *Pardes*, into which he introduced two tenant-farmers (*Arisim*). The one kept on planting trees and cutting them down, whilst the other neither planted nor cut down. With whom was the king wroth? Was it not with the one who had planted and then hewed down? Even so, whosoever studies the Torah and does not fulfil it incurs a greater penalty than he who never studied it at all. Whence do we know this? From the words of Isaiah[2]: "Let favour be shown to the wicked, for he hath not learnt righteousness"; but if a person hath learnt and carried not out his lesson, then favour should not be shown him[3].

The *Pardes* and the watch-tower.

R. Jannai (3rd c.) said: This might be compared unto a king who had a *Pardes* in which he built a high tower. The king commanded that some labourers

[1] *Lev. R.* 23, 3 ; *Cant. R.* to ii. 2.
[2] xxvi. 10. [3] *Deut. R.* 7, 4.

be placed there to tend his work, and promised that whosoever performed his task conscientiously should receive his hire in full, but whoso was slack in his labours should be put in prison. The king represents the King of kings, and the *Pardes* the world, into which the Holy One, blessed be He, placed Israel to keep the Law, making with him the condition that whosoever kept the Law, his should be the joy of Eden's garden, but whoso observed it not should incur the pain of *Gehinnom*[1].

The *Pardes* and its labourers.

What is the meaning of the text[2] "Lest thou shouldst ponder the path of life, her ways are movable that thou canst not know them"? R. Abba b. Kahana (3rd and 4th c.) explained it thus: The Holy One, blessed be He, said: "Do not sit down and *weigh*[3] the precepts of the Torah: Say not, 'Since this command is an important one I shall fulfil it, seeing that its reward is great, and since the other is a minor command, I shall not fulfil it.'" What did the Holy One, blessed be He? He revealed not to mankind the reward attaching to each precept, in order that they might perform all of them with one and the same zeal, as Scripture says, "Her ways are movable that thou canst not know them."

Unto what is this like? Unto a king who hired some labourers and brought them into his *Pardes* without disclosing the reward for working therein, so that they might not leave undone that for which the reward was small and do only that for which the reward was great. At eventide the king summoned before him each workman in turn. "Under which

[1] *Exod. R.* 2, 2.

[2] Prov. v. 6, ארח חיים פן תפלס.

[3] Based on the usage of the same root פלס in ושקל בפלס Is. xl. 12.

tree didst thou work?" enquired he of the one. "Under this tree," replied he. "It is a pepper tree," said the king, "the wages for tending it are a gold piece." "Under which tree didst thou work?" enquired he of the second. "Under this one," he replied. "As it is a white blossom, its wages shall be only half a gold piece," was the royal answer. Thereafter he called a third, asking him: "Under which tree didst thou work?" "Under that other one," he replied. "It is an olive tree," said the king, "and its wages are 200 *zuzim*[1]." Then said the workmen: "Shouldst thou not have told us for which tree the reward was greatest so that we might have tênded that one?" "Ah," replied the king, "had I told you this, how could the whole of my *Pardes* have been tended?"

Even so was it that the Holy One, blessed be He, did not reveal the reward for the performance of His precepts, except in the case of two of them—the reward for the highest among the more important ones and for the lowest among the less important. The command to honour one's parents is of the highest importance, and the reward for it is length of days, even as it is said: "Honour thy father and thy mother, that thy days may be long[2]"; and among the lowest in importance is the duty of letting the mother-bird go[3]; and what is the reward assigned to this latter? Also length of days, even as it is said: "Thou shalt in any way let the dam go...that it may be well with thee and that thou mayest prolong thy days[4]."

1 "*zuz*" is a silver coin equal to one-fourth of a *shekel*.

2 Ex. xx. 12.

3 שילוח הקן.

4 Deut. xxii. 7; *Deut. R.* 6, 2 *et cet. loc.*

The *Pardes* and the watch-man.

The conception of the *Pardes* as a mirror of the world, and the practice of setting watchmen to guard it, gave rise to a further series of similes and parables. The watchman in the simile stands for man in general. It is just in this connection that we get the famous *Mashal* of the blind and the lame, a parable which some non-Jewish writers have characterised as mechanical, unreal and impossible, but which a recent Jewish scholar has nevertheless shown to be quite consistent with oriental custom[1].

(The Emperor) Antoninus said to Rabbi (*sc.* R. Judah the Prince, 2nd and 3rd c.): The body and the soul can free themselves from the Judgment. How so? The body will say, "It is the soul that hath sinned, for from the day that she departed from me, I have been lying in the grave silent as a stone." And the soul will say, "It is the body that hath sinned, for from the day I quitted it I have been flitting in the air like a bird." And Rabbi replied: I will tell thee a parable. Unto what is this like? Unto a human king possessed of a beautiful *Pardes*, which had in it some fine early figs. He placed therein two watchmen, of whom one was lame and the other blind. Then said the lame to the blind, "I see some luscious early figs in the garden, come and carry me on thy back and we shall delight ourselves with them." The lame mounted the shoulders of the blind, and gathered some of the fruit, and they ate it together. After a time the owner of the *Pardes* came and said unto them, "Where are those fine early figs?" The lame said,

[1] *Vide* I. Abrahams, *Studies in Pharisaism and the Gospels* (1st series), p. 97. The parable of the blind and the lame is taken from the lost Apocrypha of Ezekiel; *vide O. L. Z.* xv, pp. 254 and 449.

"Have I then legs to walk with?" The blind said, "Have I eyes to see?" What did the king? He made the lame to ride upon the back of the blind and sentenced them together. Even so will the Holy One, blessed be He, bring the soul, cast it into the body and judge the two together; as it is said, "He calleth to the heavens from above and to the earth that He may judge His people[1]." He calleth to the heaven above for the soul, and to the earth for the body, to judge His people[2].

Keeping watch.

The most effective way of watching the *Pardes* was from without, so that the whole of it might come within the ambit of the watchman's vision. This supplied the Rabbis with the following illustrative simile:

"Enter not into the path of the wicked, and go not in the way of evil men. Avoid it, pass not by it, turn from it and pass away[3]."

R. Ashé (352–427) said: Unto what may this be compared? Unto a man watching a *Pardes*. When he surveys it from without, the whole of it is being watched; but when he surveys it from within, only the part that is in front is under view, but that which is behind is not kept under watch[4].

Paying the watchmen.

For popular exposition of the incident recorded in Numbers, ch. xi (the appointment of the Elders to assist Moses), the Rabbis used the following parable:

This resembles a king, who had a *Pardes*. He hired a watchman, and paid him the wages for guarding it. After a time the watchman said unto the king: "I cannot guard the *Pardes* all alone; appoint others to

[1] Ps. l. 4.
[2] *Synhedrin*, 91 *a*; *Lev. R.* 4, 5.
[3] Prov. iv. 14–15.
[4] *Yebamoth*, 21 *b*.

keep watch with me." Then said the king unto him: "It is unto thee that I have given the whole *Pardes* to guard, and thee have I charged with the keeping of its fruit, and now thou sayest, 'Bring me yet others to keep watch with me.' Behold I will certainly bring others to keep guard with thee, but know thou, that not of my own shall I recompense them for keeping guard; but out of the wages that I have given thee shall they receive their reward."

Even so did the Holy One, blessed be He, say unto Moses when he pleaded, "I am not able to bear all this people alone[1]." "Unto thee have I vouchsafed the spirit and wisdom to supervise my children. I sought no one else, so that thou mightest be alone in this honour. Now thou seekest for others. Know thou that nothing shall be taken away from mine, but I will take of the spirit which is upon thee and place it upon them[2]."

The *Pardes* of metaphysical speculation.

The idea of the *Pardes* as a metaphysical image, representing the realm of esoteric thought, is met with in Tannaitic times and is interesting not only for itself, but also by reason of its association with the problems clustering round the development of speculative philosophy in Palestine.

"Four entered the *Pardes*" [*i.e.* engaged in esoteric speculation], says the Midrash, "Ben Azzai, Ben Zoma, Aḥer and R. Akiba. Ben Azzai peered [into the divine secrets] and died. In regard to him the text says: 'Precious in the sight of the Lord is the death of His saints[3].' Ben Zoma cast a glance and was stricken. In reference to him it is said:

[1] Num. xi. 14. [2] Num. xi. 17; *Num. R.* 15, 25.
[3] Ps. cxvi. 15.

'Hast thou found honey? Eat so much as is sufficient for thee[1].' Aḥer penetrated inward and cut down the shoots [in the garden of religion][2]. Concerning him Scripture says[3]: 'Suffer not thy mouth to bring thy flesh[4] into sin.' R. Akiba entered in peace and came out in peace. Of him it is said: 'Draw me, we will run after thee[5].'"

1 Prov. xxv. 16.

2 Explained by some to mean: He poisoned the minds of the young people.

3 Eccl. v. 5.

4 "Thy flesh," *i.e.* thy disciples who are like thy children, thy flesh and blood.

5 Cant. i. 4; *Tosefta Ḥagigah*, II, p. 234; Bacher, *Ag. Tan.* I, 340. Cf. the following: R. Eliezer the Great used to say, "Peer not into the vineyard of the Holy One, blessed be He; if thou hast looked in, do not enter; if thou didst enter, have no enjoyment from it; and if thou didst derive some enjoyment from it, eat not of its fruits. For if thou didst peer and enter, if thou didst enjoy and eat therefrom, thou wilt in the end be cut off from the world" (*Tanna di be Eliahu*, ch. 7). Jewish commentators explain the expression "entered into the *Pardes*" in various ways. Rashi says: They ascended into heaven with the aid of the Ineffable Name. *Tosafoth* and *Aruch* add: They did not actually ascend into heaven, but gave the appearance of doing so. The Midrash, in joining this Aggadah to the exposition of the text from Cant. i. 4, "the king brought me into his chambers," taking "chambers" in the sense of mysteries, and the Talmud bringing it into juxtaposition with the speculations on the divine chariot מעשה מרכבה, show that the "Pardes" like the "Chariot" and the "Chambers" meant for them the sphere of esoterics. *Vide* Freudenthal, *Alex. Polyhistor.* p. 75, where he shows this to be one of the traces of Hellenistic influence upon Palestinian life and thought.

פרדס indicates Hellenistic Theosophy: in fact Philo often uses "Paradise" as an image for theosophical enquiry (51, 46 *Quaest.* in Gen. i. 6 f.). Cf. 2 Corinthians xii. 4, the Paradise contained "the tree of knowledge." פרדס, *Pardes*, is a *Notarikon* applied in Jewish literature to the four methods of Biblical exegesis, *viz.* פשט the "plain" interpretation; רמז the "allusive"; דרש the "homiletic"; סוד the "mystic" or "Cabbalistic."

III

TREES

In Biblical imagery.

The tree plays an important part in the metaphorical imagery of the Bible; and this imagery starts with the lowest part of the tree, the roots. The rooting of the tree and the spreading of its roots are used as symbols of stability, as figures of success and ensured prosperity, just as the withering of the roots is emblematical of decay. Thus, *e.g.*, Israel "will cast forth his roots as Lebanon[1]." "In the days to come shall Jacob take root[2]."

The man who trusteth in the Lord shall be "as a tree planted by the waters and that spreadeth out its roots by the river[3]." And similarly, the man whose delight is in the Law of God "shall be like a tree planted by the rivers of water[4]."

On the other hand, in his threat against Philistia[5], the Prophet says, "And I will kill thy root with famine, and he shall slay thy remnant." Again, Hosea, in describing Ephraim as smitten, declares[6], "Their root is dried up, they shall bear no fruit"; and Ezekiel, in proclaiming the divine judgment upon Jerusalem for its revolt against Babylon in favour of Egypt, exclaims[7], "Thus saith the Lord God: Shall it prosper? Shall he not pull up the roots thereof that it wither?"

[1] Hos. xiv. 6. [2] Is. xxvii. 6. [3] Jer. xvii. 7 and 8.
[4] Ps. i. 3. [5] Is. xiv. 30. [6] ix. 16.
[7] xvii. 9.

But apart from the roots, the tree itself as a whole is frequently used by the Prophets and Poets of the Bible in a figurative sense.

In Biblical imagery the tree is typical of man. "For man is the tree of the field[1]." According to its position, growth and development it denotes either the righteous or the unrighteous individual (one who trusts in the Lord or who relies upon man)[2]. Again, it symbolises Israel, "for as the days of a tree shall be the days of My people[3]"; while its stock (from which fresh shoots shall spring) signifies the permanent and ever-living element in Israel—the holy seed[4].

The tree is further used as a literary metaphor for Wisdom—for the Law, "She is a tree of life to them that lay hold upon her[5]"; a vast collection of trees —the forest or thicket—typifies a hostile army, Israel's enemies[6].

The tree in Midrashic simile.

In Midrashic poetry the use of these tree-similes is continued by the Rabbis. Some of their points of comparison are in the nature of an amplification and development of the Biblical ideas; whilst others are new figures constituting original conceptions of the Rabbinic age.

In the metaphorical language of the Bible, as we have noted above, the tree represents the Torah. In Rabbinic imagery this conception is greatly amplified and expanded.

Spreading roots.

Thus: the deep-striking roots of the tree are symbolical of the penetrating words of the Torah. "And as nails well-fastened [*lit.* well-planted], so are the words of the masters of collections[7]." And why

[1] Deut. xx. 19. [2] Jer. xvii. 5–8. [3] Is. lxv. 22.
[4] Is. vi. 13. [5] Prov. iii. 18. [6] Is. x. 33–4 *et cet. loc.*
[7] Eccl. xii. 11, וכמסמרות נטועים.

is the expression of "planting" used in the simile? Even as the roots of a tree spread in all directions, so do the words of the wise penetrate the whole body[1].

The shoot.

The figure of beautiful shoots is employed already in the Bible to symbolise the faithful ones who, as the product of the divine handiwork, help to glorify God's name: "The branch of My planting" Isaiah lovingly calls regenerated Israel[2].

In Midrashic poetry the shoot is made to typify the scholar and worthy man.

R. Simeon bar Abba (3rd and 4th c.) came to R. Ḥanina, saying: Write me a letter of commendation so that I may seek my livelihood outside the Holy Land. R. Ḥanina replied: "To-morrow I may go to thy fathers [*i.e.* die] and they will say unto me: 'We had one beautiful shoot in the land of Israel, and thou didst permit it to depart therefrom[3].'"

The fruit-bearing and fruitless tree.

The contrast between the fruit-bearing trees, such as the olive, the fig, or the vine, and the unproductive bramble, is used figuratively in the parable of Jotham[4].

[1] *Num. R.* 14, 4. R. Nathan, 3rd c., the term used for "the roots spread" is משתרשים. In *Pesikta R.* ch. III, Friedmann states that in the previous edition he found the abbreviation משתי' which he assumed to be משתילים, a reading which he accepts, and calls attention to the Biblical phrase והיה כעץ שתול Ps. i. 3. But as משתילים is not found intransitively in this sense and as in all parallels to this passage we find either משתרשים or נשרשים, it might perhaps be better to assume that the abbreviation also stood for משתרשים.

[2] Ch. lx. 21, cf. lxi. 3.

[3] *Jer. Moed Katon,* III *init.* 81 *c*; cf. *Taanith,* 5 *b*, "May all shoots taken from thee be like unto thyself." Cf. in this connection the symbolic representation of an assembly of scholars by a multitude of trees in the following Rabbinic adage (*Berachoth,* 57 *a*, below), "Whosoever dreams that he has entered a forest will become the President of the *Kallah* (*i.e.* the assembly of scholars)."

[4] Judg. ix.

In the Midrash the two classes of trees bear a similar symbolic significance, and their characteristics are played upon with considerable effect. The fruit-bearing trees denote the worthy scholars, whose knowledge is crowned by their good deeds or even the ordinary man who is morally worthy, whilst the fruitless trees stand for the unworthy scholars or others whose knowledge is not reflected in their deeds.

Thus said R. Joḥanan (3rd c.): What is the meaning of the text[1] "For the tree of the field is man"? Is then man a tree of the field? But since it is written[2], "For thou shalt eat of it, and thou shalt not cut it down," and since further it is written[3], "Thou shalt destroy and cut it down," how are the two sayings to be reconciled? If one is a worthy student, came the answer, thou shalt enjoy him and not cut him down [even as the fruitful tree is to be preserved], but if he is not worthy, thou shalt destroy and cut him down [even as it is permitted to cut down a fruitless tree][4].

R. Joshua of Sichnin (4th c.) said in the name of R. Levi (3rd and 4th c.): The trees that bear edible fruit were asked: "Why are not your voices heard?" "We have no need thereof," they replied, "our fruits are our witnesses." Then they asked of the fruitless trees, "Why are you so noisy?" and they replied, "Would that we could make our voices heard louder still so that we might attract attention[5]!"

1 Deut. xx. 19. 2 *Ibid.* 3 *Ibid.* v. 20.

4 *Taanith*, 7 *a*; Bacher, *Pal. Am.* I, 239; cf. Matt. iii. 10, vii. 19.

5 *Gen. R.* 16, 3; Bacher, *Pal. Am.* II, 424; R. Huna explains: The fruit-bearing trees, being heavily laden with fruit, make no noise, but the fruitless trees, being light, do make a noise. Cf. Eccl. vii. 6, "As the crackling of thorns under a pot, so is the laughter of the fool," and the

Rich in roots and laden with branches.

Again, the tree rich in roots typifies the man full of practical deeds, the man of action, whilst the tree laden with branches is symbolic of the man possessed of wisdom. He (*sc.* Eleazar b. Azariah, 1st and 2nd c.) used to say: He whose wisdom exceeds his works, to what is he like? To a tree whose branches are many, but whose roots are few; and the wind comes and plucks it up and overturns it upon its face, as it is said: "And he shall be like a lonely juniper tree in the desert, and shall not see when good cometh; but shall inhabit the parched places in the wilderness, a salt land and not inhabited[1]." But he whose work exceeds his wisdom, to what is he like? To a tree whose branches are few but whose roots are many, so that even if all the winds in the world come and blow upon it, they cannot stir it from its place, as it is said[2]: "And he shall be as a tree planted by the waters; and that spreadeth out its roots by the river, and shall not perceive when heat cometh, but his leaf shall be green and shall not be troubled in the year of drought, neither shall it cease from yielding fruit[3]."

The root and the branches.

There is a striking metaphor essentially Midrashic, concerning the root and branch of a tree, which the Rabbis have read into a simple Bible text.

The verse, "It shall leave neither root nor branch[4],"

comment in *Eccl. R. ad loc.* the thorns crackle, as if to let people know that they are something of importance, מימר אוף אנן קיסין.

[1] Jer. xvii. 6. [2] Jer. xvii. 8.

[3] *Aboth*, III, 22; in slightly different form in *Aboth di R. Nathan*, 22; Bacher, *Ag. Tan.* I, 229–30. The idea of comparing study and practice to firm and infirm structure occurs also in Matthew vii. 24–7, though the figure is a different one; *vide* I. Abrahams, *Studies in Pharisaism*, I, p. 92 (1st Series).

[4] Mal. iii. 19.

is thus interpreted in Midrashic poetry: The root signifies the soul; the branch denotes the body[1].

The conception of the branches of a tree as denoting man's offspring is a natural one and not unfamiliar to Bible readers. Thus, *e.g.*, Isaiah[2] speaks of the knife of destiny remorselessly severing and cutting down the spreading branches, and the Psalmist[3] idealises children as the shoots of the olive tree. In Midrashic poetry the use of this figurative conception is continued.

When R. Naḥman bar Jacob (Bab. Am., d. 356) took leave of R. Isaac (of Palestine who was a guest at his house in Babylon), he asked for a blessing. The latter replied: I will tell thee a parable. Unto what may this thing be likened? Unto a man walking in the wilderness. Hungry and thirsty and weary, he found a tree with sweet fruit, casting a pleasant shadow; and underneath it a running brook. He ate of its fruit, drank of its waters and sat in its shadow. On taking his leave, he exclaimed: "O tree, wherewith shall I bless thee? Should I say to thee, May thy fruit be sweet, surely thy fruits *are* sweet; that thy shadow be pleasant, thy shadow *is* indeed pleasant; that a brook do water thee, lo, a brook already runs by thee. But my blessing is, May all thy shoots be like unto thee." Even so is it in thy case. Wherewith shall I bless thee? With Torah? Thou hast Torah. With riches? Thou hast riches. With children? Thou art blest with children. But my blessing is, May thy offspring be like unto thee[4].

[1] *Synhedrin*, 110*b*. [2] xviii. 5. [3] cxxviii. 4.

[4] *Taanith*, 5 *a*; *vide* I. Abrahams, *loc. cit.* I, p. 103, who rightly draws attention to this "gracious" parable as a contrast to Matthew xxi. 19.

The tree rooted in a clean place, with its branches overhanging an unclean spot, is a figure for the righteous man who, though living on earth, has his soul joined to heaven: conversely the tree rooted in an unclean place, but whose branches reach out into a clean spot, represents the life of the wicked on earth.

R. Eleazar b. Zadok (1st c.) said: To what are the righteous like in this world? To a tree which stands in a clean place, while one of its branches projects into an unclean place; when the branch is cut off, the whole tree stands in a clean place. Even so does the Holy One, blessed be He, bring chastisements upon the righteous in this world, to clear away the slight sin attaching to them, in order that they may behold the world to come, as it is said[1]: "And though thy beginning was small, yet thy latter end shall greatly increase." And to what are the wicked like in this world? To a tree which stands in an unclean place while a branch protrudes into a clean place; when the branch is cut off the whole tree stands in an unclean place. Even so does the Holy One, blessed be He, grant blessings in great abundance unto the wicked in this world to compensate them for their small virtues, in order to bring them to the lowest depths, as it is said[2]: "There is a way which seemeth right unto a man, but the end thereof are the ways of death[3]."

The felling of trees.

The image of the felling of trees is used by Isaiah in a general sense in connection with the famous

[1] Job viii. 7. [2] Prov. xiv. 12.

[3] *Kiddushin*, 40 *b*; Bacher, *Ag. Tan.* I, 53; in a shorter form in *Aboth di R. Nathan*, ch. 39.

prophecy of the destruction of Assyria: "Behold, the Lord, the Lord of hosts, shall lop the boughs with terror; and the high ones of stature shall be cut down and the lofty shall be laid low. And he shall hew down the thickets of the forest with iron, and Lebanon shall fall by a mighty one[1]."

In Midrashic literature this figure is used in developed form with a somewhat similar object. The process of felling the trees typifies the attempts, some of them more successful than others, to destroy Israel.

To what may this matter be likened? To a man who comes to fell a tree. He who has had no experience in the felling of trees keeps lopping off each branch separately and soon grows weary. But the experienced man uncovers the roots and then lops them off. Even so said the wicked one [*i.e.* Balaam], "Why should I curse every single tribe? Let me rather root out the whole." When he set to work, he found them too hard [too firm to uproot]; therefore said he[2], "For from the top of the *rocks* I see him[3]." [From the top I see him like rocks.]

And very often man himself supplies the instrument of his own overthrow. R. Isaac bar Eleazar (3rd and 4th c.) said: Hence the proverb[4]: Every joist [to be felled] requires an axe [which is made usable through the wooden handle]; the worm which destroys the wood comes out of the wood itself [*i.e.* the teacher is beaten by his own pupil[5]].

[1] Ch. x. *vv.* 33–4. [2] Num. xxiii. 9. [3] *Num. R.* 20, 19.

[4] כל כשורתא בעיא מלאי ססא דקיסא מיניה וביה acc. to the reading of the Meïri.

[5] A pupil of Shammai contributed to the overthrow of his own master's teaching; *Jer. Beṣa*, 61 *c*, top; cf. *Tanna di be Eliahu Rabba*, XXIX, אין האילן נעקר אלא בבן מינו. For the origin of the prov. *vide Gen.*

A falling tree.

The figures of the falling of a tree and its consequent injury to a neighbouring one, as well as that of the smaller trees setting fire to the larger ones (the latter figure being reminiscent of the parable of Jotham[1]), are used respectively as symbols of the evil and good effects of close companionship.

On the text "(God hath appointed me another seed) instead of Abel; for Cain slew him" the Midrash says: Because of the sin he committed against Abel, Cain was killed. This is like unto two trees that were near each other. When the wind smote down the one tree, it fell on its neighbour and laid it low. Even so (when it is said) "instead of Abel for Cain slew him[2]" it means because of the sin committed on Abel Cain was slain[3].

Burning wood.

R. Naḥman bar Isaac (Bab. Am., d. 356) said: Why are the words of the Torah likened unto a tree, as it is said[4]: "She is a tree of life to them that lay hold upon her"? To tell thee that just as a small tree sets fire to the large one, even so do young scholars set on fire the minds of older scholars. Hence the saying of R. Ḥanina: Much have I learned from my teachers; more from my companions; most from my disciples[5].

R. 5, 10, "As soon as iron was created the trees began to tremble, whereupon it said unto them, 'Wherefore do you tremble, let none of you serve me (as a handle) and no injury shall befall any of you.'"

[1] Judg. ix. 15. [2] Gen. iv. 25.

[3] *Gen. R.* 23, 5. Rather obscure. The Rabbis no doubt tried to explain the apparently superfluous phrase כי הרגו קין in the mouth of the mother, and they interpreted it as mirroring psychologically the mother's thoughts. The new-born child was a compensation not only for Abel, but also for Cain, inasmuch as Cain, after committing the crime of fratricide, was to her as dead morally as his brother Abel. For a similar idea cf. Rebekah's exclamation "Why should I be bereaved of *both* of you in one day?" (Gen. xxvii. 45) when she heard of Esau's designs on Jacob's life. [4] Prov. iii. 18.

[5] *Taanith*, 7 *a*, cf. the parable of Jotham (Judg. ix) and also the

A striking metaphor, taken from the grafting of a new branch on a tree, and based upon the etymological suggestion of a Bible text, is employed by the Rabbis to express the attachment of heathen elements to Israel: Grafting.

R. Eleazar (b. Pedath, 3rd c.) said: What is the meaning of the text[1] "And in thee shall all the families of the earth be blessed"? The Holy One, blessed be He, said unto Abraham, Two good shoots[2] have I to engraft on thee, Ruth the Moabite and Naomi the Ammonite[3].

Resin derived from trees, and carefully preserved, supplies a strange biological metaphor to denote the human embryo. Resin.

"All the souls of the house of Jacob, which came into Egypt were threescore and ten[4]." Jochabed, whilst still unborn, is included to complete the number 70. R. Berechiah (4th c.) said: It is like unto the resin, which scarcely begins to ooze, when arrangements are made to collect it[5].

following Talmudic proverb: Two dry firebrands and one moist between them, the dry burns the moist, *i.e.* one pious man in the company of the wicked is ruined together with them (*Synhedrin*, 93*a*).

1 Gen. xii. 3.

2 שתי ברכות, a play upon ונברכו in the text.

3 *Yebamoth*, 63 *a*; *Yalkut*, *Gen.* § 65; in *Baba Kama*, 38 *a*, where it speaks of the claim to preservation on the part of Moab on account of the descent of Ruth and Naomi, the expression used is שתי פרידות (two pigeons). The term ברכה is also used in the Talmud in the sense of a pair of pigeons. For a parallel use of the natural imagery of grafting in the olive yard see the parable in Rom. xi. 16 ff., where the "wild" branch of the olive tree is inserted into the "good" stock; *i.e.* the Gentile, believing, is grafted in and becomes part of the living organism. In this passage of the N.T. the olive represents the collective body, whose life began with the call of Abraham—the root—the great Father of Faith.

4 Gen. xlvi. 27.

5 *Gen. R.* 94, 9; Bacher, *Pal. Am.* III, 373.

Some specific trees in Biblical and Rabbinic poetry: (1) The cedar.

But apart from the similes which cluster round the tree in general, many forms of comparison in the literature of the Midrash, no less than in the Biblical writings, are drawn from specific trees.

The cedar is a familiar figure in Biblical poetry and is used both as metaphor and simile. As metaphor it denotes chiefly power and pride; as simile it is associated also with the idea of moral strength and righteousness. It typifies rulers, whether of Israel[1] or of other nations. It represents the king of Judah[2] as well as the power of mighty Assyria[3]. It is a figure for towering height[4] as well as arrogance[5]. It symbolises the flourishing of the righteous man[6] and in a wider sense the prosperity of righteous Israel[7]. It depicts in a more idyllic sense the sturdy appearance of the ideal lover[8].

In the poetry of the Rabbis this tree chiefly connotes, both in metaphor and simile, moral strength. It typifies men of righteousness, men of renown, whose reputation spreads far and wide.

R. José b. Ḥalafta (Tanna, 2nd c.) said: I have planted five cedars in Israel [*i.e.* I begat five sons who acquired renown][9].

Commenting upon the text "The righteous shall flourish like the palm tree, he shall grow like a cedar in Lebanon[10]," R. Tanḥuma (b. Abba, 4th c.) opened his discourse as follows: Wherefore are the righteous compared to the palm and to the cedar,

1 Zech. xi. 1. 2 2 Kings xiv. 9. 3 Ezek. xxxi. 3 ff.
4 Amos ii. 9. 5 Is. ii. 13. 6 Ps. xcii. 13.
7 Num. xxiv. 6. 8 Cant. v. 15.
9 *Shabbath*, 118 *b*, cf. *The Story of Aḥikar*, I, 9: "And my son grew and shot up like a cedar."
10 Ps. xcii. 13.

and not to any other trees? It is because thou findest from experience that in the case of trees generally one cannot say from a distance, This is such and such a tree. And why not? Because they are short of stature (and hence indistinguishable). But the palm and the cedar, being tall of stature, are visible from afar. Even so are the righteous discerned and distinguished a long way off[1].

When R. Samuel b. Isaac died, the lament was made: The cedars of the land of Israel have been uprooted[2].

Bar Kippuk's (3rd c.) funeral oration at the death of Rabina ran as follows: If the flaming fire has fallen among the cedars, what shall the wall hyssop do[3]?

Its inflexibility.

But in these Midrashic writings the figurative use of the cedar is somewhat expanded. Its natural hardness and consequent inflexibility are made to symbolise the unbending and therefore breakable character of man.

On that day[4] R. Simeon b. Eleazar (2nd and 3rd c., a pupil of R. Meïr) entered his spacious house of study and preached: A man should always be as pliant as a reed and not as hard as a cedar. How is it with the reed? All the winds come and blow

[1] *Tanḥuma* to *Lech Lecho*, Buber, p. 34.

[2] אתעקרון ארזייא דארעא דישראל, *Jer. Abodah Zarah*, III, 42 *c*, top.

[3] *Moed Katon*, 25 *b*, quoted in Seliḥa for יו"כ Musaph, beginning ברית כרותה.

[4] It was the day when he returned from the Academy to his native town: He met an exceedingly ugly man who saluted him. Being in a very joyful and proud mood, Simeon did not return the man's greeting and even mocked him on account of his ugliness. When, however, the man said to him, "Go and tell the Master Who created me, how ugly His handiwork is," the Rabbi perceived his error and besought the man for pardon. *Vide Aboth di R. Nathan*, ch. 41, and more fully in *Taanith*, 20 *a*, *b*.

against it, and it sways to and fro with them. When the winds have been lulled, the reed resumes its normal position. Wherefore the reed has been deemed worthy to provide a pen for the writing of a scroll. The cedar, however, does not remain in its place. As soon as the south wind blows, it uproots it and overturns it; and what is the end of the cedar? The cutters come and chisel and carve it, they use it for covering the houses and the remainder they throw into the fire. Hence it was said: "Let a man be as soft as a reed and not as hard as a cedar[1]."

R. Samuel b. Naḥman (3rd c.) said in the name of R. Jonathan b. Eleazar (3rd c.): Better the curse wherewith Ahijah the Shilonite cursed Israel than the blessing with which Balaam blessed them. Ahijah cursed them by foretelling that "The Lord will smite Israel as a reed is shaken in the water[2]." Balaam, the wicked, blessed them by likening them to the cedar, as it is said: "Like cedars[3]." How is it with the cedar? It does not grow in a place of water, its stump produces no new shoots, and its roots are not many. And, though when all the ordinary winds in the world blow against it, they do not move it along with them, yet as soon as a south wind blows, it overturns it[4].

Cutting down the cedar.

Again, the noise made in cutting down a cedar is used figuratively for the cry of the soul in struggling to release itself from its bodily frame.

[1] *Aboth di R. Nathan*, ch. 41. [2] 1 Kings xiv. 15. [3] Num. xxiv. 6.

[4] *Taanith*, 20 *a*; Bacher, *Pal. Am.* I, 65. According to *Tosafoth*, beginning מה ארז זה, the words "by the waters" עלי מים, which would render his pronouncement a real blessing, were not used by Balaam, but were added by the angel. Hence the point of the simile. The two words are omitted also in the *Yalkut*. The *Gemara* adds: Man should ever be as pliable as the reed and not as hard and inflexible as the cedar.

R. Levi (3rd and 4th c.) said: Three things emit a sound, which travels from one end of the universe to the other, a sound which no creature within these vast bounds can perceive. These are, the course of the day, the fall of the rain, and the soul's leave-taking from the body....

R. Samuel, the brother of R. Phineas bar Ḥama, was dying at Sepphoris. R. Phineas had his comrades seated by his side. Some remark was made, and they began to laugh, whereupon R. Phineas said unto them: Behold the soul of this man's [*i.e.* my] brother is cutting cedars and lopping trees! And yet ye sit laughing and know it not[1].

(2) The apple tree.

The apple tree appears but seldom in Biblical literature, being confined practically to the Song of Songs[2] which, as already stated, has received an allegorical interpretation from the earliest days[3]. In Midrashic literature the imagery connected with this tree is also limited to the poetic and almost exclusively allegorical exposition of the Song of Songs.

The natural development of this tree in its different stages has been made symbolic of Israel's attitude at the foot of Sinai.

Shadeless.

The shadeless apple tree, offering no protection from the extreme heat of the midday sun, suggests the

Gen. R. 6, 7; in *Midrash Sam.* ch. 9, § 3, Buber, p. 74, the reading is "was at Sichnin," which is apparently the correct reading, as R. Phineas himself was at Sepphoris and far away from his dying brother; *vide* Hyman, *Toledoth Tannaim v' Amoraim*, vol. III, p. 1014, *sub nom.* Phineas.

[2] ii. 3; vii. 9.

[3] Some explain Prov. xxv. 11 "A word fitly spoken is like *apples of gold* in settings of silver" as referring to real and not artificial fruit, *vide* Wünsche, *Die Bildersprache d. Alten Testaments*, Leipzig, 1906, p. 111.

overpowering glow of the Revelation, in which Israel alone of all nations consented to abide.

R. Huna and R. Aḥa said in the name of R. José b. Zimra (3rd c.): How is it with the apple tree? All flee from it at the time of dry heat (midday); and why so, because it gives no shade[1] for anyone to sit under. Even so the heathens fled, because they would not dwell in the shadow of the Holy One, blessed be He, on the day of the giving of the Law. One might have thought that this was the case also with Israel, therefore is it written[2]: "I sat down under his shadow with great delight." I delighted in him and seated myself down. I it was who delighted in him, but not the nations[3].

Its budding and blossoming.

The early budding and blossoming of the tree before the shooting forth of its leaves is symbolic of Israel's ready, nay precipitate, acceptance of the Law, when they pledged themselves to a complete fulfilment of the precepts before knowing the detailed demands that would be made upon them.

R. Ḥama bar Ḥanina (3rd c.) said: What means the verse "As the apple tree among the trees of the wood, so is my beloved among the sons[4]"? Why is Israel compared to the apple tree? To tell thee, just as in the apple tree the fruit grows before the leaves, so did Israel's "we will do" precede his "we will obey[5]."

1 *I.e.* no big shadow like many another tree.

2 Cant. ii. 3.

3 *Cant. R. ad loc.*; Bacher, *Pal. Am.* I, 116; also in *Pesikta*, 103 *b*. In *Midr. Prov.* to xv. 17 the tradent is a different person.

4 Cant. ii. 3.

5 Ex. xxiv. 7; *Shabbath*, 88 *a*; Bacher, *Pal. Am.* I, 453; no doubt "fruit" here means the same as "blossom." Rashi, *ad loc.* says חנטת פרותיו. In *Cant. R. ad loc.* a similar statement is given in the name of

The season of the ripening of the fruit of the apple tree was noted by the Rabbis to coincide with the month of Sivan, and was therefore made to symbolise the occasion of Israel's receiving the Law.

Its ripening period.

R. Azariah (4th c.) gave two explanations: Even as the apple tree does not mature its fruit till Sivan, so did the Israelites give forth a good savour in Sivan. The apple tree takes fifty days from the time it brings forth its blossoms till it ripens its fruit; even so fifty days elapsed from the time of Israel's departure from Egypt till they received the Law[1].

The tasteful and well-flavoured fruit of the apple tree is a figurative expression for the savoury and palatable words revealed at Sinai.

Sweet-smelling and tasteful.

"As the apple tree among the trees of the wood, so is my beloved among the sons[2]." R. Judah bar Simeon (4th c.) said: How is it with the apple tree? Thou givest an *As* for its price[3] and smellest in it many fragrant odours, even so did Moses say unto the Israelites: "If you so desire you can be redeemed by a small thing[4]." "As the apple tree among the trees of the wood, so is my beloved among the sons[5]." Just as the apple tree is visible to the naked eye and has both

R. Aḥa berabi Z'era, with "blossom" instead of "fruit." The apple tree produces its blossoms before its leaves; even so did the Israelites in Egypt promise belief before hearing; hence it is said (Ex. iv. 31) "And the people *believed*; and when they *heard* that the Lord had visited the children of Israel and that he had seen their affliction then they bowed their heads and worshipped"; *Cant. R.* to ii. 3.

1 *Cant. R.* to ii. 3; Bacher, *Pal. Am.* III, 462. According to the Baraitha *Bechoroth* 8 *a*, the fig tree produces fruit after fifty and the apple tree after sixty days.

2 Cant. ii. 3.

3 איסר, an adaptation of *assarius*, *As*, a Roman coin, usually $\frac{1}{24}$th of a *Denar*.

4 *Cant. R.* to ii. 3.

5 Cant. ii. 3.

8—2

taste and fragrance, even so is it with the Holy One, blessed be He; "His mouth is most sweet; yea he is altogether lovely[1]"; He appeared unto the heathens, but they would not accept the Law, for it was in their eyes like a worthless thing, although it has taste and savour; it has taste, as it is said[2], "O, taste and see that the Lord is good"; it has nourishment, as it is written, "My fruit is better than gold, yea than fine gold[3]"; and it has savour, as it is said[4], "And the smell of thy garments is like the smell of Lebanon." But Israel said, "We know the power of the Law, therefore we shall not move away from the Holy One, blessed be He, and His Law." "Under its shadow I delighted to sit, and its fruit was sweet to my taste[5]."

In a narrower sense, although carrying on the same idea, the fruit of the apple tree is made to figure the popular exposition of the Rabbinic teachers comprised under the term "*Aggadoth.*"

R. Isaac Nappaḥa (3rd and 4th c.) in his introductory discourse said: The text "Comfort me with apples[6]" symbolises the *Aggadoth* (popular lectures) whose savour and taste are like unto the apples[7].

(3) The pomegranate. The only Biblical metaphor associated with the pomegranate is in the Song of Songs[8] where the temples of the beloved are compared to this fruit cut open. In Midrashic poetry several similes are drawn from the pomegranate with its numerous kernels which are visible through the transparent rind.

[1] Cant. v. 16. [2] Ps. xxxiv. 8. [3] Prov. viii. 19.
[4] Cant. iv. 11. [5] *Exod. R.* 17, 2. [6] Cant. ii. 5.
[7] *Soferim*, XVI, 4, *vide* also *Cant. R. ad loc.* where it is given anonymously; see Bacher, *Pal. Am.* II, 212.
[8] iv. 3.

Explaining the Biblical description of the phenomena of Nature in connection with the Egyptian plague of the hail-storm—"So there was hail and fire flashing up amidst the hail[1],"—the Rabbis use the following figure in illustration: It resembled a split (*i.e.* fully ripened) pomegranate whose seeds are visible from without (shining through)[2]. Its transparent seeds

This fruit with its characteristic fulness of seeds is symbolic of the man full of virtue and of the scholar replete with knowledge. Full of seeds.

R. Simeon b. Lakish (3rd c.) said: The fire of *Gehinnom* has no power even over the sinners in Israel. This can be deduced by *a priori* argument from the golden altar. This altar had a layer of gold only as thick as a *denarius*, yet the fire burning upon it for many years could not affect it. How much more is this the case with the sinners in Israel who are as full of precepts as a pomegranate is full of seeds, as it is written[3]: "Thy temples are like a pomegranate split open"? Read not "thy temples" but "the empty ones among thee[4]."

"And the pomegranates bud forth[5]." The text refers to the authors of the Talmud, explained Raba[6].

"Thy temples are like a pomegranate split open behind thy veil[7]." R. Abba b. Kahana and R. Aḥa (3rd and 4th c.) discoursed as follows: One said: The least learned in the three rows [of disciples in front

1 Ex. ix. 24.

2 פרטתא דרמונא *Pesikta* ויהי ביום 3 *b*; *Exod. R.* 12, 4; R. Judah, contemp. of R. Neḥemiah. In *Exod. R.* the reading is פרנותא which should be פרטתא.

3 Cant. iv. 3.

4 *I.e.* explain the Hebrew רַקָּתֵךְ to mean ריקנין שבך; *Ḥagigah*, 27 *a*.

5 Cant. vii. 13.

6 *Erubin*, 21 *b*.

7 Cant. iv. 3

of the Sanhedrin] is as replete with knowledge as this pomegranate [is full of seeds]: It were superfluous to speak thus of those who sat among the Sanhedrin themselves. The other said: The least learned among the Sanhedrin is as replete with knowledge as this pomegranate: It were superfluous to speak thus of those who sat under the olive, the vine and the fig tree, and occupied themselves with words of the Torah[1].

The fruit and the shell.

The pomegranate has suggested also a striking and original metaphor to convey the harmless nature of R. Meïr's relations with his master, Elisha b. Abuyah (or "Aḥer"—the sceptic, "the Faust of the Talmud" as he has been called); for, say the sages, Rabbi Meïr in finding a pomegranate, ate the fruit thereof, and threw away the husk[2].

As the pomegranate used to adorn the holy vestments in the Temple[3] we may here add another metaphorical expression connected with ritual adornment[4].

Circlet and blossom.

"Circlet and blossom" is a Rabbinic metaphor for excellence and beauty. Rabbi Ḥanina and R. Marinus the son of Hoshayah Rabbah (Bab. Am., 3rd and 4th c.) both said in the name of Abba Nehorai: Whenever someone used a well-ordered argument before R. Tarphon (2nd c.) he exclaimed: "Circlet and blossom[5]!"

[1] *Cant. R.* ch. 4, 6, elsewhere in the same chapter with some variations. Bacher, *Pal. Am.* II, 499; about the rows of disciples *vide Synhedrin* 37 *a* and Rashi *ad loc.*

[2] *Ḥagigah*, 15 *b*; others put it thus: R. Meïr absorbed Aḥer's study like one who eats a date—he ate the fruit and threw away the stone.

[3] *Vide* Ex. xxviii.

[4] *Vide* Ex. xxv. The circlet on the candlestick is generally taken to have been in the shape of a pomegranate.

[5] כפתור ופרח.

And when one used an irrelevant argument he would say: "My son shall not go down with you[1]."

The bush plays no part in Biblical imagery. But the special selection of this plant as the medium for the divine revelation to Moses was in itself sufficient to kindle the imagination of the Rabbis, who made the bush the subject of interesting similes. (4) The thorn bush.

The nature of the bush—hard, prickly, deceptive, and therefore hurtful—is made to typify Israel's servitude in Egypt.

R. Simeon b. Joḥai (2nd c.) said: Why did the Holy One, blessed be He, quit the high heavens in order to speak to Moses [about Israel's redemption from servitude] from the midst of the bush? Because, even as the thorn bush is the hardest of all trees, and no bird entering therein comes out intact, but is torn limb from limb, so was Israel's servitude in Egypt harder than all the servitudes in the world; for neither man-servant nor maid-servant, except Hagar alone, had ever succeeded in leaving Egypt, as it is said[2]: "And Pharaoh gave men charge concerning him [*i.e.* Abraham] and they sent him away and his wife and all that he had[3]." Hard and prickly.

[1] לא ירד בני עמכם *Gen. R.* 91, 9; Bacher, *Ag. Tan.* I, 356; בְּנִי is taken in the sense of בִּינָתִי, my "understanding," my "consent": some Rabbis explain the original text (Gen. xlii. 38) in the same way. Jacob said to Reuben, "My consent" cannot go with you. I cannot agree to your proposal. In connection with this metaphorical idea may be taken the following expression of a later Rabbi: On the text (Is. xxvii. 6) "Israel shall bloom and bud," Rab Joseph taught: This signifies the scholars of Babylon who make blossoms and flowers for the Torah, *i.e.* adorn the Law with their exposition (*Shabb.* 145 *b*).

[2] Gen. xii. 20.

[3] *Mechilta*, fragment in Appendix to Friedmann's edition, p. 119 *b*. Bacher, *Ag. Tan.* II, 117; somewhat modified in *Exod. R.* 2, 5, and given in the name of José b. Ḥalafta: "All that he had" implying also the Egyptian maid Hagar whom he had acquired during his stay in Egypt.

R. Phineas the Priest the son of R. Ḥama (4th c.) said: Just as in the case of the bush, when a man lays his hand upon it he does not feel its prickly nature, but when he removes his hand he finds it torn, even so when Israel went down to Egypt they were unnoticed by any one, but when they went out it was with signs, with wonders and with war[1].

Its lowliness.

The lowliness of this plant among the trees symbolises the (temporary) degradation of Israel in the land of bondage, and also the divine humility in the revelation to Moses.

R. Eleazar (*sc.* b. Arach) said: Why did the Holy One, blessed be He, reveal Himself from the high heavens and speak with him [*sc.* Moses] from the bush? Because, as the bush is the lowliest of all trees in the world, even so did Israel descend to the lowest degree and the Holy One, blessed be He, went down with them and redeemed them, as it is said: "And I went down to deliver him from the land of Egypt[2]."

The same Rabbi said: The Omnipresent might have revealed Himself from the height of mountains, from the topmost of the everlasting hills, or from the cedars

[1] *Exod. R.* 2, 5; Bacher, *Pal. Am.* III, 333; cf. the following variants: R. Judah bar Shalom (4th c.) said: "Even as in the case of the bush, the birds enter into it and do not feel its prickles, but when they depart they find their wings plucked; so at the time of Israel's going down to Egypt, *etc. ibid.*; *vide* Bacher, *Am.* III, 437; in *Yalkut Exod.* § 169, the Nature touch is more explicit. Even as in the case of the bush, whosoever puts his hand into it is not hurt *because its thorns are bent downwards*, but when he wants to remove his hand, the thorns catch him and he cannot draw it out (*sc.* unhurt); even so did the Egyptians first receive Israel kindly, but when Israel wished to go forth they did not allow them.

[2] *Mechilta*, fragment in Appendix to Friedmann's edition, p. 119 *b*; in slightly modified form in *Exod. R.* 2, 5; cf. Philo, *Life of Moses*, bk I, p. 16, "The burning bush—a symbol of the oppressed people; and the burning fire—a symbol of the oppressors."

of Lebanon, yet He humbled Himself and spake from the midst of the bush, and thereunto applies the saying of King Solomon[1], "He that is lowly of spirit shall attain to honour"; for among the trees thou canst find nothing more lowly than the bush. Hence Scripture says[2]: "For though the Lord is high, yet regardeth He the lowly[3]."

The particular number of the leaves on the bush suggests to the Rabbis the number of the Patriarchs. Its leaves.

R. Naḥman the son of R. Samuel b. Naḥman (3rd c.) said: Among the trees, some grow one leaf, others two, others again three. But the bush has five leaves. The Holy One, blessed be He, said unto Moses: "The Israelites shall not be redeemed except through the merits of five, *viz.*, those of the three Patriarchs, thy merit and that of Aaron[4]."

The use of the bush for fences typified God's people becoming the fence of the world. Its use for fences.

R. Joḥanan (3rd and 4th c.) said: The bush is used for making a fence round the garden, even so does Israel form a fence to the world (guarding and protecting it against moral deterioration).

Its growth by the waters, both in the garden and by the river side, denotes Israel flourishing by the waters of the Torah. Its growth by the water.

The bush grows beside all waters. Even so the people of Israel wax great only through the merit of the Torah, which is called "water," as it is said[5]: "Ho, every one that thirsteth, come ye to the waters."

The bush grows both in the garden and by the river; In the garden

[1] Prov. xxix. 23. [2] Ps. cxxxviii. 6.

[3] *Mechilta di R. Simeon b. Joḥai*, ed. Hoffmann, p. 2.

[4] *Exod. R.* 2, 5. [5] Is. lv. 1.

and by the river. even so does Israel exist both in this world and in the world to come.

Producing thorns and roses. The production by the bush of both roses and thorns symbolises the people of Israel as comprising within itself both the righteous and the wicked[1].

There are other non-productive trees of a general character, having a symbolic significance in the poetry of the Midrash.

(5) The sycamore tree. The sycamore tree[2] on account of its barrenness typifies ignorance and worthlessness.

Resh Lakish (3rd c.) said: Saul was like a block of a sycamore tree (*i.e.* a man barren of thought, empty of merits)[3].

"A poor man that oppresseth the weak[4]," such is Jephtha, who was a shoot of a sycamore tree (*i.e.* poor in the knowledge of the Law)[5].

(6) The tamarisk. The tamarisk, for its strength and height, symbolises the great and the learned.

On the text "And Abraham planted a tamarisk tree in Beer Sheba[6]" R. Azariah in the name of R. Judah bar Simon (4th c.) said: The "tamarisk" denotes the Sanhedrin, even as it is said[7]: "Now Saul was sitting in Gibeah, under the tamarisk tree in Ramah[8]."

1 *Exod. R.* 2, 5.

2 In the Bible a symbol of plenty—2 Chron. i. 15, cf. ix. 27 and 1 Kings x. 27.

3 *Jer. Abodah Zarah,* II, 40 *c*: גרופית של שקמה ; גרופית = a little stump or shoot.

4 Prov. xxviii. 3.

5 גרופית, *Tanḥuma B'ḥukothai, ad fin.* ed. Buber.

6 Gen. xxi. 33.

7 1 Sam. xxii. 6.

8 Ramah was a seat of judgment; *Gen. R.* 54 end, *vide Tosefta Sotah,* 11, 12, where the tamarisk of Ramah is explained to mean the Beth-Din of Samuel, and Rashi to 1 Sam. xxii. 6, where tamarisk is taken as a symbol of Samuel himself; Bacher, *Pal. Am.* III, 181. For the association

"It hangs on high tamarisks" is a metaphorical expression used by the Rabbis to convey that the saying originates from great men[1].

"The tamarisks [*i.e.* the old, the eminent] among the Babylonian scholars are but like the pigeons [the young] among the Palestinians[2]," was the proverbial utterance of R. Ḥama b. Bisa (3rd c.) the father of Hoshayah.

(7) The carob tree.

The carob tree is employed as a figure for the man of beautiful hair and handsome appearance. Absalom showed himself handsome by his hair. R. Ḥanina (*sc.* b. Ḥama, 3rd c.) said: His hair was like a big carob tree[3].

It is used also as a symbol of poverty in a striking passage dealing with Repentance. The following was taught in the name of R. Eleazar: The Sword and the Book were sent down from heaven wrapt up together, and the Holy One, blessed be He, said, "If you keep that which is written in this book you shall be delivered from the sword...." In the name of R. Simeon b. Joḥai the teaching was as follows: The loaf and the stick were sent down wrapt up together

of a tree with the judgment seat cf. "Deborah was sitting under a palm tree and the children of Israel came up to her for judgment" (Judg. iv. 5). This was also between Ramah and Bethel. Cf. also the Sanhedrin and the "threshing floor" arrangement of their judgment seat.

1 דתליא באשלי רברבי; *Beṣa*, 27 *a*; *Abodah Zarah*, 7 *b*; cf. the following (*Pesaḥim*, 112 *a*), Rabbi Akiba said to R. Simeon b. Joḥai: If you desire to hang, hang thyself on a tall tree (*i.e.* if you must refer to an authority, select a good one).

2 אשלי דיינין שבגליות גזלי דיינין שבארץ ישראל; *Jer. Baba Meṣia*, I, end, 8 *a*; cf. the saying, *Jer. Nedarim*, VII, 40 *a*, "the small group of scholars in the land of Israel is dearer to me than the great Sanhedrin in other lands."

3 כחרובית *Jer. Sotah*, I, 17 *b*, top; *Num. R.* 9, 24; *Midrash Sam.* ch. 13.

from on high, and God said, "If you keep the Torah, there is bread to eat, but if you do not, there is the stick with which to beat."

This may be deduced from the Bible text[1], "If ye be willing and obedient, ye shall eat of the good of the land; But if ye refuse and rebel, ye shall be devoured with the sword[2]" [or eat carob][3]. R. Aḥa said Israel needs carob [*i.e.* poverty] to be forced to repentance[4] [*i.e.* only when Israel are reduced to such a state of poverty that they must eat carob do they repent of their evil ways].

(8) The acacia. The acacia, whose utility begins when it is cut down, is made to symbolise the career of usefulness which follows upon affliction.

"Go speak [bring destruction] to Pharaoh king of Egypt[5]." The proverb says: In acacias there is no profit except you cut them down [*i.e.* a wicked man can only be converted by suffering][6].

[1] Is. i. 19. [2] חרב תְּאֻכְּלוּ.

[3] וַחֲרָבִין תֵּאכֵלוּ, *i.e.* be impoverished.

[4] *Lev. R.* 35, 6, cf. the saying of R. Akiba, יאה מסכנותא לברתיה דיעקב *ad loc.*, and יאה עניותא ליהודאי *Ḥagigah*, 9 *b*.

[5] Ex. vi. 11 (according to the Rabbis the words of the message are not indicated, the latter half of the verse denoting the result "and he *will* let the children of Israel go out of his land." They therefore explain דַּבֵּר, "speak," as connected with דֶּבֶר, "destruction." Hence the point of the proverb).

[6] *Exod. R.* 6, 5 *finis*.

IV

VITICULTURE

VITICULTURE was a well-established industry known and understood by the people of Palestine from the very earliest times. It is therefore natural that the subject should occupy a prominent place in the metaphorical imagery of the Bible.

In the imagery of the Bible.

The Psalmist[1] depicts, under the image of the transplanted vine, the transfer of the people of Israel from their unfavourable condition in the land of Egypt to the more congenial surroundings of the Promised Land. And Israel's exposure to the merciless attack of plundering nations is portrayed under the picture of the utter destruction of the vineyard and the vine[2].

Similar figures are used with equal poetic force by the Prophet-Poets of the Bible; by Isaiah in particular, in his beautiful Parable of the Vineyard, and elsewhere[3]; by Hosea[4], who speaks of Israel "as the luxuriant vine which put forth fruit freely"; and by Jeremiah[5], who in the name of God laments the fact that "many shepherds have destroyed My vineyard, trodden My portion under foot, and made My pleasant portion a desolate wilderness"; whilst the Prophet Ezekiel[6] makes elaborate use of the figure of the vine, once in a flourishing condition, but now sud-

[1] Ps. lxxx. 9–11.
[2] *Ibid.* *vv.* 13, 14.
[3] Ch. v; cf. ch. xxvii. 2–6.
[4] Ch. x, *v.* 1.
[5] xii. 10.
[6] xix. 10–14.

denly plucked up, as a symbolic representation of the City of Jerusalem, reduced from its position of pristine glory to a state of utter desolation.

The same Prophet[1] uses a similarly elaborate parable of the growing vine—but the picture is marked with some touches of artificiality—in describing the vacillating attitude of Israel in placing itself under the protection of different nations. And he likewise employs the figure of the withered vine[2] to symbolise the inhabitants of Jerusalem given over to fire and flame.

But the writers of the Bible, apart from utilising the vineyard and the vine as a whole for didactic purposes, have employed also more specific aspects of the vine and its products for the purpose of popular illustration.

The complete and simultaneous falling of the faded leaves of the vine as well as the fig tree, is a figure used by Isaiah, who is very fond of this kind of simile, to describe the utter destruction of the hostile hosts[3].

The grape in the process of development, "when the blossom is over and the flower becometh a ripening berry[4]," in its progressive stages of growth, from unripe[5] to ripe[6], in its varying conditions of bitter[7], sour[8] and sweet, often enters into the imagery of the Bible.

Like refreshing grapes in a desert land, so welcome to God was the finding of Israel, says Hosea[9].

Like the disappearance of the clusters, after the gleaning of the vintage, is the departure from the

[1] Ezek. xvii. 1–10. [2] *Ibid.* xv. 2 ff. [3] Is. xxxiv. 4.
[4] Is. xviii. 5. [5] Jer. xxxi. 29. [6] Is. lxv. 8.
[7] Deut. xxxii. 32. [8] Ezek. xviii. 2. [9] ix. 10.

earth of the upright and the goodly man, declaims Micah[1]; whilst the unexpected finding of new wine in an odd cluster which saves the vine from destruction, "for there is a blessing in it," is made by Isaiah[2] to symbolise the saving of many from destruction for the sake of God's servant.

The figure of the wine-press and the wine-store is also used with striking effect by the Prophets of the Bible. The treading of the wine-press, the trampling of the grapes under foot, and the staining of the worker's garments by the splashing of the blood-red wine, suggested the bold image of God meting out vengeance upon the virgin daughter of Judah[3] as well as upon the nations who oppressed Israel[4].

The settling of the wine upon the lees, without being disturbed by tilters, or being emptied from vessel to vessel, so that the wine retains its flavour, is used both by Jeremiah[5] and Zephaniah[6] as a figure for those in Israel and among other nations who are over-confident and at ease.

And the handing round of the cup of undiluted wine with its effect upon him who quaffs it to the bitter end is employed by the writers of the Bible to symbolise the cup of punishment dealt out by God both to Israel and the other nations.

Viticulture in Rabbinic simile.

That the Rabbis should continue to utilise the simile of the vineyard and of its products for the purposes of instruction was but natural. For viticulture was still prevalent and popular in the days of the Rabbis, even as it had been in the period of the Prophets and the Psalmists.

1 vii. 1–2. 2 lxv. 8. 3 Lam. i. 15.
4 Is. lxiii. 3. 5 xlviii. 11–12. 6 i. 12.

The possession of vineyards both near home and in distant parts was a feature of the life of the people.

R. Simeon b. Ḥalafta said: Unto what may this be likened? Unto one man living in Galilee and possessing a vineyard in Judea, and another living in Judea and owning a vineyard in Galilee. He who dwelt in Galilee used to go to Judea to hoe his garden and the one from Judea went to Galilee to hoe his. On coming together they said unto each other: "Instead of thee coming to my domain, take charge of my garden which is situated within thy region, and I shall in return guard thy property which is within my confines."

Even so when David said[1], "Keep me as the apple of the eye," the Holy One, blessed be He, said unto him[2], "Keep My commandments and live." Thus said the Holy One, blessed be He, unto Israel, "Keep ye My precepts, the precept of reading the *Shema* morning and evening, and I shall guard you," even as it is written[3] "The Lord shall keep thee from all evil; He shall keep thy soul[4]."

The vineyard and the vine: a type of Israel.

Some of the Rabbis of the Midrash, harking back to the Psalmists' use of the vine metaphor, still think of the vine as symbolic of Israel. But their description of the vine-growing process is more elaborate in its details, and these are clearly set forth with the object of homiletic exposition.

Transplanting the vine.

Thus R. Tanḥuma b. Abba (Amora, 4th c.) introducing the discourse on the text "Thou didst pluck

[1] Ps. xvii. 8. [2] Prov. iv. 4. [3] Ps. cxxi. 7.

[4] *Tanḥuma Kedoshim*, Buber, p. 38*a*, § 57. In *Yalkut* to Ps. xvii. § 671, this is given in the name of R. Ḥiyya.

up a vine out of Egypt[1]," said: Why is Israel likened unto the vine? How is it with the vine? When its owners try to improve it, what do they do? They transplant it from one place to another, and it improves. Even so did the Holy One, blessed be He. When He wished to make Israel known in the world, what did He do? He plucked them out of Egypt and brought them into the wilderness, where they began to prosper and accepted the Law by proclaiming "everything that the Lord hath spoken we will do and obey." Their fame then spread in the world, as it is said[2]: "And thy renown went forth among the nations for thy beauty[3]."

Preparing the soil.

The preparation of the soil for the cultivation of the vine, the transfer and orderly arrangement of the plants, are made typical of the varied stages in Israel's early history. "Thou didst pluck up a vine out of Egypt[4]." How is it with the vine? says an anonymous Rabbi. It is not planted in a place of rugged slabs of earth[5], but the clods are first broken under it[6] and then it is planted. Even so, "Thou didst drive out nations and didst plant them [Israel]." Again, the more thoroughly the soil beneath the vine is sifted and cleared, the better is its growth and quality. Even so was it with Israel. "Thou clearedst all kings before them," and then they took deep root and filled the land[7].

Arranging the plants.

The vine is not planted haphazard[8] but in regular rows[9]; even so was Israel arranged in serried ranks[10],

1 Ps. lxxx. 9. 2 Ezek. xvi. 14.
3 *Exod. R.* 44, 1 *et cet. loc.*; Bacher, *Pal. Am.* III, 490.
4 Ps. lxxx. 9. 5 טרשים. 6 בולשין אותה מתחתיה.
7 *Ibid.* v. 9. 8 ערבוביא. 9 שורות שורות.
10 דגלים דגלים.

"Every man by his own standard with the ensigns of their fathers' houses[1]."

Growth and development of the vine.

The growing vine taken as a whole presents to one Rabbi of the 3rd century a symbol of Israel with its different social grades and their relationship to the outside world. R. Simeon b. Lakish said: This nation is likened unto a vine. Its branches stand for landowners[2]; the clusters of grapes for the Disciples of the Wise[3]; the leaves for the *Ammé-Ha'aretz*; the rods or thin branches[4] for the empty ones in Israel [the meritless, men devoid of all discipline and virtue]. And this is the message which they were wont to send from Palestine [to the people of Babylon]: "Let the bunches of grapes pray for the leaves" [*i.e.* the scholars for the uncultured], since were it not for the leaves the clusters could not exist[5].

The vine is the meanest of all trees and yet [in its developed state] it rules over all the other trees[6]; even so is it with Israel; he seems low in this world now, but in time to come his inheritance will extend from end to end of the world[7].

How is it with the vine? One branch [or twig] sprouts forth from it and overtops many trees[8]. Even so is it with Israel; one righteous man descends from them and rules from one end of the world to the other [*e.g.* Joseph, Joshua, David, Solomon, and Mordecai][9].

1 *Lev. R.* ch. 36, 2.

2 בעלי בתים. Rashi, *ad loc.* explains this as 'men of substance, benevolent and generous.'

3 אשכולות, "clusters," being explained, *Sotah*, 47 *a*, as איש שהכל בו, a man possessing all knowledge.

4 קנוקנות.

5 *Ḥullin*, 92 *a*, *vide* Bacher, *Ag. Am.* I, 375.

6 שולטת בכל האילנות.

7 *Lev. R.* 36, 2 anonym.

8 שרביט אחד יוצא ממנו ומכבש כמה אילנות.

9 *Ibid.* anonym.

The vine hangs on a reed[1]. Even so does Israel gain support through the merit of the Law which was written with a reed. The vine trails along steps and terraces[2] and is made to overspread tall cedars[3]. Even so does Israel overtop in numbers all kingdoms of the earth[4].

Just as the vine lives[5], says R. Tanḥuma b. Abba (4th c.), and supports itself upon the dead [withered and dried up] trees, even so does Israel live and thrive, relying upon the [merit of the] dead [*i.e.* the Patriarchs][6].

The destruction of the vineyard.

As in the Bible, so also in Midrashic poetry the spoliation of the vineyard symbolises the oppression and attempted destruction of Israel.

This might be compared unto a king [or prince] who had a vineyard which three enemies attacked together. The first began plucking among the small single bunches, the second continued the work of havoc by thinning the clusters. The third tried to uproot the vines. Even so did Pharaoh order: "Every son that is born ye shall cast into the river[7]." Nebuchadnezzar then tried to diminish the scholars: "The craftsmen and the smiths were departed from

[1] נשענת על גבי קנה. [2] עולה על כל מסע ומסע.

[3] מדלין אותו על גבי ארזים גדולים.

[4] *Ibid.* anonym. For other examples of figurative application of the trailing vine cf. the following. R. Tanḥuma said: This wine even its mother [*i.e.* the vine] could not support it [it trails on the ground], and wilt thou be able to support it? This vine is supported by many reeds and beams and yet it cannot stand erect, and wilt thou be able to support it [after thou hast drunk thereof]? (*Lev. R.* 12, 4). A vine of gold trailing over wooden pillars was placed at the entrance of the Temple, and whosoever brought a free-will offering of a leaf, a berry or a cluster hung it thereon (*Ḥullin*, 90 *b*). [5] Another variant "is sapful."

[6] *Lev. R.* 36, 2; *Exod. R.* 44, 1 *et cet. loc.*; Bacher, *Pal. Am.* III, 490.

[7] Ex. i. 22.

Jerusalem[1]": whilst Haman sought to uproot the whole vineyard, as it is written[2]: "To destroy, to slay, to cause to perish all Jews."

R. Abin (4th c.) said: This may be likened unto a king who had a vineyard. Enemies entered into it, cut it down and ruined it[3]. Who is it that needs to be consoled? The vineyard or its owner? Even so the Holy One, blessed be He, said: "Israel is my vineyard"..."Who needs to be consoled? Is it not I[4]?"

This may be likened unto robbers who entered the royal vineyard and crushed the vines. The king came, and finding the vineyard in ruins, was filled with anger and attacked the rogues. He did not invoke the aid of any thing or person, but went and cut them down and tore them up, as they had done to the royal vineyard. Even so when the Egyptians visited the children of God with hard judgments, the Holy One, blessed be He, was filled with wrath against them and smote them[5].

Watching the vineyard.

To guard against spoliation, watch was kept over the vineyard, as over the field, garden and orchard. This watching over the vineyard is used in Rabbinic parable. "Remember what Amalek did unto thee by the way when ye came forth out of Egypt[6]." R. Levi (3rd c.) said: He attacked them on the way like robbers. Unto what may this be compared? Unto a king who had a vineyard. He surrounded it with a fence and placed there a dog that was wont to bite,

[1] Jer. xxix. 2.

[2] Esther iii. 13; *Gen. R.* 42, § 3; *Lev. R.* 11, § 7; *Esther R.* Intro. § 11. In *Lev. R.* the reading is "He sought to stamp out, to exterminate the last germ or root of Israel," ביקש לקעקע ביצתן של ישראל.

[3] וקיצצוהו ופיסקוהו.

[4] *Pesikta*, p. 128 *a*, *b*.

[5] *Exod. R.* 30, § 17.

[6] Deut. xxv. 17.

for, thought he, whosoever shall come and break the fence the dog shall bite him. After a time the king's son came, broke the fence and was bitten by the dog. Whenever the king desired to recall the son's sin in breaking the fence he would say unto him: "Dost thou remember how the dog bit thee?"

Even so, whenever the Holy One, blessed be He, desired to recall Israel's sin committed at Rephidim when they said, "Is the Lord among us or not[1]?," He said unto them, "Remember what Amalek did unto thee by the way[2]."

A later Rabbi used a slightly modified version of this parable in explanation of the same event.

R. Aḥa said: This might be compared unto one who entered by night to steal grapes from the vineyard where the watchman was his friend. As soon as the watchman observed him and saw that it was his friend, what did he do? He let loose upon him the dog that was there and then he stood up and rescued him from it. And whenever the watchman desired to remind his friend that he had come to steal grapes, he would say unto him, "Remember how I rescued you from the dog." Even so Scripture might have said, "Remember ye what ye did at Rephidim." And why does it say, "Remember what Amalek did unto thee"? He recalled it to them in indirect manner[3].

The vine and vineyard as symbols of the world.

Besides representing Israel, the figure of the vine and the vineyard served in the imagery of the Rabbis to symbolise the world. We find this use already in the Tannaitic period. Rabbi Eliezer b. Hyrcanus, one of the most prominent Tannaim of the 1st and

[1] Ex. xvii. 7. [2] *Tanḥuma Teṣe*, *Pesikta Zachor*, p. 26 *b*.
[3] *Pesikta R.* p. 55 *b*.

2nd centuries, saw in the vine of which Joseph dreamt[1] an allegorical representation of the world, its "three branches" symbolising the three Patriarchs, its "shooting buds and blossoms" denoting the Matriarchs, and "the clusters bringing forth ripe grapes" signifying the tribes[2].

This conception was continued by a Tanna of a later age. R. Eleazar bar Simon (2nd c.), the Talmud relates, was appointed by the Roman Government as chief of the body-guard or executioner[3], and being rebuked by R. Joshua b. Korḥa with the stinging remark: "O, Vinegar, son of wine, how long wilt thou deliver the people of our God unto slaughter?," he answered in excuse of his conduct: "I am only destroying the thorns out of the vineyard." To which R. Joshua rejoined: "Let the owner of the vineyard [*i.e.* God] himself come and destroy the thorns out of the vineyard[4]."

Redemption of the vineyard.

Like unto a vineyard is the whole world and the fulness thereof[5], said R. Abbahu (3rd and 4th c.). And what constitutes the act of redemption[6]? The benediction we pronounce before partaking of worldly enjoyments[7].

For all earthly possessions are in reality not ours. Man may enjoy them whilst he lives, but in quitting this earth he must surrender them all.

[1] Gen. xl. 10. [2] *Ḥullin*, 92 *a*; Bacher, *Ag. Tan.* I, 149. [3] ארכיליפורן.

[4] *Baba Meṣia*, 83 *b*; cf. *Jer. Maasroth*, III, 50 *d*, middle; *vide* also *Pesikta*, Buber, pp. 91–2 and notes *ad loc.*

[5] העולם כלו ומלואו עשוי ככרם.

[6] The fruit of a newly-planted tree was forbidden for the first three years. In the fourth year it was still regarded as "holy," and could be eaten only in the Holy Land, unless it were redeemed for its value in money. *Vide* Lev. xix. 23, and cf. Deut. xx. 6.

[7] ומהו פדיונו ברכה, *Jer. Berachoth*, 9 *d*, *Midrash Tillim* to Ps. xvi. *init.*

Geniba (Bab. Am., 3rd c.) said: This might be compared unto a fox who found a vineyard which was fenced round on all sides, but had one little hole in it. He sought to enter but could not. What did he do? He fasted three days until he became thin and emaciated. He then entered through that hole, ate and grew sleek. Wishing to leave, he could in no way pass through. He then fasted another three days until he again grew thin and meagre and reduced to his former state, and then went forth. On quitting it he turned his face and gazed back upon the place, saying, "O vineyard, vineyard, how goodly art thou, and how goodly is the fruit which thou producest; all thy contents are beautiful and praiseworthy, but what enjoyment has one from thee? In the state in which one enters he must leave it." Even so is it with this world [and its dwellers]. "As he came forth of his mother's womb, naked shall he go back as he came[1]."

The vineyard as symbol of Jerusalem.

In addition to Israel and the world, the vine in Rabbinic imagery, as in the Bible, symbolises Jerusalem—the Holy City with its Sanctuary and Service. R. Eleazar of Modiim[2] says: "The vine[3]" symbolises Jerusalem; "the three bunches" represent the sanctuary, the king and the High Priest; "the buds and blossoms as it were shooting forth" denote the young priests in training[4]; and "the clusters thereof bringing forth ripe grapes" indicate the drink-offerings[5].

[1] Eccl. v. 14; *Kohel. R. ad loc.*

[2] A scholar of the second Tannaitic generation, *i.e.* 1st and 2nd centuries.

[3] Gen. xl. 10.

[4] פרחי כהונה suggested by כפורחת in the text.

[5] *Ḥullin*, 92 *a*; Bacher, *Ag. Tan.* I, 200.

Again R. José (b. Ḥalafta, 2nd c.) explains "the choicest of vine" (Is. v. 2) as signifying the Sanctuary; "the tower in the midst of it" (*sc.* the vineyard) as symbolising the altar; and "the vat hewn therein" as typifying the *Shittim* (*i.e.* the pits by the side of the altar into which the remainder of the libations was poured)[1].

The vine symbolic of the Law.

The vine also represents the Law.

R. Joshua (b. Ḥananiah, 1st and 2nd c.)[2] said: "The vine[3]" symbolises the Torah; "the three branches" typify Moses, Aaron and Miriam. The "buds and blossoms shooting forth" denote the Sanhedrin, and the "clusters bringing forth grapes" represent the righteous in every generation[4].

These four main metaphorical conceptions gathering around the vineyard and the vine, *viz.* Israel, the World, the Holy City and the Law, run like a golden thread throughout the range of imagery associated with this familiar object of Nature. They are traceable in the figurative representations of every aspect of viticulture.

The vine in bud and blossom.

Thus the vine in bud and blossom is made to refer typically to Israel, the Temple Service and the Houses of Study and Prayer.

"The vines are in blossom, they give forth their fragrance[5]," is explained by some Midrashic authors as a poetic allegory, referring to Israelites who survived the three days of the Egyptian plague

[1] *Sukkah*, 49 *a*; Bacher, *Ag. Tan.* II, 174; cf. the exposition of "the vines in blossom give forth their fragrance," Cant. ii. 13, as denoting "the drink-offerings," *Cant. R. ad loc.*

[2] The colleague of R. Eliezer. [3] Gen. xl. 10.

[4] *Ḥullin*, 92 *a*; Bacher, *Ag. Tan.* I, 149.

[5] Cant. ii. 13.

of darkness, who repented and were redeemed[1]. It is interpreted by others as denoting the drink-offerings brought to the Sanctuary[2]. Again the text[3] "Let us get up early to the vineyards" is expounded by Raba (3rd and 4th c.) as an allegory for the Synagogue and the Houses of Study: the words "Let us see whether the vine hath budded" as a figure for the men versed in the text of the Scriptures (*i.e.* the Biblical scholars)[4]. And the expression "whether the vine blossom be open" is interpreted as a symbol of the scholars learned in the Mishnah[5], and according to some also as a type of the Synagogue and study houses[6].

The products of the vine: the grapes ripe and unripe.

And the same series of metaphors is associated with the products of the vine—the grapes and the wine, which typify chiefly Israel and the Torah.

R. José b. Judah of Chephar Babli (a Tanna, 2nd c.) said: He who learns from the young, unto what may he be likened? Unto one who eats unripe grapes. And he who learns from the old, unto what may he be likened? Unto one who eats ripe grapes[7].

How is it with the vine? Whosoever eats of its unripe fruit will have his teeth set on edge; so it is with Israel, whosoever comes and joins battle with them will in the end get his deserts at their hands. Pharaoh came and warred with Israel, and received retribution at their hands; the thirty-one kings did battle with Israel and they all paid the penalty[8].

We have already noted above, in the case of the

[1] *Cant. R. ad loc.* [2] *Ibid.* [3] Cant. vii. 13.

[4] Some explain "the budded vine," Cant. vi. 11, as typifying the Synagogue and Houses of Study. *Vide Cant. R. ad loc.*

[5] *Erubin*, 21 *b.* [6] *Cant. R. ad loc.* [7] *Aboth*, IV, 26.

[8] *Midrash Samuel*, ch. 16; *vide* also *Lev. R.* 36, § 2.

metaphorical imagery of the vine as a whole, that the clusters of grapes represented the Disciples of the Wise[1]. This figure is of frequent occurrence in the poetry of the Midrash, as the following examples will show. The Mishnah says[2]: With the death of R. José b. Joeser of Zeredah and Joseph b. Joḥanan of Jerusalem the "clusters" ceased [*i.e.* the men who possess everything[3]] even as it is said[4]: "[Woe is me! for I am the last of the summer fruits, as the grape gleanings of the vintage]; there is no cluster to eat." To this another Baraitha is adduced[5]: All clusters that sprang up in Israel since the days of Moses to the death of Joseph b. Joeser of Zeredah had no stain on them; from that time onward there was some stain on them.

The clusters of grapes.

The clusters [*i.e.* men learned in the Law and without evil report] from the days of Moses until the death of José b. Joeser were as learned in the Law as Moses our Teacher; thenceforth they were not as learned as he, said R. Jehudah in the name of R. Samuel[6].

How is it with the vine? It has both fresh and withered grapes[7]; even so is it with Israel. There are among them men versed in the Scriptures[8], men learned in the Mishnah, in the Talmud [Halachah] and in the Aggadah[9].

How is it with the vine? It has both big and small clusters of grapes, and the bigger [*sc.* more heavily

1 The saying of R. Simeon b. Lakish in *Ḥullin*, 92 *a*.

2 *Sotah*, 47 *a*; cf. *Temurah*, 15 *b*.

3 Rashi, *ad loc.*; Torah the fear of sin and *Gemilluth Ḥasadim*.

4 Mic. vii. 1.

5 *Tosefta B. K.* ch. 8, and *Temurah*, 15 *b*.

6 *Vide Temurah*, 15 *b*, and marginal references.

7 יש בה ענבים יש בה צמוקים.

8 בעלי מקרא.

9 *Lev. R.* 36, 2.

laden] cluster appears to hang lower than the lighter cluster. Even so is it with Israel; the more strenuously one toils in the Torah, and the more learned he is than his neighbour, the more humble is he[1].

How is it with the vine? Its leaves cover and protect the clusters of grapes[2]; even so is it with Israel; the *Ammé-Ha'aretz* among them guard and protect the Disciples of the Wise[3].

Nebuchadnezzar was like the second class of enemy, who enters into the king's [or prince's] vineyard and begins thinning the clusters[4] [*i.e.* Nebuchadnezzar diminished the scholars by persecution]; as it is said: "The craftsmen and the smiths were departed from Jerusalem[5]."

Like bunches of grapes tied together with bunches of grapes is the marriage between a scholar and a scholar's daughter. Like bunches of grapes intertwined with berries of thorns is a scholar married to an ignorant man's daughter[6].

The metaphorical conceptions of the vineyard and the wine as referring to Israel and the Torah are continued in the further processes associated with the grape.

Pressing out the wine.

Thus, *e.g.*, with the pressing out of the wine.

How is it with the vine? At first it is trodden under foot and then it is served up on the table of kings; even so is it with Israel; they are despised in this world, but will be highly prized in the world to come[7].

[1] *Lev. R.* 36, § 2, in exposition of Ps. lxxx. 9, anonym.

[2] העלים שלה מכסין על האשכולות.

[3] *Lev. R. ibid.*

[4] מזנב באשכולות.

[5] Jer. xxix. 2; *Gen. R.* 42, § 3; *Lev. R.* 11, 7; the craftsmen and smiths are used as metaphors for scholars.

[6] *Pesaḥim*, 49 *a*.

[7] *Lev. R.* 36, § 2.

The heated mass of grapes for the press.

Again, there is a bold eschatological simile taken from the heated mass of grapes, which may here be mentioned. King David prayed that he might dwell in God's tent for ever (*lit.* through both worlds)[1]. Did then David expect to live for ever? Or is it possible for man to live in two worlds? ask the Rabbis. To which they reply: David prayed that he might become worthy of having his words repeated in his name in the Synagogues and Houses of Study after he had departed this life. And of what worth would this be unto him? they further ask. And they reply that the uttering of an adage in the name of him who had said it makes the lips of the dead author vibrate again.

R. Isaac bar Zeiri (4th c.) said: What is the meaning of the text[2] "And the roof of thy mouth like the best wine that glideth down smoothly for my beloved, moving gently the lips of those that are asleep"? They are like unto a heated mass of grapes. How is it with the heated mass of grapes? As soon as one applies his fingers to it, it drips; even so is it with the lips of the righteous; as soon as a tradition is quoted in their name, their lips mutter in the grave[3].

Wine: a symbol of Torah.

If the grapes denote the scholar, the wine both in its natural state and in its prepared form represents the Law. And this latter image is developed in various ways.

Old and new wine.

Wine improves with age. It gains in quality the

[1] Ps. lxi. 5. [2] Cant. vii. 10.

[3] Given in different forms and in the names of varied tradents, *vide Jer. Berachoth*, II, 4 *b* bottom; *Bechoroth*, 31 *b*; *Yebamoth*, 97 *a*; *Synhedrin*, 90 *b*.

longer it remains in the jar; even so does the knowledge of the Law grow in quality with the scholar's advancing age[1].

R. José b. Judah of Chephar Babli (2nd c.) said: He who learns from the young, unto what may he be likened? Unto one who...drinks wine from its vat. And he who learns from the old, to what may he be likened? Unto one who drinks old wine[2].

"I will cause thee to drink of the spiced wine[3]!" This signified the Talmud, which is mixed with Mishnayoth, like an apothecary's preparation[4]. Spiced wine.

The words of the Torah are like spiced wine. Even as spiced wine contains an admixture of wine, honey and pepper, so do the words of the Torah embody the strength, sweetness and pungency typified by these three ingredients[5].

Sweet wine in Midrashic poetry is also a figurative expression for happy events that rejoice the heart, for good and noble deeds, as well as for the righteous among men; similarly the wine that has turned sour is suggestive of misfortune, degeneration and sin. Wine sweet and sour.

How is it with the vine? It produces vinegar as well as wine, both of which require a "benediction" to be said before they are drunk. Even so is Israel in duty bound to pronounce a blessing for the evil as well as for the good[6].

"Send thee men[7]." This may be likened unto a rich man who had a vineyard. When he saw that the wine was good he said: "Bring the wine into *my*

[1] Cf. Job xii; *Sifré Deut.* to xi. 22, § 48 anonym.
[2] *Aboth*, 4, 26, quoted above. [3] Cant. viii. 2.
[4] *Cant. R. ad loc.*, *vide Soferim*, xv, 7.
[5] *Pesikta*, *Baḥodesh*, p. 102.
[6] *Lev. R.* 36, 2. [7] Num. xiii. 1.

house," and when he noted that the wine had turned sour, he said, "bring the wine into *your* house." Even so was it with the Holy One, blessed be He; when He saw that the deeds of the elders were worthy and honest, He claimed them for Himself, as it is said[1], "Gather unto *Me* seventy men." But when He saw the spies who were destined to sin, He assigned them unto Moses, "Send *thee* men[2]."

The same metaphorical conception of wine as Torah is contained in the further imagery connected with the product of the vine, as well as its storing.

Effects of wine.

Even as wine rejoices the heart, so do the words of the Torah[3].

Said R. Ḥama bar Ukba (pupil of R. José b. Ḥanina, 3rd c.): Even as wine tells its tale on the human countenance, so do the words of the Torah imprint their stamp upon the student of the Law. People point with the finger and say, "This one is a Disciple of the Wise[4]."

How is it with the wine? Whosoever drinks of it his face brightens; even so "a man's wisdom maketh his face to shine[5]," when he is asked and is able to answer; "but the boldness of his face is changed" when he is asked and cannot reply[6].

The wine-store.

R. Judah b. Ilai (2nd c.), in commenting on the text, "He brought me into the banqueting house[7]," said: The congregation of Israel exclaimed: "The Holy One, blessed be He, brought me into a large cellar of wine [*i.e.* to Sinai]. He gave me there the

[1] Num. xi. 16.
[2] *Num. R.* 16, 4. In *Tanḥuma, ad loc.*, the reading is "likened unto a king and his tenants."
[3] Cf. Ps. xix.
[4] *Cant. R.* to Cant. i. 2.
[5] Eccl. viii. 1.
[6] *Midrash Sam.* ch. 16.
[7] Cant. ii. 4.

banners of Torah, of precepts and good deeds, and I accepted them with great love[1]."

"Let him kiss me with the kisses of his mouth, for thy love is better than wine[2]."

R. Eleazar said: This may be likened to a king who had a cellar of wine; when the first guest came, he mixed a cup and gave it to him; when the second came he did the same, but when the king's son came he gave him the whole cellar. Even so was Adam commanded concerning six precepts...Noah had an additional one given to him, so too did Abraham, Isaac and Jacob each receive an additional precept. But upon Israel was enjoined every positive and negative precept[3].

The storing of wine.

The mode of storing wine supplied the Rabbis of the Midrash with many similes. R. Judah the Prince said: Look not at the vessel[4], but at what it contains. Many a new vessel is full of old wine [*i.e.* many a young man is replete with deep learning] and many an old vessel has not even new wine in it[5].

Even as wine cannot be preserved either in vessels of gold or silver, but is laid up in the commonest of vessels, *viz.* earthenware vessels, so can the words of the Torah abide only with the humble in spirit[6].

This simile is enunciated in a slightly modified form by R. Hoshaya (1st Amoraic Generation, c. 200 C.E.). And as an illustrative incident the Rabbi adduces

1 *Cant. R. ad loc.*, Bacher, *Ag. Tan.* I, 211. The same idea, though varied in the second part, is expressed by R. Abba in the name of R. Isaac, Bacher, *Ag. Am.* II, 224; and by Rabbi Joshua of Sichnin in the name of R. Levi, Bacher, *Ag. Am.* II, 385.

2 Cant. i. 2.

3 *Cant. R. ad loc.*, Bacher, *Ag. Am.* II, 36, *vide* notes *ad loc.*

4 Which is the usual custom; cf. Matt. ix. 17; Mark ii. 22.

5 *Aboth*, IV, 27.

6 *Sifré* to Deut. xi. 22, § 48 anonym.

an interesting conversation between the Emperor Hadrian's daughter and R. Joshua b. Ḥananiah, in which the apparent incongruity between the splendid scholarship of the Rabbi and his plain personal appearance was reconciled by quoting the prevalent wise practice of storing the best of wine in the commonest of earthenware vessels.

The daughter of the Emperor said to R. Joshua b. Ḥananiah, "To think of such pre-eminent learning in such an ugly container!" "But," asked the Rabbi, "Does not your father store wine in an earthenware vessel?" "In what else should he store it?" she exclaimed. "Surely you in your high position should store it in vessels of gold and silver," answered the Sage. She went and suggested it to her father, who thereupon put the wine into vessels of gold and silver. The wine turned sour. When the report reached him, the king enquired of his daughter as to who had made that suggestion to her. "R. Joshua b. Ḥananiah," she replied. The Rabbi was called and asked why he had told her so. Whereupon he replied, "According to her exclamation was my answer." "But," retorted the king, "are there not also comely persons who are at the same time learned in the Law?" To which the Rabbi replied, "Had these been less comely they might have been more learned still[1]."

Wine and vinegar.

Wine stored in cellars often became sour and turned into vinegar, and this fact formed the basis of a considerable number of Midrashic similes.

"The whole earth was of one language[2]" [*i.e.* they were all alike—tarred with the same brush]. This

[1] *Taanith*, 7 *a*; *Nedarim*, 50 *b*; *vide* Bacher, *Ag. Tan.* I, 182 f.

[2] Gen. xi. 1 [אחת] שׂפה=שׁפה, an Aramaic expression for selling wine.

might be compared unto one who had a cellar full of wine. He opened one cask and found it vinegar. He opened a second and found it the same, and so on with the third. These samples, he said, prove that all the wine is bad[1].

"Noah was in his generation a man righteous and whole-hearted[2]." This might be likened unto one who had a wine-cellar. He opened a cask and found it vinegar [*i.e.* quite sour]; he opened a second and found it the same; he opened a third, and found that it had turned somewhat sour[3]. When told that the wine was sour he enquired: And is there one better than this? "No," came the reply.

Even so was Noah righteous in his generation, but had he lived in the generation of Moses or of Samuel, he would not have been regarded as righteous[4].

R. Ḥanina, expounding the same text and wishing to convey a similar idea of the relative righteousness of Noah, adduced a parable of R. Joḥanan (3rd c.). He (Noah) was like unto a cask of wine which lay stored away in a cellar full of vinegar. Whilst it remained in its place its flavour kept good, but when the cask was removed it lost some of its flavour[5].

"Vinegar the product of wine" [*i.e.* degenerate

[1] הא מְשְׁפּוּ דכולא בישא *Gen. R.* 38, 6; cf. *Yalkut Gen.* § 62. Some read מסתיא, "it is sufficient," *sc.* proof. משפו is a term for the wine which has been strained and clarified from dregs, *vide Baba Meṣia*, 60 *a*, and Rashi, *ad loc.* Any remains of dregs turn it quickly into vinegar. The phrase הא משפו דכולא בישא might therefore mean, This is a clarification which is totally bad.

[2] Gen. vi. 9.

[3] מצאה קוסס.

[4] *Gen. R.* 30, 9, R. Judah contemp. of R. Neḥemiah; as the proverb has it בשוק סמייא צווחין לעווירא סגי נהור. "In the street of the totally blind they call the partially blind rich of light."

[5] *Synhedrin*, 108 *a*.

scion of a distinguished sire, bad son of a good father]. "Why dost thou hand over to slaughter the people of God?" was the message sent by R. Joshua b. Korḥah to R. Eleazar b. Simon, when unlike his father Simon, the enemy of the Romans, Eleazar accepted office under their rule[1].

There were two stages in the life of the Persian King Cyrus: before he became sour [*i.e.* before he changed for the worse], and after he had become sour[2].

The sampling of wine.

The possibility of the wine having turned sour as well as the variety in the qualities of wine gave rise to the custom of sampling. This sampling of the wine was often used figuratively among the scholars in the Academies of Learning.

"Go and smell at his jar[3]," said Raba to R. Adda b. Ahaba (Bab. Am., 3rd c.) [*i.e.* examine his mental capacity, test him whether he is a scholar or not[4]].

Tapping and drawing the casks.

Some Rabbinic similes are taken also from the tapping and drawing of the casks and the straining of the wine.

On the text "And the bones of Joseph Moses took with him[5]" (*sc.* from Egypt to bury at Shechem), the Rabbis spoke in parable: Unto what may this be likened? Unto robbers who entered a cellar of wine. They took a jar and drank of it. The owner of the cellar looked in at them and said, "May it [the wine you drank] be pleasant unto you, may it be sweet

[1] See p. 134, *Baba Meṣia*, 83 *b*; cf. *Jer. Maasroth*, 50 *d*; *Pesikta*, 92 *a*; Bacher, *Ag. Tan.* II, 309; cf. the following: Mar Ukba (an Amora of the 4th c.) said, "In this matter I am in comparison with my father—like vinegar the product of wine" [*i.e.* a degenerate son!], *Ḥullin*, 105 *a*.

[2] קודם שהחמיץ; לאחר שהחמיץ *Rosh Hashanah*, 3 *b*.

[3] פוק תהי ליה בקנקניה.

[4] *Baba Bathra*, 22 *a*.

[5] Ex. xiii. 19 and Jos. xxiv. 32.

unto you, may it agree well with you. You have drunk the wine, put the cask back in its place." Even so did the Holy One, blessed be He, say unto the tribes: "Ye have sold Joseph, return the bones to their place[1]."

"And Jacob said to Simeon and Levi, Ye have troubled me[2]." The Rabbis put it (metaphorically) thus: The jar was clear and you have spoilt it [*i.e.* by killing the Shechemites].

Rabbi Judah bar Simon said (*sc.* Simeon and Levi's reply was as follows) The jar was spoilt but we have clarified it[3].

"God hath found out the iniquity of thy servants[4]." R. Levi (3rd and 4th c.) says: Like one who drains the cask and sets it on its lees[5].

Straining the wine.

Again a Tannaitic sage in analysing and describing the characteristics and capacities of students of the Law employed the following wine metaphors:

There are different natures [with regard to receptive and retentive faculties] among those who sit at the feet of the wise: (1) the "funnel[6]" that takes in through one way and lets out through the other [*i.e.* a scholar that learns and forgets easily][7]; (2) The "strainer[8]," which lets the wine pass and keeps back the lees [*i.e.* a scholar who abandons the useful and retains the useless][9].

[1] *Gen. R.* 85, 3; *Exod. R.* 20, 9; R. Levi, 3rd and 4th c.; Bacher, *Pal. Am.* II, 419. In a more contracted form in *Mechilta Beshallaḥ init.* and *Deut. R.* 8, 4.

[2] Gen. xxxiv. 30.

[3] *Gen. R.* 80, 12 *ad fin.*

[4] Gen. xliv. 16.

[5] *Gen. R.* 85, 2. In another place given in the name of R. Isaac: The metaphor is obviously suggested by מצא, "found," being taken in the sense of מצה, "drained," cf. שתית מצית Is. li. 17.

[6] משפך.

[7] *Aboth*, v, 15, 18, more fully in *Aboth di R. Nathan*, ch. 40.

[8] משמרת.

[9] *Aboth*, *ibid.*

And there is one striking simile taken from the carting about and distribution of the wine.

Carting and distribution.

"And the Lord was with Joseph." This would imply that He was not so much with the other sons of Jacob. [Discoursing on this] R. Judah [4th c.] said: This might be compared unto a driver[1] who had charge of twelve kine laden with wine; when one of them entered into the shop of an idolater, the driver left the eleven and followed after the one. Then said they unto him, "Why dost thou leave the eleven and follow after the one?" And he replied: "These are in the open street, and I have no fear that the wine will become ritually unfit for use[2]." Even so is it with these [*i.e.* Jacob's sons]; the others are grown-up and under the supervision and control of their father, but this one [*i.e.* Joseph] is still young and under his own control; therefore "the Lord was with Joseph[3]."

There is a considerable number of euphemistic metaphors suggested by the vineyard and the products of the vine.

Wine euphemisms.

"He turneth not by the way of the vineyards[4]" is explained by Judah ben Simeon bar Pazzi[5] as a euphemism[6].

R. Jonah said in the name of R. Krispa: A

1 בהמי.

2 יין נסך, *i.e.* wine known or suspected to have been manipulated by an idolater; and as such forbidden to Jews.

3 Gen. xxxix. 2; *Gen. R.* 86, 4; Bacher, *Pal. Am.* III, 267.

4 Job xxiv. 18.

5 Palestinian Amora and Aggadist of the beginning of the 4th cent. who was fond of using parables.

6 שלא היתה בעילתן לשום בנים *Jer. Yebamoth*, 7 c; Bacher, *Pal. Am.* III, 174 (note). In *Gen. R.* 30, 2, it is explained anonymously as שלא היתה כונתן למטעת כרמים.

maiden who is of age is like unto an open wine-jug[1].

The presumption is that no man drinks out of a cup unless he has first examined it, *i.e.* that none will marry without having ascertained the girl's suitability for marriage[2].

"And ye shall not go about after your hearts[3]." Rabbi (2nd and 3rd c.) said (in reference to conjugal infidelity): One must not drink of one cup while thinking of another cup[4].

[1] בוגרת כחבית פתוחה *Jer. Kethuboth*, 1, *init.* 24 *d.*
[2] *Kethuboth*, 75 *b*–76 *a.*
[3] Num. xv. 39.
[4] *Nedarim*, 20 *b*; *vide Sifré Deut.* § 349, שמעון ולוי בכוס אחד שתו

V

THE FIG

In Biblical simile.

In the poetry of the Bible the cultivated fig tree provides numerous interesting examples of metaphor and simile. The attention devoted to its cultivation and growth as well as its nutritive results are used to typify the reward granted to him who waits upon his master[1]. The first ripe fruit—the early fig—which was considered a great delicacy, and was eagerly seized upon by the passer-by, was frequently employed by the Prophets as a subject of simile. The discovery of Israel, and his immediate adoption by divine Providence, are likened to the finding of the first ripe fruits of the fig tree in its first season[2]. And the same figure is used by Nahum[3] to express the swiftness with which Nineveh's strongholds shall be shaken and made to surrender.

The fig falling from the tree (like the falling leaves from the vine) is made to symbolise the downfall of hosts[4].

In contrast to the delicious early figs, the image of the "vile figs that cannot be eaten, for they are so evil" is used by Jeremiah to depict the effects of the sword, of famine and of pestilence[5]; and the same Prophet employs the combination of the two figures to describe the opposite effects of good and evil. Under the type of the two baskets of figs—the good

[1] Prov. xxvii. 18. [2] Hos. ix. 10; cf. Is. xxviii. 4. [3] iii. 12.
[4] Is. xxxiv. 4. [5] Jer. xxix. 17.

and the bad—God foreshadows the restoration of them that are in captivity, and the desolation of Zedekiah and his followers[1].

The fig in Midrashic poetry.

In the poetry of the Midrash the similes relating to the fig tree are drawn chiefly from its shape and growth, its penetrating roots, the imposing sweep of its branches, the usefulness of all its parts, and the fading of its leaves; the ripening of its fruit in different stages, at different periods and in varying qualities; the deferred plucking of the figs to their due seasons, and their being pressed into cakes for later use.

The growth of the fig tree.

The growth of the fig tree is used as a natural figure in describing the extension of the Holy Land and the Holy City. In order to render more vivid and more picturesque Ezekiel's conception of a Jerusalem of the future "broadened and widening upward[2]," a Rabbi of the 2nd century poetically adds: The land of Israel will in time to come extend and rise on all its sides like the fig tree, which is narrow below, and the gates of Jerusalem will reach even unto Damascus[3].

The land of Israel, continues a third-century sage in exposition of a prophecy of Jeremiah, will in the future extend and rise on all its sides like the fig tree, which is narrow below and wide above, and the exiles shall come and take rest under it[4].

[1] Jer. xxiv.

[2] Ezek. xli. 7.

[3] R. José b. Durmaskith (a woman of Damascus) in a controversy with R. Judah, a disciple of R. Akiba. *Sifré* to Deut. i. 1; *Pesikta*, 143 *a*; Bacher, *Ag. Tan.* I, 395.

[4] R. Joḥanan (3rd c.) in *Cant. R.* to vii. 5, who bases it on Jer. xxx. 18: "And the city shall be builded upon her own mound," where עַל תִּלָּהּ is explained as meaning כתאנה על תלה.

In exposition of the Psalmist's description of the City of God as "Fair in situation" or "Beautiful in elevation[1]," R. Ḥanina b. Papa (3rd and 4th c.) said: [The text may be explained to mean a city] "Beautiful in its branches[2]"; resembling the fig tree, which is rooted in the earth and rises straight; its branches shoot forth from every side, and it is beautiful. In this sense does the Psalmist call Jerusalem "beautiful in its elevation[3]."

Its penetrating roots.

The figure of the penetrating roots of the fig tree is used to illustrate and expound a text of the Bible[4]: "And they brake all their bones in pieces." As with a pestle[5] add the Rabbis in explanation; and like the roots of the fig tree which though soft yet break through rock and stone[6].

The fig tree judged by its branches.

The way in which the branches of the fig tree denote its quality is used in the Midrash to illustrate a Biblical maxim. "Instead of thy fathers shall be thy sons[7]," says Scripture. It is the branch [of a fig tree] which confirms [the reputation of] that tree, explain the Rabbis [*i.e.* a good son of a good father][8].

The utility of all parts.

The utility of nearly all the parts of the fig tree is employed by a Rabbi to explain the motive underlying one of the earliest of Jewish rites. R. Judan (4th c.) said: Just as the fig tree has nothing useless, save the peduncle only[9], and when this is removed the last imperfection is taken away, even so did God

[1] יפה נוף Ps. xlviii. 3.

[2] Hebrew נוף means "a branch" as well as "elevation."

[3] *Pesikta R.* ch. 41 *init.*; Friedmann, p. 172 *b*; Bacher, *Pal. Am.* II, 525.

[4] Dan. vi. 25. [5] כהדין פסטילום.

[6] *Yalkut Sam.* § 103, cf. *Shoḥer Tob* to Ps. lxxviii. 11, and *Midrash Samuel*, Buber, p. 80, note 17.

[7] Ps. xlv. 17. [8] *Cant. R. init.* to i. 1, § 6. [9] עוקצה בלבד.

say unto Abraham, "Thou hast no imperfection save the foreskin; remove this, and thus take away thine only blemish. Walk before me and be perfect[1]."

Ripening of the figs at different periods.

The ripening of the figs at different periods was utilised by the Midrashic preachers in their exposition of the phenomena of creation, as recorded in the Book of Genesis. R. Neḥemiah (2nd c.) said: It was with the order of the world's creation as it is with the gatherers of figs. Each phenomenon of creation shone forth and became visible in its due season.

R. Berechiah (4th c.) explained this saying of R. Neḥemiah as follows: It is written, "And the earth brought forth[2]," *i.e.* something which was already existing and stored up[3].

Plucking in due season.

The plucking of the fig in due season supplied the Rabbis with a cheering simile, calculated to bring comfort to the mourner in the hour of his bereavement.

R. Neḥemiah (2nd c.) said: When the fig tree is plucked in due season, it is good both for the tree and for the fig, but when it is gathered out of its time, it is bad both for the tree and for the fig. The following incident will serve as a confirmation of this truth[4]:

R. Ḥiyya Raba (2nd and 3rd c.) and his disciples—and according to others R. Simeon b. Ḥalafta (2nd c.)

[1] Gen. xvii. 1; *Gen. R.* 46, 1. [2] Gen. i. 12.

[3] *Gen. R.* 12, 4. The figs, more than is the case with other fruit, are plucked one after another, each one in its season. Even so the hosts of heaven and earth although created together with the heaven and the earth, appeared each one as it was called forth in its season.

[4] דא אלמא=דילמא, a heading used in the Palestinian dialect for introducing a story as an illustration corresponding to the Hebrew מעשה.

and his disciples, and according to others again, R. Akiba (2nd c.) and his disciples—sat and taught under a fig tree. The owner of the tree was wont to rise early and pluck his figs. "Let us change our place, lest he suspect us," said they, and seated themselves in another place. On the morrow the owner of the tree rose early to pluck his figs. Not finding the Rabbis, he made search, and on discovering them he said: "My Masters, one kindly act had you been doing me, and now you withhold it." "Heaven forfend!" they replied. "Why then have you left your place and gone to another?" said he. "Because we thought you were suspecting us." "Heaven forfend!" replied he. "Let me tell you wherefore I used to rise early to pluck my figs. It was because when the sun shines on them they become wormy." Then said they: "Well does the owner of the fig tree know when is the right time for his tree to be plucked and he plucks it. Even so does the Holy One, blessed be He, know when the hour for the departure of the righteous has come and He takes him away[1]."

When R. Joḥanan came to the verse[2] "Behold, He putteth no trust in His saints" he wept. If He trusteth not His saints, in whom then doth He put his trust?

[1] *Kohel. R.* to 5, 11, and in somewhat modified forms in *Jer. Berachoth*, II, 5 *c* top; *Gen. R.* 62, 2 and *Cant. R.* to vi. 2 דודי ירד לגנו, "My beloved is gone down to his garden to the beds of spices to feed in the gardens and to gather lilies." In *Gen. R.* 62, 2 and in *Cant. R.* to vi. 2 the name of the originator of the tradition is given as R. Abbahu (3rd and 4th c.). Bacher, *Pal. Am.* II, 105, note 2, explains that R. Neḥemiah in our extract is a mistake for R. Abbahu, and is introduced there because R. Neḥemiah appears frequently as the disputant with R. Juda (the Tanna). For a parallel *vide* John i. 48, where some take it to refer to the receiving of religious instruction. For the practice of studying whilst sitting under trees *vide* Büchler in *J. Q. R.* (N.S.) for 1914.

[2] Job xv. 15.

Once he was walking on the road, and he saw a man gathering figs, leaving the ripe ones and picking those that were unripe. "Are not the others better than these?" asked R. Joḥanan. Whereupon the man replied, "I am bound on a journey, the unripe figs will keep, but the others will not keep." Then said R. Joḥanan, "This makes clear the verse 'Behold, He putteth no trust in His saints[1].'"

Similes from the gathering of the fig tree and the plucking of the figs are used respectively to illustrate the method of progress in the study of the Law, and the development of Israel as a nation from the time of Abraham to the period of the Exodus.

The mode of gathering its fruits.

"Whoso keepeth the fig tree shall eat the fruit thereof[2]." Why is the Law compared to the fig tree? The majority of trees, the olive, the vine, the palm, are plucked once, but the fig tree is plucked little by little. Even so is it with the Law, one studies a little to-day, and more to-morrow, because its study cannot be completed either in a year or in two years[3].

R. Joḥanan (3rd c.) commenting upon the same text[4] said: Wherefore are the words of the Torah likened unto a fig tree? To tell thee that just as one finds figs on the fig tree, as often as he handles it[5], even so is it with the words of the Torah, as long as one meditates therein he finds in it some palatable truth[6]. A similar application of the mode of plucking the figs is used in connection with the following Bible text: "I found Israel like grapes in the

1 *Ḥagigah*, 5 *a*.

2 Prov. xxvii. 18.

3 *Num. R.* 12, 9 and 21, 15 anon.

4 Prov. xxvii. 18.

5 ממשמש בה.

6 *Erubin*, 54 *a*, *b*; Bacher, *Pal. Am.* I, 237, note 2, says that the hander down of the traditions is Ḥiyya b. Abba (3rd and 4th c.).

wilderness; I saw your fathers as the first-ripe in the fig tree at her first season[1].”

R. Judan (4th c.) said: In the fig tree the figs are first picked singly, then in twos, then in threes, until they are gathered in baskets by aid of shovels. Even so was Abraham our father at first alone[2] and he inherited the land; then there were two, Abraham and Isaac; then three, Abraham, Isaac and Jacob; and in the end the children of Israel became fruitful, increased abundantly and multiplied[3].

Figs in their different stages of growth.

There are a few Midrashic metaphors and similes (some of them euphemistic in nature) taken from the figs in the different stages of their growth and in the variety of their qualities, as the following examples will show.

The wise men, say our Aggadists, used parabolic expressions to describe the stages of a woman's physical growth. “*Paggah*,” a hard undeveloped berry; “*Boḥal*,” a fig in that stage of ripening, when the beads grow white; “*Tzemel*,” a fig in its last stage of growth[4].

In explanation of the name “Gomer the daughter of *Diblaim*[5]” Samuel (3rd c.) said: [She was so called] because she was sweet in the mouth of all like figs. R. Joḥanan (3rd c.) said: Because they all trod upon her even as figs are trodden upon [to make the pressed cake][6].

1 Hos. ix. 10. 2 Ez. xxxiii. 24.

3 Ex. i. 7; *Gen. R.* 46, 1; Bacher, *Pal. Am.* III, 259.

4 צמל, בֹחל, פגה Mishnah, *Niddah*, 47 *a*. וכן תנא דבי ר׳ ישמעאל ראויה היתה לדוד בת שבע בת אליעם אלא שאכלה פגה (רש״י שקפץ את השעה וכו׳) *Synhedrin*, 107 *a*; cf. in this connection the saying of R. José that the tree of which Adam ate the fruit was the fig tree (*Gen. R.* 15, 7).

5 Hos. i. 3.

6 דבלים being connected with דבילה, a cake of pressed figs, *Pesaḥim*, 87 *b*.

R. Levi (3rd and 4th c.) said: Two men, Abraham and Job, said one and the same thing. Abraham exclaimed: "That be far from Thee to do after this manner, to slay the righteous with the wicked" [apparently assuming that God might act thus unjustly][1]. Job argued: "It is all one—therefore I say, He destroyeth the innocent and the wicked[2]." And yet Abraham received a reward, whilst Job was punished. For Abraham swallowed the fig ripe [spoke deliberately, in prayerful mood, protesting that God would not do evil], whilst Job swallowed it unripe [*i.e.* spoke rashly, averring that God does evil[3]].

R. Ḥiyya bar Abba (3rd and 4th c.) said: There is a tangle of questions[4] in this context. Abraham exclaimed[5] "That be far from Thee to do after this manner, to slay the righteous with the wicked"; and the Holy One, blessed be He, replied: "That be so; as with the righteous so shall it be with the wicked." The punishment of the wicked shall be suspended because of the righteous. I would they were indeed righteous, but in truth they are righteous men of a lower order (like figs of a poorer quality)[6]. Figs of inferior quality.

Discoursing upon the theme "And the earth was without form and void[7]," R. Berechiah (4th c.) opened his sermon with the following text[8], "Even a child is known by his doings, whether his work be pure and

[1] Gen. xviii. 25. [2] ix. 22.

[3] *Gen. R.* 49, 9; *Tanḥuma Vayyera*; *Yalk.* Job, § 904; Bacher, *Pal. Am.* II, 398. According to the reading in *Tanḥuma Vayyera*, Buber, p. 45, בלעה בשולה and בלעה פגה instead of אמר בישולה and אמר פגה in *Gen. R.*

[4] עירבובי שאילות. [5] Gen. xviii. 25.

[6] צדיקים ניבלי *Gen. R.* 49, 9; Bacher, *Pal. Am.* II, 189.

[7] Gen. i. 2. [8] Prov. xx. 11.

whether it be right." He said: While the earth was still developing, it produced thorns[1].

"The fig tree ripeneth her green figs[2]." These, say the Rabbinic Allegorists, denote the righteous and the just[3].

[1] עד דהיא פנה אפיקת כובייא *Gen. R.* 2,1; Bacher, *Pal. Am.* III, p. 387.

[2] Cant. ii. 13.

[3] *Exod. R.* 15, 1.

VI

THE OLIVE

THE olive tree with its products is used figuratively in the prophetic and poetic literature of the Bible. The green olive tree "fair" and "beautiful" with its branches spreading out and "of goodly fruit" is used both by Hosea[1] and Jeremiah[2] to typify Israel. The Psalmist employs it as a figure for the man who trusts in the mercy of God for ever and ever[3] and also as a simile of family life[4]—a picture of children sitting round their parents' board. In Biblical imagery.

The product of the olive tree likewise supplies a number of Biblical similes replete with poetic effect. The oil for anointing, used not alone in sacred ceremonial "upon the head that ran down upon the beard[5]," but also for ordinary health purposes "unto the bones[6]"; its qualities of preciousness, smoothness and softness are used as comparisons in the Psalms[7], the Song of Songs[8], and the Wisdom books of the Bible[9].

The (?premature) casting of the flower of the olive tree is applied by Job[10] to depict the condition of the man who trusts in vanity; and the gleanings that remain when the olive tree is beaten and its fruit is gathered are made by Isaiah[11] to represent the remnant of Israel. The olive tree figures also most

[1] xiv. 7. [2] xi. 16. [3] Ps. lii. 10. [4] Ps. cxxviii. 3.
[5] Ps. cxxxiii. 2. [6] Ps. cix. 18. [7] *Loc. cit.* and Ps. lv. 22.
[8] i. 3. [9] Prov. v. 3; Eccl. vii. 1. [10] xv. 33.
[11] xvii. 6, cf. xxiv. 13.

prominently in the well-known vision of Zerubbabel and Joshua, the lay and ecclesiastical heads of the returned exiles from Babylon[1].

The olive in Midrashic simile.

In Midrashic poetry the Biblical similes derived from the olive tree and its oil are expanded by the Rabbis, who added to keenness of vision into the world of nature an exalted sense of national pride and religious fervour. Apart from the imagery associated with the natural phenomena of the tree itself, the process of the gathering of the olives is made to reflect Israel's treatment by the nations and his own attitude of mind under such ordeal. The nature and qualities of the oil itself are made to mirror the characteristics and ideals, the hopes and destinies, of Israel as a people, as well as of some of his early ancestors. The olive and its products are used also to describe the effect of the words of the Law—"the oil of the Torah"—and of the students and disciples, who spread its knowledge, kindle its light and illumine the darkness.

The evergreen olive tree.

The Bible speaks metaphorically of Israel as the olive tree. This is expounded by a Rabbi of the third century.

R. Joshua b. Levi said: Why has Israel been compared to the olive tree[2]? To tell thee that even as the leaves of the olive tree do not drop either in the days of sun or in the season of rain, so will Israel never be utterly undone either in this world or in the world to come[3].

Nature of its fruit-yielding.

R. Isaac Nappaḥa (3rd and 4th c.), using the same Bible text, weaves around the nature of the growing

[1] Zech. iv. 3. [2] Jer. xi. 16.

[3] *Menaḥoth*, 53 *b*; Bacher, *Pal. Am.* I, 144; *vide Berachoth*, 57 *a*, "Whoever beholds an olive tree in his dream will enjoy a good name."

olive tree a poetic figure of Israel's survival after the destruction of the Temple.

R. Isaac said: At the time when the Sanctuary was destroyed the Holy One, blessed be He, found Abraham standing in the Temple....With lamentation and weeping he was saying unto himself, "Perhaps, Heaven forfend, there is no salvation for Israel." At that moment there went forth a heavenly voice[1], saying unto him: "The Lord called thy name, a green olive tree, fair, with goodly fruit[2]." Even as this olive tree is tardy in yielding its fruit, so will Israel behold his goodly destiny in the latter end[3].

A similar poetic extension is given in Midrashic literature to the Biblical image in which the olive plants are made to typify children. The development of this idea by the Rabbis is based upon a special characteristic distinguishing this particular plant.

The grafting of olive plants.

Says R. Levi (3rd c.): "Thy children [shall be] like olive plants round thy table[4]." Even as the olives are not affected by grafting [for when they are grafted on to another tree their fruit is in no way impaired] so shall thy children comprise no unworthy offspring[5].

The fully-laden olive plants.

Another Rabbi expounded the verse[6] as follows: How is it with the olive tree? It produces various

[1] *Bath-Kol.* [2] Jer. xi. 16.

[3] *Menaḥoth*, 53 *b*; Bacher, *Pal. Am.* II, 250, in note 2 says: It takes about ten years to get the first supply from a newly-planted tree, and about thirty years till it produces a full crop.

[4] Ps. cxxviii. 3.

[5] *Jer. Kilaim*, 27 *b* below, ch. I, Halachah 7; Bacher, *Pal. Am.* II, 383; in *Midrash Tehillim*, *ad loc.*, the author is given as R. Joshua b. Levi, a Palest. Amora of the first half of the 3rd century which Bacher suggests as probable instead of R. Joshua of Sichnin in the name of R. Levi.

[6] Ps. cxxviii. 3.

kinds of olives; some to be eaten fresh; others to be dried; and others again for the extraction of oil; and the oil of the olive burns more brightly than all other oils. Its leaves do not drop either in the days of summer or in the season of rain. Even so are the children of proselytes. Some of them are learned in the Scriptures, others in the Mishnah; some are men of commerce, others are men of wisdom and understanding; others again know a thing in due season; and the children of all such live for ever[1].

The gathering of the olives and the production of oil.

The gathering of the olives and the production of oil supply an elaborate simile for Israel's oppression by the nations. "The Lord called thy name, a green olive tree, fair, with goodly fruit[2]."

The olive, while yet on the tree, is marked out for shrivelling[3]; afterwards it is taken down and beaten[4]; after which it is transferred into the vat, put into the mill and ground[5]. A net is then put around[6] and stones are placed thereon; only then the olives produce their oil. Even so is it with Israel. The heathen comes buffeting him from place to place, putting him into prison, binding him with chains, and surrounding him with soldiers[7]. Then does Israel repent and the Holy One, blessed be He, answers him[8].

R. Joḥanan (3rd c.) said: Why is Israel likened unto the olive[9]? To tell thee, that just as the olive does not bring forth its oil except through pounding, so does Israel not return to the right path except through chastisement[10].

[1] *Num. R.* 8, 9. [2] Jer. xi. 16. [3] מגרגרין אותו

[4] ונחבט. [5] טוחנין אותו. [6] מקיפין אותן בחבלים.

[7] For טרטיוטין read סטרטיוטין=אסטרטיוטין=στρατιώτης. Brüll, in *Jahrb.* v, 127, suggests reading="tortum," *i.e.* instruments of torture.

[8] Anonym. *Exod. R.* 36, 1. [9] Jer. xi. 16.

[10] *Menaḥoth*, 53 *b*; Bacher, *Pal. Am.* I, 247.

In Midrashic poetry the nature and qualities of oil symbolise in varied manner the condition of Israel and his position in the world. Nature and qualities of oil.

Discoursing upon the text "Thy name is as ointment poured forth[1]," the Rabbis say: Just as the oil tastes bitter at the first and sweet at the last, even so does Scripture say of Israel, "Though thy beginning was small, yet thy latter end shall greatly increase[2]."

Even as the oil is rendered better through more pounding so is Israel brought to repentance through trial and tribulation.

Just as the oil does not mix with other liquids, so does Israel not mingle with other nations, even as it is written, "Thou shalt not make marriages with them[3]." It will not mix.

All other liquids can be mixed with one another; oil cannot be diluted but remains distinct; even so does Israel not mix with the heathens[4].

"Unstable as water" is the simile used by Jacob of Reuben[5]. Why like water? asks the Midrash. And the reply is as follows: When a man has a pitcher full of water, and the water is poured out, nothing is left therein. But if he has a pitcher full of oil or of honey [and he pours it out] something still remains. Even so, says R. Jeremiah (4th c.), putting an unfavourable construction[6] upon the text, Reuben left himself no merit; whilst R. Nathan (3rd c.), Its adhesiveness.

[1] Cant. i. 3.

[2] Job viii. 7; in *Deut. R.* 7, 3 the application of the simile (נמשל) is....even so is it with the words of the Law. At the first a man endures pain for them, but at the last he enjoys their goodness.

[3] Deut. vii. 3.

[4] Anonym. *Exod. R.* 36, 1.

[5] Gen. xlix. 4.

[6] לפגם.

construing the text favourably[1], says Reuben cleared himself of all sins[2].

Its use for illumination.

Even as the oil brings light unto the world, so is Israel a light unto the world, as it is said[3], "And nations shall come to thy light, and kings to the brightness of thy rising[4]."

R. Judan (4th c.) said: "Thy name is as ointment poured forth[5]." Thy name shall illumine everyone who occupies himself with the oil of the Torah. This is the opinion of R. Judan, for it is said[6], "And the yoke shall be destroyed because of the anointing oil." The yoke of Sennacherib broke, because Hezekiah and his associates occupied themselves with the oil of the Torah[7].

Its buoyancy.

Even as oil rises above all other liquids, so will Israel be above all other nations, as it is said[8]: "And the Lord thy God will set thee on high above all the nations of the earth[9]."

1 לשבח.

2 *Gen. R.* 99, 6 anonym.; *Tanḥuma, ad loc.*, with addition of deductions and names of authors; *vide* Bacher, *Pal. Am.* III, 103.

3 Is. lx. 3.

4 In *Deut. R.* 7, 3 the comparison runs: ...So are the words of the Torah; in *Exod. R.* 36, 1 the simile is continued thus: ...So does the Sanctuary illumine the whole world, as it is written (Is. lx. 3), "And nations shall walk by thy light"; therefore are our ancestors called the green olive tree, for they illumine all with their faith.

5 Cant. i. 3.

6 Is. x. 27.

7 *Cant. R. ad loc.*; Bacher, *Pal. Am.* III, 257 and 263. In note 3, p. 263, Bacher quotes the saying of Berechiah in *Tanḥuma* to יתרו *init.*, שמן (read שמך) מאיר למי שעוסק בשמנה של תורה and adds that the sense of תורק is not clear; but perhaps it is connected with מרק, to scour, brighten; cf. נחשת מרוק, bright brass, 2 Chr. iv. 16.

8 Deut. xxviii. 1.

9 Compare the following from *Num. R.* 18, 16: R. Levi (3rd and 4th c.) said: Why did Korah strive against Moses? He said: I am the son of oil (בן יצהר)...and into whatsoever liquids you pour the oil, it rises to the top [*sc.* even so ought I to rise to the highest rank]; Bacher, *Pal. Am.* II, 370.

Even as oil floating on another liquid, when the cup is full, does not flow over with other liquids[1], so will the words of the Law not flow over [the lips] when mingled with words of frivolity.

How is it with the oil? When thou hast in thy hand a cup filled with oil and there falls into it a drop of water it replaces a drop of oil. Even so when a word of the Torah enters the heart, a word of scoffing is banished, and when a word of scoffing enters the heart, a word of the Law is removed.

One may mix all liquids without knowing which is below or which is above, but oil, even though it be mixed with all the liquids in the world, will always emerge at the top. Even so was it with our ancestors. When they did the will of God, they took their place above the nations[2].

Even as the oil [when poured out] gives forth no echoing sound[3], so does Israel suffer in silence, giving forth no resounding cry in this world, but as to the world to come it is written[4]: "And thou shalt be brought down and shalt speak out of the ground[5]." Absence of resonance.

But the oil is typical also of the Torah and of good deeds. As oil means life to the world, so do the words of the Torah[6].

"Let thy garments be always white; and let not thy head lack ointment[7]." R. Joḥanan b.

[1] Reading בשאר for כשאר according to Jastrow *s.v.* זרזף. The passage might also mean: oil even in a full cup does not flow over like other liquids, just so will words of the Law not bubble forth like words of frivolity.

[2] Anonym. *Exod. R.* 36. 1. [3] אין לו בת קול. [4] Is. xxix. 4.

[5] *Cant. R. ad loc.* This extract is introduced by ד"א and follows immediately after the saying of R. Judan. Possibly it is to be ascribed to this author.

[6] *Deut. R.* 7, 3; *vide Berachoth*, 57 *a*, "Whosoever sees olive oil in his dream should look forward to the light of the Torah."

[7] Eccl. ix. 8.

Zakkai said: This speaks of precepts, good deeds and Torah[1].

Sweet olive oil and bitter olive leaves.

The sweet olive oil typifies the sages of Palestine, whose relations with each other are invariably agreeable, whilst the scholars of Babylon are as bitter to one another in Halachah as are the leaves of the olive tree[2].

The scented oil supplies some interesting similes in Midrashic writings. It typifies respectively Noah, Abraham and the good men generally. It symbolises also the pleasantness of the Bible text when sweetened by Aggadic interpretation.

Scented oil.

"And the smell of thy ointments is better than all manner of spices[3]." R. Samuel bar Naḥman (3rd c.) said: How is it with the oil? In itself it is odourless, but when perfumed it becomes permeated with many odours; even so is it with a verse of Scripture. By applying to it an exposition, thou wilt find therein many palatable shades of meaning[4].

The flask of scented oil.

R. Simon ben Lakish (3rd c.) said: Noah was righteous even in his own generation [which was wicked]. How much more righteous would he have been in a

[1] *Kohel. R. ad loc.*; Bacher, *Ag. Tan.* I, p. 39, esp. note 2.

[2] *Synhedrin*, 24 *a*. R. Isaac (3rd and 4th c.); *vide* Bacher, *Pal. Am.* II, 223. "Bitter as an olive leaf" was a well-known saying. Cf. *Erubin*, 18 *b*, and *Synhedrin*, 108 *b*, by Jeremiah b. Eleazar (3rd c.): The dove in bringing back the leaf of an olive tree said [symbolically], יהיו מזונותי מרורין כזית, "Let my food be as bitter as an olive leaf provided only it come from Thy [the Lord's] hand, rather than be as sweet as honey and I be dependent upon human gifts"; in *Gen. R.* 33, 6 (author R. Abbahu, 3rd and 4th c.); *Lev. R.* 31 *ad fin.* and *Cant. R.* to iv. 1 (author R. Aibo) in slightly different form, רמז רמזה לו אמרה לו לנח מוטב מר מזה מתחת ידו של הקב"ה ולא מתוק מתחת ידך, *vide* Bacher, *Pal. Am.* III, 66.

[3] Cant. iv. 10.

[4] טעמים; the Hebrew word טעם has the double meaning of "taste" and "reason"; Cant. iv. 10; *Cant. R. ad loc.*; Bacher, *Pal Am.* I, 500.

generation which was righteous? Said R. Hoshayah (3rd c.): How may the explanation of Resh Lakish be brought home by a simile? It may be likened to a flask of scented oil[1] lying in a sordid spot. Even there it sent forth its perfume; how much more would it have shed its sweet odours in a fragrant spot[2]?

"Thine ointments have a goodly fragrance[3]." R. Joḥanan (3rd c.) expounded this verse in reference to Abraham our father. When the Holy One, blessed be He, told him "Get thee from thy land and from thy kindred," to what was he like? To a flask of scented oil lying in a corner, whence its perfume could not spread abroad. Then came someone, moved it from its place, and its perfume spread on all sides. Even so did the Holy One, blessed be He, say to Abraham: "Thou art possessed of many good deeds, many precepts have been entrusted to thee. Move about from place to place in this wide world and then shall thy name become magnified in My world[4]."

"Thine ointments have a goodly fragrance[5]." To what may the disciple of the wise be compared? To a flask of scented oil; when open, its odour goes forth; when closed, its odour does not go forth. (The teacher of the Torah enhances his name only when

[1] פולייטון, *φουλιατον*, *foliatum*, *i.e.* an ointment or oil prepared from leaves of spikenard.

[2] מקום הבוסם, *var.* מבושם, *Synhedrin*, 108 *a*; in a somewhat modified form in *Gen. R.* 30, 9, in the name of R. Neḥemiah, where the readings are צלוחית של אפרסמון and מונחת בין הקברות.

[3] Cant. i. 3.

[4] *Cant. R. ad loc.*; in *Gen. R.* 39, 2 the reading is אפופילסימון. The ointment of spikenard is frequently referred to in the New Testament.

[5] Cant. i. 3.

he gives forth his teaching to disciples and does not keep it sealed within himself[1].)

"A good name is better than precious ointment[2].' How far does precious ointment spread? From the sleeping-chamber to the dining-hall[3]. But a good name extends from one end of the world to the other, as it is said, "And the fame of David went out into all lands[4]."

[1] *Abodah Zarah*, 35 *b*, R. Naḥman the son of R. Ḥisda (3rd and 4th c.).

[2] Eccl. vii. 1.

[3] מקיטון לטרקלין (= κοιτών).

[4] 1 Chron. xiv. 17; *Exod. R.* 48, 1 *init.*

VII

THE PALM

THE evergreen date-palm[1] was plentiful in Palestine in ancient times, and its qualities are frequently referred to figuratively in the poetical books of the Bible. Like the cedar, another evergreen tree, the palm is used to symbolise the prosperity of the righteous man, who "shall flourish like a palm tree[2]." Its towering branch represents the leaders of men[3]. Its tall, slender, graceful stalk typifies the beautiful female figure[4]; it also depicts the idols, which are "as upright as the palm tree, but speak not[5]." In Biblical imagery

A design of a palm, together with one of the vine, was used, no doubt with symbolic significance, in the Temple of Solomon[6]. It figured also in the plan of Ezekiel's Temple[7] and appears with somewhat similar symbolism on Jewish coins of the Maccabean period. The representation of the branch of the palm tree was also used on tombstones[8].

In Midrashic poetry the imagery of this plant-simile is continued, though the mode of comparison is somewhat varied. The palm in Midrashic poetry.

Following the Biblical conception which saw in the palm the representation of the righteous man and leader, the Rabbis perceived in it the figure of a certain type of scholar.

[1] Called by the Arabs "the sister of man."
[2] Ps. xcii. 13. [3] Is. ix. 13, xix. 15. [4] Cant. vii. 7–8.
[5] Jer. x. 5. [6] 1 K. vi and 2 Chron. iii. [7] Ezek. xl. *passim*.
[8] Possibly with ref. to Ps. xcii. 13 and similar passages.

"Thou art a mountain palm[1]" was an expression used by R. Eliezer b. Hyrcanus of his colleague R. Ishmael.

"The branches of palm trees[2]" symbolise the disciples of the wise, who force themselves[3] to learn Torah from one another[4].

The palm also typifies Israel. "I said, I will go up to the palm tree[5]." This, says R. Jonathan b. Eleazar (3rd c.), signifies Israel[6].

Again it denotes some specific personages, and is even made to typify God Himself.

"The branches of the palm tree[7]" symbolise (according to various Rabbinic exegetes) (*a*) The Holy One, blessed be He[8]; (*b*) Isaac[9]; (*c*) Rebekah[10].

They represent Rebekah: For even as the palm has both edible fruit and prickles, so did Rebekah rear up a righteous man and a wicked one[11].

These last palm images are utilised by the Rabbis in connection with the symbolism of the "Four

[1] דקל הרים *Sifra Tazria*, to Lev. xiii. 47; Bacher, *Ag. Tan.* I, 103, explains it as meaning "too narrow" in the interpretation of Holy Writ, even as the mountain palm produces few and weakly fruit. Jastrow in Dict. explains it as "too rash"; *vide Menaḥoth*, 84 *b*, top; a variant in R. Shimshan to *Negaim*, 11, 7, is דוקר—cutting through mountains, sophistical. *Yalkut Lev.* § 552 reads עוקר; Levi explains it as follows: Just as the דקל הרים, on account of the dry soil in which it grows, throws off its fruits before its time, even so you can retain but little of your learning.

[2] Lev. xxiii. 40, כַּפּוֹת תמרים.

[3] שכופין א"ע ללמוד תורה אלו מאלו.

[4] *Lev. R.* 30, 11 anonym.

[5] Cant. vii. 9.

[6] *Synhedrin*, 93 *a*; Bacher, *Pal. Am.* I, 74.

[7] Lev. xxiii. 40.

[8] Adducing as a support the text (Ps. xcii. 13), "The righteous shall blossom as the palm," which apparently they explain to mean "so as to approach the divine who is symbolised by the palm."

[9] With play upon the word כַּפּוֹת, which resembles the word כָּפוּת = bound. שהיה כָּפוּת ועקוד ע"ג המזבח, referring to the binding of Isaac in Gen. xxii.

[10] *Lev. R.* 30, 10 anonym.

[11] *Lev. R.* 30, 10.

Plants[1]" which are taken bound together as part of the ritual observance on the Feast of Tabernacles, and of which the palm branch is one. Examples of the symbolic significance of the other constituents—the citron, the myrtle and the willow of the brook—will be given in their respective places.

But the following parable associated with the religious symbolism of the palm branch may here be mentioned.

R. Abin (4th c.) said: This might be compared to two litigants who entered before the Judge, and it was not known which had won the cause. But when one of them went forth with a palm branch in his hand it became known that he had been successful. Even so Israel and the other nations enter on *Rosh Hashanah* (New Year's Day) and lodge their complaints before the Holy One, blessed be He, and it is not known who proves the victor. But when Israel march forth before the Holy One, blessed be He, with their palm branches and citrons in their hands, we know that they had won on the Day of Judgment. Wherefore, Moses warned Israel and commanded them to take unto themselves on the first day the fruit of the goodly tree and the branches of the palm trees and the willows of the brook, and rejoice before the Lord[2].

Many of the palm similes in Midrashic poetry are based upon its natural properties and characteristics which the Rabbis analyse and describe.

Its shoots and sap cells.

The palm produces no less than three new shoots[3].

1 ד׳ מינים.

2 *Lev. R.* 30, 2.

3 Buber reads אנבונין (connected with אנביה שגיא), some read אלבנין; in *Yalkut*, Ps. *ad loc.* the reading is אנבובין.

Even so Israel is not wanting in three righteous men[1].

Just as the palm and the cedar have their middle parts [sap cells] directed upwards, even so is the heart of the righteous directed towards the Holy One, blessed be He[2].

"And she sat under a palm tree[3]," says the Bible text of Deborah. Why did she hold session under a palm tree? asks the Midrash. R. Simeon b. Abishalom (Pal. Am.) said, in order to ensure privacy. Some explain it differently thus: even as the palm tree has only one "heart" [*i.e.* sap cells only in the stem, but none in the branches] so did Israel of that generation have one heart directed to their Father in Heaven[4].

Some qualities of the palm.

Just as the palm and the cedar have neither cavities nor excrescences[5], even so do the righteous have neither cavities nor excrescences in their character[6].

As with the palm and the cedar, whosoever climbs to the top of them and neglects to take measures for his safety, falls down and dies; even so, whosoever springs upon Israel will in the end receive his punishment at their hands [*e.g.* Pharaoh for his attempt on Sarah][7].

[1] *Num. R.* 3, 1 anonym.; for the idea of the varying number of righteous men, one, *three*, 30, 31, 36, 45, as constituting by their merit the support of the world, see Marmorstein, *Midrash Ḥaserot we Yeterot*, p. 30, note 123.

[2] *Gen. R.* 41, 1; anonym. in exposition of Ps. xcii. 13.

[3] Judges iv. 5.

[4] *Megillah*, 14 *a*; this comparison is quoted in the name of R. Levi in connection with Ps. xcii. 13. *Sukkah*, 45 *b*; Bacher, *Pal. Am.* II, 322.

[5] עקומים and סיקוסים (=σύκωσις).

[6] *Gen. R.* 41, 1 anonym. in exposition of Ps. xcii. 13 "The righteous shall flourish like the palm tree. He shall grow like a cedar in Lebanon."

[7] *Ibid.*

Just as the palm has taste but no smell, so is it with Israel; among them are men possessed of Torah but without the fragrance of goodly deeds[1].

Just as the palm has nothing useless, since the dates are used for food, its branches for Prayer and Praise, its dried twigs for a covering, its bast for the making of ropes, its leaves for sieves, its planed trunks for ceiling a house; even so is it with Israel. He has no useless member, for amongst them are men versed in the Bible, in the Mishnah, in the Talmud and in the Aggadah[2].

Just as the palm and the cedar cast a long-drawn shadow, so is the reward of the righteous long-deferred[3].

Just as the palm and the cedar have feelings of longing[4] so also do the righteous, and what is the object of their longing? The Holy One, blessed be He[5].

The palm tree bears fruit, even so do the righteous bear fruit[6].

[1] *Lev. R.* 30, 12 anonym. on the text "the branches of palm trees," Lev. xxiii. 40.

[2] *Gen. R.* 41, 1; anonym. in ref. to Ps. xcii. 13. Similarly in *Num. R.* 3, 1, where it concludes: Even so in Israel there are righteous, upright and pious men, learned in the Law, and even their degenerates (סוריהן) are benevolent.

[3] *Gen. R.* 41, 1; anonym. based on Ps. xcii. 13; in Bacher, *Pal. Am.* III, 767, this part is ascribed to Isaac bar Adda (Bab. Am., 3rd c.), ref. *Shoḥer Tob* to Ps. xcii. 13.

[4] *I.e.* a passion for grafting. And the following incident is adduced in the name of R. Tanḥum. A palm tree was planted at Ḥammthan (a mile from Tiberias) but produced no fruit. A palm-gardener passing by and noticing the tree said: This palm is looking longingly towards an odoriferous palm tree at Jericho (the city of palms) and desires to be grafted. As soon as they had the grafting done to it, the palm brought forth fruit.

[5] *Ibid.*

[6] *Num. R.* 3, 1; R. Huna, 4th c.

The palm when once uprooted cannot be replaced; even so is it with the righteous: once dead, their places can no more be filled[1].

Dates and prickles.

The palm produces dates and prickles, and whosoever wishes to collect the dates, must be prepared to be hurt by the prickles; even so is it with the righteous: whosoever is not on his guard against them [finds] their bite the bite of the fox, their sting the sting of the scorpion, and their hissing the hissing of a burning serpent[2].

Raba (3rd and 4th c.) said: Fever, except that it is the messenger of the angel of death, is as beneficent as are prickles for the palm tree (since they guard and protect it)[3].

Species of dates.

There occur Midrashic similes taken not from the palm tree but from its produce.

As the palm tree produces juicy dates and Nicholas dates, dates of an inferior quality, and also prickles[4], even so it is with the Israelites: they have among them men versed in the Law, as well as men unversed in it and men who are boorish[5].

The palm tree yields inferior dates[6] which are not brought into the storehouse, as well as dates which are brought into the storehouse. Even so was it with the Israelites in the wilderness: some of them entered into the land, others did not enter[7].

Sticky dates.

The adhesiveness of dates is used to explain a mystic idea embodied in a Bible text. In explanation of the verse "But ye that did cleave unto the Lord your God are alive every one of you this day[8]," the

[1] *Num. R.* 3, 1. [2] *Ibid.* anonym., cf. *Aboth* 2, 15. [3] *Nedarim*, 41 *a*, *b*.
[4] סולין – נובלות – ניקלווסין – רטובים. [5] עמי הארץ and בורים.
[6] נובלות. [7] *Num. R.* 3, 1 anonym. [8] Deut. iv. 4.

Rabbis add: Like two dates which adhere to one another [though separable][1].

The following proverbs may here be cited:

The bad palm will travel to meet a barren cane [*i.e.* like meets like][2].

Whosoever eats the tender bark of the palm branch shall be beaten with the peeled branch itself [*i.e.* the evil a man does will punish him][3].

Hang a palm's heart about a swine and he will yet indulge in his filthy habits[4].

Also the following poetic description in the form of a series of similes:

When Moses and Aaron came and stood before Pharaoh they seemed to resemble the ministering angels. Their tall stature was like unto the cedars of Lebanon, the sockets of their eyes like the spheres of the sun, their beards like the clusters of a palm tree, the glow of their faces like unto the splendour of the sun...and their speech like unto a flaming fire[5].

[1] *Synhedrin*, 64 *a* anonym.

[2] *Baba Kama*, 92 *b*.

[3] *Lev. R.* ch. 15, 8; the same in a slightly different form in *Shoḥer Tob*, 22, Here is the palm bark and here is the peeled branch; you have eaten the bark, you will be beaten by the branch [*i.e.* the object sinned against holds the means of punishment].

[4] *Berachoth*, 43 *b*.

[5] *Yalkut Exod.* § 181.

VIII

THE NUT TREE

The symbolism of the nut tree.

THE nut holds no place in the poetic imagery of the Bible, the only reference to it being in the Song of Songs vi. 11. But in the general allegorisation of this idyll a symbolical turn was given to the phrase "Nut grove" which occurs in the above passage[1]. It typified Israel[2].

The poetic fancy of the Rabbis played about this allegorical figure in characteristic fashion, and a wealth of metaphor and simile began to cluster round the nature and properties of the nut tree as the following extracts will show[3].

The mode of planting it.

R. Joshua of Sichnin (4th c.) in the name of R. Levi (3rd and 4th c.) said, "How is it with plants generally? If you cover their roots at the time of planting, they flourish; otherwise they do not flourish. But with the nut tree, if you cover its roots at planting it does not thrive. Even so is it in the case of Israel. "He that covereth his transgressions shall not prosper[4]."

[1] It would appear that the symbolism of the nut was current in the Alexandrian school. Philo (*Life of Moses*, III, § 22) makes the nut, whose eatable part and seed are the same, the symbol of perfect virtue. He also uses it as an emblem of the soul.

[2] Hence its use in the "Ḥaroseth." Isserles in *Shulḥan Aruch*, *Oraḥ*, *Ḥayyim*, 473, 5.

[3] The symbolism of the nut-tree was continued and developed in Cabbalistic literature. *Vide* Ḥayyim Vital, *Etz Ḥayyim*, *Hechal*, VII, "Gate," 9, ch. 11.

[4] Prov. xxviii. 13; *Cant. R.* to vi. 11; Bacher, *Pal. Am.* II, 386; somewhat differently in *Pesikta R.* ch. 11 (42 *a*). When all other trees are struck they cover their roots to preserve their life. But when the nut tree is struck it uncovers its roots and lives. Even so is it with Israel, "He

Resh Lakish (3rd c.) said: The nut tree is smooth, as we are taught in the Mishnah[1]: R. Simeon says, Just as in the case of nut trees with smooth surfaces[2], whosoever climbs to the top of the tree rashly [without considering how he climbs] falls down and receives his punishment; even so whosoever lords it over the congregation of Israel, giving no heed to his obligations as guardian over them, will in the end fall and receive his retribution at their hands, as it is written[3]: "Israel is holiness unto the Lord, the firstfruits of his increase; all that devour him shall be held guilty[4]."

Its smoothness.

Israel is likened unto the nut tree[5]. The nut tree is trimmed for its own good and sends forth its shoots anew; it grows afresh like the hair and the nails, which grow again after they are cut. Even so is it with the children of Israel. Whenever they are shorn of their hardly gotten substance in this world and give it to the toilers of the Torah, it all redounds to their own good, seeing that it is returned unto them anew. They retain an affluence in this world and a goodly reward is promised to them in the world to come[6].

Trimming the nut tree.

who covereth his transgressions shall not prosper." The Cabbalists draw attention to the fact that אגוז, "nut," is בגמטריא, numerically = חט[א], "sin."

[1] *Peah.* 4. 1. [2] בחליקי אגוזים. [3] Jer. ii. 3.

[4] *Cant. R.* to vi. 11. In *Pesikta R.* ch. 11, p. 42 *b*, examples are quoted of great leaders—Moses (Num. xx. 10 f.), Isaiah (vi. 5 f.), and Elijah (1 K. xix. 10 and 24)—who were punished because they offended Israel.

[5] Cant. vi. 11.

[6] *Cant. R. ad loc.*; Bacher, *Pal. Am.* I. 143, author R. Joshua b. Levi (3rd c.). In *Pesikta R.* ch. 11, p. 43 *a*, the same author, R. Joshua b. Levi, uses another simile, *viz.* the garden, which is frequently mown down and grows again better and fairer, הגינה שאני גוזז אותה כל שעה. Cf. *Gittin*, 7 *a*, where the simile for the same lesson, based upon Nah. i. 12, וכן נגוזו ועבר, is taken from an aspect of pastoral life. It was taught in the school of R. Ishmael: whoever cuts גוז part of his belongings and

Three species of nuts.

R. Levi (3rd and 4th c.) said: There are three kinds of nuts. The *Perech* (soft-shelled eatable) nuts[1], nuts of a medium hardness, and *Kitron* (a species of hard) nuts[2]: the *Perech* nut which bursts open of itself, the medium nut which breaks when beaten, and the hard nut which is difficult to break, and which even when cracked by means of a stone is of no use at all[3]. Even so is it with the Israelites. There are some among them who do good of their own accord. These are the soft nuts. There are others who, when solicited for a good cause, give readily. These are the medium ones. And there are others again, who even when urged to do a good deed are appealed to in vain. And yet, said R. Levi, the door that is not opened for a *Mitzvah* [a holy obligation] is opened through the physician [*i.e.* when stricken with illness, even the hard-hearted are prompted to do acts of charity][4].

The structure of the nut.

Why is Israel compared to the nut[5]? R. Berechiah (4th c.) said: As the nut consists of four layers[6] with a vacant space [a court][7] in the heart of it, so was Israel ranged in the wilderness under four flags in four camps, with a Tent of Assembly in the centre[8].

devotes it to charitable purposes will be rescued from the judgment of *Gehinnom*. This might be compared to two sheep passing through water, one of them shorn and the other unshorn. The shorn one passed through in safety, the other (being heavier) did not pass in safety. תנא דבי ר׳ ישמעאל...משל לשתי רחלות שהיו עוברות במים אחת גזוזה ואחת אינה גזוזה, *vide* Bacher, *Ag. Tan.* II, 342 (note 6).

1 אגוזי פרך. 2 קטרונים.

3 According to *Yalkut*, which reads אין תועלת בו instead of אין תוחלת בו.

4 *Pesikta R.* ch. 11; Friedmann, p. 42 *b*; also in *Cant. R.* to vi. 11.

5 Cant. vi. 11. 6 מגורות. 7 סירה.

8 *Cant. R. ad loc.*, same in *Yalkut Cant.* § 992; in *Pesikta R.* ch. 11, 42 *a*. As the nut has four layers (אגורות), so when Israel went forth

In the case of all other fruits, a man may take some of them from a sack without the others, be they dates, mulberries or figs, feeling the effect. But with nuts when you draw out a few all the others are disturbed[1]. Even so is it with Israel; one man sins and all feel the consequences. [As the text has it[2]] "One man sins, and with all the Congregation wilt Thou be wroth[3]." Piles of nuts.

How is it with the nut? You have a sackful of nuts, you put in many grains of poppy seed, many grains of mustard and yet room is found for them all. In the same way numerous proselytes may come and find shelter in the tents of Israel[4].

One cannot evade paying the custom dues on nuts, because by their rattling they make themselves heard and are thus disclosed. Even so is it with the Israelites: wheresoever one of them may go he cannot say "I am not a Jew," for he is duly recognised, even as it is written: "All that see them shall acknowledge them, that they are the seed which the Lord hath blessed[5]." The rattling of nuts.

Why [is Israel] likened unto nuts? All other fruits when falling to the ground make no noise, but the nut when falling emits a penetrating sound. Even

into the wilderness, Moses arranged them under four banners (דגלים), with the Shechinah in their midst.

1 מתרעמין ומרגישין. 2 Num. xvi. 22.

3 *Pesikta R.* ch. 11, p. 42 *a*, anonym. In *Cant. R.* to vi. 11 the simile is given as follows: How is it with the nuts? You take one out of a heap and all begin to roll and get into commotion (מורדרין ומתגלגלים). Even so is it with Israel, when one of them is beaten, all feel the blow.

4 *Cant. R.* to vi. 11; in slightly different form but in same sense in *Pesikta R.* ch. 11, p. 42 *b*.

5 Is. lxi. 9; *Cant. R.* to vi. 11.

so when the righteous man dies, the report spreads and penetrates the whole world[1].

Nut-cracking.

The stone cracks the stony nut. Even so shall the Law, which is called "stone," subdue the evil inclination, which is also called "stone[2]."

"I went down into the garden of nuts"[3]. This refers to the Israelites who sanctified themselves before Mount Sinai and might be likened unto the nut. How is it with the nut? If you strike it, the whole of it crumbles[4] [and its palatableness can be judged]. Even so when the Israelites sanctified themselves they became pleasing[5].

R. Judah bar Simon (4th c.) said the nut has two rinds. Even so Israel is enjoined to observe two precepts in the performance of the rite of circumcision[6].

The shell and the fruit.

R. Azariah (4th c.) said: Just as in the case of the nut, the shell preserves the fruit, so do the *Ammé-Haaretz* [the uncultured] that are in Israel support and maintain the study of the Law, as it is written, "It is a tree of life to those who take hold of [*sc.* uphold] it[7]."

In the case of the nut, the shell is preserved so

[1] *Pesikta R.* ch. 11, p. 42 *a*.

[2] *Cant. R.* to vi. 11. The Law is spoken of as the Tables of "Stone" (Ex. xxiv. 12 *et cet. loc.*); the evil inclination is likewise referred to as "stone" (Ez. xxxiv. 26), "And I shall remove the heart of stone." The evil inclination or sin, as already stated, equals numerically "nut"; חט[א] = אגוז.

[3] Cant. vi. 11.

[4] אם הקשתו כלו מפעפע.

[5] *Yalkut Cant. ad loc.* § 992.

[6] *I.e.* מילה and פריעה (uncovering the corona), *Cant. R.* to vi. 11. In *Pesikta R.* ch. 11, p. 42 *a*, in the name of R. Abin.

[7] *Cant. R.* to vi. 11. In *Pesikta R.* ch. 11, p. 42 *a*, the conclusion is: so do the Israelites occupy themselves with the Law and their companions engage in acts of benevolence.

long as it clings to the kernel, but is cast on the dung-hill when separated. Even so is it with Israel; as long as their people cleave to the learned and listen to their teachings, they have the merit of acquiring two worlds, this world and the world to come; but if they stand apart and do not associate with the learned, then will they perish from this world[1].

The nourishment in nuts.

R. José bar Judah (2nd c.) said: Whosoever has never seen a nut and knows it not, imagines it to be nothing but shell; let him but break it and he will find therein stores of food. Even so is it with Israel. The nations who know them not say that they are smitten on account of their sins. But on examination they discover in Israel endless stores of good deeds[2].

Soiled nuts.

Raba (3rd and 4th c.) explained: Why are the scholars compared to the nut? To tell thee, that just as the kernel of the nut may be wholesome, even though the nut itself is soiled, so is the scholar's learning not to be despised even though he himself has degenerated[3].

R. Azariah (4th c.) said: If the nut falls into a dust heap you take it out, scour, rinse and wash it, and it becomes again fit for food. Even so, however

[1] *Pesikta R.* ch. 11, p. 42 *a*, anonym. *Vide Ḥullin*, 92 *a*, in connection with אומה זו כגפן נמשלה; *Lev. R.* ch. 25, where the text is emphasised, "It is a tree of life to them who '*uphold it*,'" and where reference is made to the pact between Issachar and Zebulun as typical of the association between the scholar and the merchant; *Kethub.* 111 *b* where ואתם הדבקים (Deut. iv. 4) and ולדבקה בו (*ibid.* xi. 22), "to cleave to God" are made to imply association with the learned.

[2] *Yalkut Cant.* to vi. 11 § 992.

[3] *Ḥagigah*, 15 *b*. Cf. the case of Aḥer, whose teaching R. Meïr enjoyed.

much the Israelites are soiled with sins throughout the year, the Day of Kippur comes and makes atonement for them, as it is written[1], "For on this day atonement shall be made for you[2]."

Nuts for play.

The nut serves as a plaything for a child, and as a pleasurable pastime for a king. Even so is it with Israel. When they are meritorious, "kings shall be thy nursing fathers" (fondling thee)[3], and when they are sinful, "I am become a sport and a derision" to all my people[4].

[1] Lev. xvi. 30.

[2] *Cant. R.* to vi. 11. In *Pesikta R.* ch. 11, p. 42*a*, anonym., the beginning is: All fruits when they fall on the ground and become soiled one shrinks from eating them. But with the nut if it fall, etc.

[3] Is. xlix. 23.

[4] Lam. iii. 14; *Pesikta R.* ch. 11, p. 42*a*. In *Cant. R.* to vi. 11: As the nut is a plaything for children and an entertainment (שעשוע) for kings, so is it with Israel: a "derision" in this world because of their transgressions but a "fondling" in the world to come. Lam. and Is. as above. For reference to nut-games in ancient and medieval Jewry *vide* I. Abrahams, *Jewish Life in the Middle Ages*, p. 379.

IX

THE THORN AND THE REED

Apart from the general use of thorns and thistles as symbols of barrenness, destruction and desolation[1], the natural characteristics of thorns and the thorn-hedge, which sting and bruise, cling together and obstruct, and are therefore always shunned and frequently destroyed, supply a set of obvious similes in Biblical poetry. Thorns and snares connote general obstruction[2]. They also symbolise the dangers which confront the man who walks in the way of the froward[3].

In Biblical imagery.

The hedge of thorns typifies the way of the sluggard[4], whilst the thorn piercing the hand of a drunkard is like the parable in the mouth of fools[5]. The thorns symbolise the ungodly—to be thrust away[6], the enemies of God—to be devoured[7], the idolatrous nations who are a source of constant provocation[8], the adversaries who oppose the fulfilment of the prophet's charge[9].

The prophet[10] figures the best in the corrupted state of Society of his day as a brier and a thorn-hedge. The rapidly spreading thorn-fire stands for the destruction of the wicked[11], and the crackling of thorns under a pot is used as a description for the laughter

1 *Vide* Gen. iii. 18; Is. xxxiv. 13; Hos. ix. 6.
2 Hos. ii. 8.
3 Prov. xxii. 5.
4 Prov. xv. 19.
5 Prov. xxvi. 9.
6 2 Sam. xxiii. 6.
7 Nah. i. 10.
8 Num. xxxiii. 55.
9 Ezek. ii. 6.
10 Micah vii. 4.
11 Ps. cxviii 12

of the fool[1]. The reed, as representing fragility, weakness and unreliability, is likewise an object of simile in the Bible[2].

The thorn in Midrashic simile.

The Rabbis of the Midrash draw many similes from the thorn and the thorn-bush; from their wild growth, their entangling and impenetrable nature; from their cumbersomeness, on the one hand, when growing in the field, and fit therefore only to be cut down, and their usefulness, on the other hand, as hedges to fill up gaps. The Talmudic sages, like the Biblical writers, also derive some poetic comparisons from the reed, with regard, especially, to its characteristic flexibility.

Its growth unsown and uncultivated.

The growth of thorns unsown and uncultivated, in contrast to grain which requires so much toil and effort for its production, is used in the 3rd century as a simile in the sphere of matrimony and childbirth.

R. Ḥanina b. Pazzi (3rd and 4th c.) said: These thorns are neither hoed [dug over] nor sown, but they spring up and grow of themselves; whilst in the case of wheat how much pain and how much trouble are expended until it grows up! Even so Ammon and Moab, like Ishmael, were born soon after marriage, whilst the first four mothers of Israel were barren at first[3].

The growth of rushes and flags.

The growth of rushes and flags amidst certain requisite surroundings is used already in the Bible for the purpose of comparison: "Can the rush grow up without mire? Can the flag grow without water? Whilst it is yet in its greenness and not cut down,

[1] Eccl. vii. 6.
[2] See 2 K. xviii. 21; cp. Is. xxxvi. 6; Ezek. xxix. 6-7; 1 K. xiv. 15.
[3] *Gen. R.* 45, 4; Bacher, *Pal. Am.* III, 556–7.

it withereth before any other herb; so are the paths of all that forget God; and the hypocrite's hope shall perish[1]."

In Midrashic poetry the same simile is used by Rabbi Joshua b. Ḥananiah (1st and 2nd c.). But the teaching derived from the comparison is different. "Can the rush grow up without mire? Can the flag grow up without water?" Even so Israel cannot exist without Torah[2].

The leafy reeds.

The reeds, full of knots and leaves, are used as a figurative expression to typify abundance.

On the text "And the sons of Dan *Ḥushim*[3]" Raba (Bab. Am., 3rd c.) said[4]: Perhaps this means, even as it has been taught in the school of Hezekiah [*sc.* Ḥiyya's son, 3rd c.], that they were as numerous as the leaves [or the knots] of reeds[5].

R. Nathan (2nd c.) thus explained the verse "And the land was filled with them[6]": They became like the leaves of reeds[7].

The entangling thorn-bushes.

Very interesting are the application and working out by Midrashic writers of the Biblical simile of the hedge of thorns or thorn-bushes with reference to their entangling nature and their impenetrability.

On the text "The way of the sluggard is like a hedge of thorns[8]," R. Jacob b. José (Amora of unknown period)[9] said: This verse speaks of God and of Esau. The way of the sluggard, that means of

1 Job viii. 11–13.

2 *Mechilta* to xvii. 8; Friedmann, p. 53 *b*; Bacher, *Ag. Tan.* I, 169.

3 Gen. xlvi. 23.

4 With a play upon the word חושים, which might be related to חישת קנים, a thicket of reeds.

5 *Baba Bathra*, 141 *b*.

6 Ex. i. 7.

7 *Exod. R.* 1, 8.

8 Prov. xv. 19.

9 *Vide* Bacher, *Pal. Am.* III, 770, note.

Esau. And why like a hedge of thorns? Because, just as the thorn-bush sticks to one's garments, and when cleared on one side it catches hold on another side, even so is it with the Kingdom of Esau [*i.e.* Rome]; it collects the *annona*[1], but before that is collected comes the poll-tax, and before that is completed there comes the military levy[2].

Useless thorns and thorn-bushes.

In the poetry of the Midrash as of the Bible, the useless thorn is a type of the worthless and the wicked. It also represents wrong conceptions and fallacious ideas.

R. Samuel b. Naḥman (3rd c.) said in the name of R. Joḥanan (3rd c.): Punishment comes only when there are wicked people in the world, but it begins with the righteous. Scripture says[3], "If a fire break out and catch in thorns." Where does a fire break out? Where there are thorns about. And it makes a start with the righteous first, as the text continues[4]: "So that the stacks of corn have been consumed." It does not say: "The stacks of corn *shall be consumed*," but "the stacks of corn *have been* consumed" already, a long time ago[5].

In exposition of the text, "And he [*i.e.* Jeroboam] made priests from among all the people[6]," R. Ila (Bab. Am., 3rd and 4th c.) said with a play upon the words used[7]: He made priests of the thorns

[1] ארנון, *i.e.* a tax from crop and other farmers' produce delivered in kind.

[2] The reading being either בא עליהם טריבוט or באים לעסק טירונין, τίρων, a young soldier; *Pesikta R.* ch. 10, p. 33 *b*; also *Pesikta Shekalim*, 11 *a*, *b*, with notes, and *Tanḥuma ki Tissa.*

[3] Ex. xxii. 6.

[4] *Ibid.*

[5] *I.e.* not ויאכל גדיש but ונאכל גדיש, *B.K.* 60 *a*; Bacher, *Pal. Am.* I, 68, under name of Jonathan b. Eleazar (3rd c.).

[6] מקצות העם 1 Kings xii. 31.

[7] מקצות, resembling קוצים.

among the people[1], *i.e.* of the lowest orders among the people[2].

And a like simile based upon word-suggestion is given in the following exposition of the Rabbis:

It does not say[3], "They have *passed away* from the road which I commanded them," but "they have *turned aside* quickly out of the way which I commanded them." When at Sinai they were like lilies, and roses, now [*i.e.* after the incident of the golden calf] they have become like rubble, like thorn-bushes[4].

And similarly thorns and reeds represent erroneous conceptions, as the following example will show:

Walking on thorns.

Expounding the text, "And he brought him [*sc.* Abraham] forth abroad[5]," R. Judah in the name of R. Joḥanan says, That means, he lifted him [metaphorically] above the vault of heaven, saying, "Look to the heavens," *i.e.* look *down* to the heavens away from the influence of the planets. According to the other Rabbis, God said to Abraham, "Thou art a prophet and not an astrologer." And when in the days of Jeremiah Israel wished to return to the cult of astrology, the Holy One, blessed be He, prevented them. "Thus saith the Lord, Learn not the way of the nations, and be not dismayed at the signs of heaven[6]." "Abraham your father" [God is represented as saying] "had long desired to be subject to the influence of the planets, but I would not permit him." And in reference to this R. Levi (3rd c.) said: While the

1 מן הקוצים שבעם.

2 *Jer. Gittin*, I, 43 *d*, top.

3 Ex. xxxii. 8.

4 *Exod. R.* 42, 7, סָרוּ of the text suggesting סֵרָיוֹת. Cf. סורי הגפן Jer. ii. 21.

5 Gen. xv. 5.

6 Jer. x. 2.

sandal is on thy foot, tread the thorns down [*i.e.* whilst you may, counteract the baneful influences of this cult][1].

In expounding the text, "These are the generations of heaven and earth when they were created," the Midrash dwells on the unfathomable mysteries of Creation, and proceeds:

The impenetrable thicket of reeds.

And if a man tell thee, I can penetrate into the natural order of things[2], say unto him: Thou canst not understand the ways of an earthly king, how then wilt thou comprehend the doings of the King of kings, the Holy One, blessed be He!

R. Naḥman (4th c.) said: This may be likened unto a thicket of reeds into which no man could enter, for whosoever entered therein lost his way. What did a certain wise man do? He kept on cutting down and going forward. He entered and passed out by the path thus opened out. Whereupon all commenced to pass in and out through the cut path. [*I.e.* the wise man must remove the errors which are like thorns in the field of philosophy or the realm of metaphysics[3].]

Removing and destroying the thorns.

The metaphorical conception of thorns as denoting the wicked, who are to be uprooted and destroyed, is developed in the Midrash from its use in the Bible.

R. Ishmael the son of R. José (2nd c.) went to Neapolis[4]. When the Samaritans came to him, he said: I will prove to you that you do not worship this mountain [*i.e.* Gerizim], but the images under it, for

[1] *Gen. R.* 44, 12; cf. *Aḥikar*, II, 13, "My son, whilst thou hast shoes on thy feet tread down the thorns and make a path for thy sons and for thy sons' sons"; thorns = wrong notions.

[2] לעמוד על סידורו של עולם.

[3] *Gen. R.* 12, 1; more briefly in *Cant. R.* to i. 1 § 8.

[4] On the site of the ancient Shechem.

it is written[1]: "And Jacob hid them under the oak [or terebinth] which was by Shechem." Then he (R. Ishmael) heard their voices, saying, "Let us go up early and set in order these thorn-bushes" [*i.e.* "let us kill these men, for betraying the secret"]. He understood that they were seeking to slay him, so he rose early and departed[2].

Bundles of cut thorns.

In explanation of the verse "I am thy shield[3]" R. Levi (3rd and 4th c.) said: [This assurance was given] because Abraham was afraid, saying: Among the troops I slew there may possibly have been one righteous or God-fearing man.

This might be compared to one who was passing before the king's *Pardes.* Seeing a bundle of thorns he went down and took it away. Perceiving that the king had seen him, the man tried to hide from him. "Why dost thou hide thyself?" said the king. "How many working men should I have required to gather it? Now that thou hast done it, come and receive thy reward." Even so the Holy One, blessed be He, said unto Abraham: These troops that thou didst slay were cut thorns. Hence it is written[4]: "And the people shall be as the burnings of lime, as thorns cut down that are burned in the fire[5]."

The thorn and the lilies.

R. Simlai (3rd c.) asked of R. Jonathan what is the meaning of the text "There is one that is destroyed by reason of injustice[6]," and he adduced an incident (*Ma'aseh*) to illustrate the possibility of such accidental occurrence. A man was sent to collect the taxes from the inhabitants of Tiberias and Sepphoris. When collecting at Tiberias he saw a man from Sep-

[1] Gen. xxxv. 4.. [2] *Jer. Abodah Zarah*, v, 44 *d.* [3] Gen. xv. 1.
[4] Is. xxxiii. 12. [5] *Gen. R.* 44, 4, quoted also p. 91. [6] Prov. xiii. 23.

phoris and seized him. "But I am of Sepphoris," the man protested. "I have instructions to collect at Sepphoris too," replied the tax-gatherer. But before he had completed his collection at Tiberias notice of relief from taxation reached Sepphoris, and the man of Sepphoris had thus been mulcted unjustly. This, said R. Simon (3rd and 4th c.), is like unto a sickle that moweth down thorns and has not enough; [it moweth down] at the same time a lily and still has not sufficient[1].

The useful thorn-hedge.

But in addition to continuing and elaborating the Biblical imagery which clusters round the thorn and the thorn-bush, Midrashic poetry has added one or two new conceptions to the symbolism of this plant. The thorn and thorn-bush are by no means the worthless objects which the greater number of the Biblical figures might lead us to imagine. They served also a useful purpose in providing a fence round the field. This fact supplies the Rabbis with a fresh simile, which they read into a Bible text.

A certain Sadducean said to R. Joshua b. Ḥananiah (1st and 2nd c.): Thou descendant of a thorn race[2], it is written about you (Jews): "The best of them is as a brier[3]." "You fool," he replied, "go to the end of the verse [in order to understand the whole of it] where it is written 'the most upright are better than the thorn-hedge.'" And why does the text say "The best of them is as a brier?" It means that just as the briers safeguard the gap even so do the good men among us safeguard and protect us[4].

In like manner the Midrashic writers have given

[1] *Gen. R.* 49, 8.

[2] חדקאה.

[3] Mic. vii. 4.

[4] *Erubin*, 101 *a*.

a new meaning to a Biblical simile concerning the reed.

The flexible reed.

R. Samuel b. Naḥman (3rd c.) said in the name of R. Jonathan (*sc.* b. Eleazar, 3rd c.): What is the meaning of the verse[1], "Faithful are the wounds of a friend; but the kisses of an enemy are deceitful"? Better was the curse wherewith Ahijah the Shilonite cursed Israel than the blessing wherewith the wicked Balaam blessed them. Ahijah the Shilonite cursed them by comparing them to the reed; he said to the Israelites[2], "For the Lord shall smite Israel as a reed is shaken in the water." How is it with the reed? It stands in a place of water where its stump throws out new shoots, and its roots increase; so that when even all the winds blow against it they cannot move it, but it waves to and fro with them, and when they subside it remains standing. But Balaam blessed them by comparing them to the cedar as it is said: "Like cedars by the waters[3]." And therefore, proceeds the Talmud: man must at all times be yielding like a reed and not unbending like a cedar.

Reeds single and in bundles.

On the text "And his band he established upon earth[4]" the Rabbis say: It is a common experience[5]— if a man take a bundle of reeds, can he break them at one stroke? If, however, he take them singly, he may break them. Even so dost thou find that Israel

[1] Prov. xxvii. 6. [2] 1 Kings xiv. 15.

[3] *Taanith*, 20 *a*. Bacher, *Pal. Am.* I, 65, in the name of Jonathan b. Eleazar; cf. Matt. xi. 7; Eph. iv. 14, "a reed shaken with the wind." For another simile from the flexible reed cf. the following: When he [*sc.* R. Shesheth] bent [at prayer] he bent like a cane [when it is swung] and when he erected himself [in prayer] he did so like a serpent [*i.e.* raising his head first], *Berachoth*, 12 *b*. See p. 112 *supra*.

[4] Amos ix. 6. [5] בנוהג שבעולם.

will not be redeemed [and thus become unbreakable] until they are formed into one band[1].

The thorn in proverb.

The thorn and reed are also used metaphorically in many proverbial sayings:

To throw something over the thorn-hedge is a figure for its uselessness.

"Thy good-natured advice is taken and thrown over the hedge" [*i.e.* thy advice comes too late][2].

To push one aside with a reed is a familiar metaphor for the summary dismissal of a reason or argument. The disciples said to Bar Kappara (Tanna, 2nd and 3rd c.), in reference to a reply he gave to a philosopher: "Rabbi, this man thou didst push aside with a reed [*i.e.* dismissed with a vague and paltry reply], what answer wilt thou give us[3]?"

"From a thorn-bush comes forth a rose" [*i.e.* good children often come from a bad father][4].

To place thorns in the eyes is a metaphor for giving offence. In the days of Rabbi (*i.e.* Judah Hanasi) they wanted to regard Babylonia as *Isa*[5] in relation to Palestine. Whereupon he said: "You are placing thorns between my eyes[6]."

1 *Tanḥuma Niṣabim*, p. 49; cf. Aesop's fable on the same theme.

2 *Baba Kama*, 83 *a et cet. loc.*

3 *Jer. Shabbath*, III, 6 *a et cet. loc.*; cf. the following: The disciples said to Rabbi Joshua b. Korḥah (2nd c.): This one thou didst drive away with a broken reed, *Lev. R.* 4, 6; also the disciples to R. Joḥanan b. Zakkai (1st c.) *vide Num. R.* 19, 8, *Pesikta* p. 40 *b*; cf. also *Gen. R.* 70, 5.

4 *Cant. R. init.* to i. 1 § 6, cf. תחת הנעצוץ יעלה ברוש Is. lv. 13.

5 עיסה (opposed to סלת נקיה) = a mixed family, a family suspected of containing an alien admixture.

6 *Kiddushin*, 71 *a*; cf. a familiar expression of R. Judah, *Synhedrin*, 38 *a*, where he uses the same retort to Judah and Ḥizkiah the sons of R. Ḥiyya, in reference to a statement of theirs made when in an exhilarated mood, and which they based upon Is. viii. 14, that the son of David would not come until the disappearance of the two Houses in Israel, *viz.* the Rosh-Golah in Babylon and the Nasi in the Land of Israel.

"To cut reeds in the meadows" is an expression for the illiterate. The students of the academy said to Rab Naḥman bar Gurya, when he came to Nehardea[1]: "Thy master cut reeds in the meadow[2]."

When Rab Dimi (3rd and 4th c.) came [from Palestine to Babylon], he said: "Youth is a wreath of roses; old age is a wreath of thorns[3]."

"For as the crackling of thorns under a pot, so is the laughter of the fool[4]." R. Levi the son of R. Z'era (4th c.) made this verse a text for opening his discourse[5]. None of the trees when it burns makes a noise, but thorns, when burning, crackle, as much as to say: "We too are wood[6]."

[1] A town in Babylon renowned as the seat of a college founded by Samuel.

[2] *Shabbath*, 95 *a*.

[3] *Shabbath*, 152 *a*, top. R. Dimi [= Abdima Naḥotha] was an itinerant Rabbi, who often carried Palestinian traditions to Babylonian Schools and Babylonian teachings to Palestine.

[4] Eccl. vii. 6.

[5] עביד ליה נטילת רשות.

[6] *Kohel. R. ad loc.* Bacher, *Pal. Am.* III, 548. It has been suggested that the author of this saying probably had a less pleasant enunciation than the others, who were below him in knowledge.

X

THE LILY

The imagery of the lily.

THE symbolism of the lily plays an interesting part in the poetry of the Song of Songs. The natural beauty of this flower, which is considerably enhanced by the striking contrast with its thorny environment, is again and again drawn upon in this Biblical idyll to typify the exquisite charm and inimitable beauty of the beloved bride: "As a lily among thorns, so is my love among the daughters[1]," and also of the lover in the eyes of his bride[2]. The same flower is used by Hosea[3] to symbolise Israel the beloved of the Lord.

In Rabbinic literature the similes taken from the lily are in very large measure elaborated from the Biblical figures found in the Song of Songs and in Hosea.

The choicest kind.

"I am a rose of Sharon, a lily of the valleys[4]." R. Eleazar b. Pedath (3rd and 4th c.) said: The righteous are compared to the most precious of flowers and to the best of their kind: to the most precious of flowers—"like a lily"; and to the choicest among that species—"like a lily of the valleys"; not like the lily of the mountains which withers easily, but like the lily of the valleys, which is ever green[5].

Growing among thorns.

"As a lily among thorns, so is my love among the daughters[6]."

R. Isaac (3rd and 4th c.) interpreted this text as

[1] Cant. ii. 2. [2] *Ibid.* v. 13. [3] xiv. 6. [4] Cant. ii. 1.

[5] שמרטבת והולכת *Cant. R. ad loc.*; Bacher, *Pal. Am.* II, 76.

[6] Cant. ii. 2.

pplying to Rebekah, for it is said[1]: "And Isaac was forty years old when he took Rebekah, the daughter of Bethuel the Syrian[2] of Padan-Aram, the sister of Laban the Syrian, to be his wife." If this were intended to tell us that she was of Padan-Aram, why does it say: "the sister of Laban the Syrian"? But her father was a deceiver[3], and her brother was a deceiver, and so were all the men of her place deceivers, and yet this righteous woman came from among them. To what was she comparable? To "a lily among thorns[4]."

R. Ḥanan of Sepphoris (3rd c.) explained this verse as referring to acts of benevolence. According to the custom of the world[5], if ten men enter a house of mourning, not one of whom is able to open his mouth, to recite the blessings of the mourners[6], and then one comes, opens his mouth and recites the blessing, to what is he like? To "a lily among thorns."

A single lily among the thorns.

The same applies when ten men ordinarily enter a house of feasting, not one of whom is able to open his mouth, to recite the blessing of the bridegroom[7], and one comes, and does so, to what is he like? To "a lily among thorns."

1 Gen. xxv. 20.

2 Hebrew ארמי, "Aramean."

3 רמאי by transposition of letters.

4 *Cant. R. ad loc.*; *Gen. R.* 63, 4; *Lev. R.* 23, 1; Bacher, *Pal. Am.* II, 243.

5 בנוהג שבעולם.

6 A form of such blessing of comfort to the mourners is given in *Kethuboth*, 8 *b*, "Our brothers, who are wearied and distressed by this mourning; set your hearts to consider this: such happenings are of time immemorial, going back to the days of creation. Many have drunk [*sc.* of the cup of sorrow] and many yet will drink, like the drinking of the first shall be the drinking of the last. Our brothers, may the Master of consolations console you; Blessed be He, Who comforts the mourners."

7 For the "Seven Benedictions" still recited at marriage ceremonies and wedding feasts *vide* Jewish Prayer Book, Singer, p. 299

Or when ten ordinary men enter the Synagogue, not one of whom is able to recite the prayers, and lead the congregation in the reading of the *Shema*[1], and then one comes and performs his task, to what is he like? To "a lily among thorns[2]."

Plucking the lily.

R. Eleazar (b. Pedath, 3rd c.) interpreted this verse[3] as applying to the redemption from Egypt. Just as the lily when set among thorns cannot easily be plucked by its owner, so was the redemption of Israel a hard task for the Holy One, blessed be He. Hence it is written[4], "Or hath God essayed to go and take him a nation from the midst of another nation by trials, by signs and by wonders," etc.[5]

Clearing the thorns around the lily.

R. Aibo (4th c.) interpreted this verse as referring to Israel's ultimate redemption. How is it with the lily? When set among thorns it is difficult for the owner to pluck it. What does he do? He brings fire and burns down that which surrounds it and then plucks it. Even so, "The Lord has ordained concerning Jacob that they that are round about him shall be his adversaries[6]," as hostile[7] as Ḥallamish is to Naveh[8], as Jericho to Naaran[9], as Susitha[10] to Tiberias,

[1] לפרום על שמע, *vide* Elbogen, *Der Jüd. Gottesdienst*, p. 26.

[2] *Cant. R. ad loc.*; cf. also *ibid.*, the simile of Israel the single lily or rose saving the whole *Pardes*, *i.e.* the world.

[3] Cant. ii. 2. [4] Deut. iv. 34.

[5] *Cant. R. ad loc.*; Bacher, *Pal. Am.* II, 76. [6] Lam. i. 17.

[7] Hostility between a Jewish settlement and a neighbouring non-Jewish locality.

[8] Ḥallamish, a place E. of Gadara in Galilee, and inhabited by hostile Gentiles; נוה in *Lev. R.*, correct reading for גווה in *Cant. R.* In Naveh lived R. Tanḥum ר׳ תנחום דמן נוי, *Shabbath*, 30 *a*; R. Shila ר׳ שילא דנוהא, *Lev. R.* 34, 9; R. Abimi אבימי נותאה, *Abodah Zarah*, 36 *a*; *vide* Neubauer, *Géographie du Talmud*, p. 245.

[9] Corr. reading נערן.

[10] Susitha was a place occupied by Gentiles, סוסיתא עיר שרובה גוים, *Jer. Rosh Hashanah*, II, 1, *vide* Neubauer, p. 238.

as Castra to Ḥaifa[1], as Lydda[2] to Oni. Hence it is said[3], "This is Jerusalem; I have set her in the midst of the nations, and countries are round about her." On the morrow [*i.e.* in the future] when the end comes, what will the Holy One, blessed be He, do? He will bring fire and burn down all about her. Hence it is said[4]: "And the peoples shall be as burnings of lime; as thorns cut down, that are burned in the fire." What is written here[5]? "The Lord will lead him alone[6]."

Gathering the lilies.

"My beloved is gone down to his garden to the beds of spices, to feed in the gardens and to gather lilies[7]."

R. José b. Ḥanina (3rd c.) said: "My beloved"—that is, the Holy One, blessed be He, [is gone down] "to His garden"—*i.e.* the world, "to the beds of spices," *i.e.* Israel, "to feed in the gardens"—these are the Synagogues and Houses of Study, "and to gather lilies"—*i.e.* to gather to Himself [by death] the pious ones from among Israel[8].

The wind-tossed lily.

R. Ḥanina the son of R. Abba [3rd c.] explained

[1] The following Rabbis lived at Ḥaifa: Abba, Arni, Isaac Nappaḥah and Abdimi.

[2] For Lydda (in Tannaitic times a place of *Talmidé-Ḥachamim*) and the nature of its inhabitants in the Amoraic period *vide Shabbath*, 10 *a*, מאכל לודים; *Gittin*, 47 *a*, ריש לקיש זבין נפשיה ללודאי; *Tosefta Yebamoth*, IV, 5, when a לסטים confesses to having killed a Jewish person בכניסתו ללוד.

[3] Ezek. v. 5. [4] Is. xxxiii. 12. [5] Deut. xxxii. 12.

[6] *Cant. R. ad loc.*; *Lev. R.* 23, 5; Bacher, *Pal. Am.* III, 78 note; Rab in *Yebamoth*, 16 *b*, and Rab Jehudah *Kiddushin*, 72 *b*, apply the verse from Lam. to the hostility in Babylon between Humania and the Jewish town of Pum Nahara.

[7] Cant. vi. 2.

[8] *Cant. R. ad loc.* In *Jer. Berachoth*, 5 *b*, *c*, "to feed in the gardens," *i.e.* the nations of the world; "to gather lilies," *i.e.* the pious among the nations, in order to plant them among Israel. In Bacher, *Pal. Am.* I, 401, 440 (notes), also in name of R. Simeon b. Lakish.

this verse from the Song of Songs[1] as referring to the ruling powers[2]: Just as in the case of the lily when set among thorns, at one time a north wind goes forth and inclines it towards the south[3] and then the thorn pricks it; at another time a south wind comes forth and bends it towards the north, and once more the thorn pricks it[4], but withal its heart [*i.e.* petals] is always directed upward, so indeed is it with Israel. Although the ruling power may collect from them *annonæ*[5] and *angariæ*[6], yet their heart is ever directed toward their Father in Heaven, as it is said[7], "Mine eyes are ever towards the Lord[8]."

Another Rabbi gave a similarly poetic Nature-interpretation to other lily texts of the Bible. "I will be as the dew unto Israel, he shall blossom as the lily[9]." The Holy One, blessed be He, said unto them, "Everything depends upon you. Even as the lily puts forth blossoms and its heart is turned upward, so shall your heart, when you are doing penitence before Me, be directed upwards like the lily. At that hour will I bring the Redeemer...." Hence the Psalmist's invocation[10]: "To the Chief Musician set to *Shoshannim*" [lilies][11].

The tender lily.

Poetic simile also clusters round the numerous

[1] Cant. ii. 2. [2] מלכיות.

[3] *Cant. R.* reads "towards the North."

[4] This part is omitted in *Cant. R.*

[5] אנוניות = annual produce.

[6] אנגריות, forced service. In *Cant. R.* the reading is בורסגניות, which Jastrow corrects into כרוסרגוריות = χρυσάργυρον, the gold and silver tax, levied by Constantine the Great.

[7] Ps. xxv. 15.

[8] *Lev. R.* 23, 5. In *Cant. R. ad loc.* the author is R. Huna—4th cent.

[9] Hos. xiv. 6. [10] Ps. lxxx. 1.

[11] *Shoḥer Tob* to Ps. xlv. § 3.

other characteristics of the lily. In explanation of the text, "Set about with lilies[1]," the Midrash says: This alludes to the words of the Law which are as tender as the lilies[2].

On the verse "I am a lily of the valleys[3]" R. Abba b. Kahana (3rd and 4th c.) said: The congregation of Israel[4] exclaimed before the Holy One, blessed be He, I, even I, am still beloved, though plunged in the depths of troubles[5], and when the Holy One, blessed be He, lifts me out of my deep sorrow I shall be filled with the sap of good deeds like the lily[6].

The lily in sun and dew.

In connection with the freely expounded text from the Song of Songs already referred to[7], R. Abun (4th c.) said: How is it with the lily? When the heat comes upon it, it is withered, but when the dew falls it blooms again. Even so as long as the shadow of Esau exists, Israel [if one may use the expression] seems to be withered in this world, but in time to come, the shadow of Esau shall pass away and Israel shall continue to be full of sap, as it is said[8]: "I will be as the dew unto Israel."

Sweet-smelling and dainty.

Just as the lily cannot be passed by, says another

[1] Cant. vii. 3, סוגה בשושנים.

[2] *Shoḥer Tob* to Ps. ii.; author R. Judan, 4th cent. In *Cant. R. ad loc.* anonym.

[3] Cant. ii. 1. [4] כנסת ישראל.

[5] חבצלת (אני)=חביב צל, *i.e.* "I am beloved," חביב, though "in the shade" צל.

[6] *Cant. R. ad loc.*; Bacher, *Pal. Am.* II, 498. The expression מרטבת מעשים טובים, "filled with the sap of good deeds," is frequently used; *e.g.* R. Aḥa (4th c., Bacher, *Pal. Am.* III, 149) in same section, and in *Shoḥer Tob* to Ps. lxxx. 1: Israel says to God "When Thou fixest deep thine eyes upon me I am filled with the sap of good deeds like a lily and break forth into song"; and R. Berechiah (4th c.) in *Shoḥer Tob* to Ps. i. § 20.

[7] Cant. ii. 2. [8] Hos. xiv. 6. *Esau* (*Edom*) typifies *Rome*.

poetic Sage, if only because of its fragrance[1], so Israel cannot be set at nought, if only because of the precepts and good deeds which he performs[2]. Just as the lily is valued only for its fragrance, so were the righteous created only for the redemption of Israel.

Just as the lily is brought up on the royal table [*i.e.* considered a delicacy] at the beginning and end of the meal[3], so is Israel of equal worth both in this world and in the world hereafter.

Just as the lily is recognisable among the plants, so is Israel distinguishable among the nations, as it is said[4]: "All that see them shall acknowledge them that they are the seed which the Lord hath blessed."

A Sabbath flower.

Just as the lily is set apart for Sabbath and Festivals, so is Israel assigned for future redemption[5].

The redness of the colour of the lily or rose is used as a euphemistic metaphor in the Midrash: What I have seen was like in appearance unto a red lily[6].

A single lily saves the garden.

And there is the following parable based upon the worth of this flower, a parable already quoted in the chapter dealing with the *Pardes*. "As a lily among the thorns, so is my love among the daughters[7]." R. Azariah (4th c.) in the name of R. Judah, in the name of R. Simeon, said: This might be compared unto a king who possessed a *Pardes*, in which were planted a row of fig trees, a row of vines, a row of pomegranate trees and a row of apple trees. He handed it over to

1 אינה בטלה אלא על גב ריחה.

2 One of the commentators suggests the reading אינה ניטלת is not taken up and used.

3 Certain varieties of the lily, *e.g. lilium pomponium*, are edible.

4 Is. lxi. 9.

5 *Cant. R. ad loc.*; *Lev. R.* 23, 6; Bacher, *Pal. Am.* III, 411.

6 כשושנה אדומה *Cant. R.* to vii. 3.

7 Cant. ii. 2.

a tenant-farmer and went away. After a time the king returned and looked into the garden to see what had been done and found it full of thorns and thistles. He brought in woodcutters[1] to raze the plantation. He then noticed therein one rose-coloured lily[2]. He picked it up, smelt it, and his soul was refreshed. "For the sake of this lily," said the king, "the *Pardes* shall be saved." Even so the world was created only for Israel. After twenty-six generations the Holy One, blessed be He, looked into His world to see what had been done there. He found it all in deluge and devastation. He brought cutters to raze it, as it is said: "The Lord sat as King at the flood[3]." Then He noticed a rose-coloured lily—that is Israel. He took it up and smelt it, *i.e.* He tested the Israelites when He set them in array to receive the Ten Words: and his soul was refreshed, when the Israelites said, "We will do and obey." Then said the Holy One, blessed be He: "Because of this lily the *Pardes* shall be saved. Through the merit of the Law and its students the world shall be saved[4]."

[1] קַצָּצִים. [2] שושנה אחת של ורד. [3] Ps. xxix. 10.

[4] *Cant. R. ad loc.*; cf. *Lev. R.* 23, 3; *vide* Bacher, *Pal. Am.* III, 169, *sub* Judah b. Simeon.

XI

THE MYRTLE

In Midrashic poetry.

IN the Bible no metaphorical or symbolic significance attaches to the Myrtle. But its prescribed use in Jewish ritual, as one of the Four Plants appointed for the Feast of Tabernacles[1], together with the fact that this myrtle shrub has a place in the mystic vision of Zechariah[2], was sufficient to clothe it with a certain poetic symbolism; and a few metaphors and similes were made to cluster round the myrtle in Midrashic poetry.

The myrtle tree.

The myrtle trees are a type of the righteous. It has been taught in a Baraitha:—R. Meïr (2nd c.) says: Her name was Esther, and why was she called Hadassah, "the Myrtle"? Because of the righteous, who are called "Myrtles"; and so it is said[3], "And he stood among the myrtle trees[4]."

The boughs and their leaves.

"The boughs of the thick tree[5]," which the Halachah takes to mean "myrtle boughs," typify the Holy One, blessed be He, says R. Akiba (Tanna, 50–132)[6].

[1] Lev. xxiii. 40. [2] i. 8–11.

[3] Zech. i. 8.

[4] *Megillah*, 13 *a*; Bacher, *Ag. Tan.* II, 39.

[5] Lev. xxiii. 40.

[6] *Pesikta*, 184 *a*. This poetic conception agrees with his Halachic interpretation of this observance. R. Akiba ruled that myrtle leaves which formed only one verticil satisfied the ritual requirements in regard to the specified plant. Hence the myrtle naturally typified the One and Only God. R. Ishmael, on the other hand, and probably others with him, required a triple verticil from the leaves in order to satisfy the ritual demands. Hence no doubt the reason for the other similes.

According to other Rabbis they symbolise the three rows of students that sat before them (*i.e.* the Great Sanhedrin)[1]. And again, "The myrtle trees that were in the bottom[2]" typified, according to R. Joḥanan (2nd and 3rd c.), Ḥananiah, Mishael and Azariah in Babylon[3]. According to R. Berechiah (4th c.) they are symbolic of Israel in the depths of exile[4].

Abounding with leaves.

There is a further simile suggested by the leaves of the myrtle tree.

"The boughs of thick trees[5]." These symbolise (according to various Rabbinic exegetes) Jacob or Leah; even as the myrtle abounds with leaves so was Jacob (and equally so Leah) blessed with many children[6].

Redolent but tasteless.

The odour and taste of the myrtle likewise supplied the Midrashic writers with objects for simile. Commenting upon the verse "The boughs of thick trees[7]," they say: Just as the myrtle has fragrance but no taste, even so is it with Israel; there are among them men with a knowledge of the Torah, but without good deeds[8].

In interpreting the text "And he brought up Hadassah[9]" the Rabbis add: Just as the myrtle is sweet in smell, but bitter in taste, even so was Esther sweet to Mordecai, but bitter to Haman[10].

1 *Lev. R.* 30, 11 anonym. 2 Zech. i. 8–11.

3 *Synhedrin*, 93 *a*; Bacher, *Pal. Am.* I, 307.

4 *Ibid.*, "depth" is a term for Babylon; *vide* Bacher, *Pal. Am.* III, 361. Read שהיה מבקש להדמות לאותן שנקראו הדסים, לישראל שהן נתונין במצולה. This Midrashic imagery is continued in later Jewish literature. The three verticils symbolise the three patriarchs (*Zohar*, III, 35 *a*; *Tikkunim*, 3 *b*). Cabbalistically the shrub, with its three whorls, also typifies the *Sefiroth*, might, power and glory.

5 Lev. xxiii. 40. 6 *Lev. R.* 30, 10 anonym.; *Pesikta*, 184 *a*.

7 Lev. xxiii. 40. 8 *Lev. R.* 30, 12 anonym. 9 Esther ii. 7.

10 *Esther R. ad loc.*

The myrtle in the desert.

There is a fine Midrashic simile taken from the growth of the myrtle in the desert land.

R. Joḥanan (3rd c.) said: Whosoever learns Torah and does not teach it, is like unto a myrtle in the wilderness [where its very loneliness makes it forgotten and unused]. Some say, Whosoever learns Torah and teaches it even in a place where there is no disciple of the wise [*i.e.* where there is no receptive ear] is like unto a myrtle in the wilderness and therefore possessing a special value[1].

Among thorny bushes.

And there is a further simile suggested by its growth among the thorny bushes.

"And the boys grew[2]." R. Levi (3rd c.) said: This might be compared to a myrtle and a rose bush growing side by side; when they became big and blossomed forth, the one gave forth a fine fragrance, and the other a thorn[3]. Even so was it with Esau and Jacob. For thirteen years both of them went to and from the school. After thirteen years, the one turned to the Houses of Study and the other to the houses of idol-worshippers[4].

"The four species."

At this point it may be appropriate to add the symbolic interpretation of the remaining two objects, which together with the palm and myrtle—already dealt with—form the "*Aguddah*," the union of four species, used in the ceremonial of the Feast of Tabernacles, *viz.* the "fruit of the goodly tree" (*Ethrog*

[1] *Rosh Hashanah*, 23 *a*; Bacher, *Pal. Am.* I, 235. [2] Gen. xxv. 27.

[3] זה נותן ריחו וזה חוחו.

[4] *Gen. R.* 63, 10; Bacher, *Pal. Am.* II, 345; note also the following proverb: "A myrtle among willows remains a myrtle still, and people call it a myrtle" (*Synhedrin*, 44 *a*); quoted by R. Abba to illustrate the dictum of R. Abba bar Zabda that an Israelite, though he has sinned, remains an Israelite still.

or citron) and the willows of the brook (*'Araboth*). The *Ethrog* is made to typify in turn the Holy One, Abraham and Sarah[1]; to symbolise by its taste and fragrance that section of Israel which possesses the taste of Torah and fragrance of good deeds[2]; to signify by its beauty the members of the Great Sanhedrin, whom the Holy One has graced with old age[3].

And the willows of the brook, which wither before the other three species, typify respectively Joseph who died before his brothers, or Rachel, whose demise preceded that of her sister[4]; they symbolise those in Israel who have neither the taste of Torah nor the fragrance of good deeds[5]; they signify the two scribes that stood before the *Dayanim*—the Judges of the Jewish Court[6]. Moreover, in their external appearance the *Lulab* (palm) resembles the human spine; the myrtle the eye, the *Ethrog* the heart, and the willow the mouth[7].

[1] *Lev. R.* 30, 9 and 10. [2] *Ibid.* 30, 12. [3] *Ibid.* 30, 11.
[4] *Ibid.* 30, 10. [5] *Ibid.* 30, 10. [6] *Ibid.* 30, 11.
[7] *Ibid.* 30, 14. The symbolism of the "four plants" is largely made use of in the liturgic poetry of the Feast of Tabernacles.

XII

PASTORAL

Biblical figures.

PASTORAL similes, as might well have been expected, abound in the Bible. They are used principally to typify the relationship between God and His people and to record certain episodes in the early history of Israel.

God is the Shepherd, and Israel "the people of His pasture and the flock of His hand[1]." He led them tenderly "like a flock" out of Egypt[2], and with kindly solicitude shepherded them through the wilderness[3].

In the course of their history He entrusted the care of His "beautiful" flock to human shepherds, the prophets and leaders of every age. "As for me, I have not hastened from being a shepherd after thee," says Jeremiah[4].

But the children of Israel, like "the straying sheep[5]," often wandered away altogether shepherdless, or worse still trusted themselves to "selfish, negligent and misleading shepherds who scattered and drove the flock away[6]"; "shepherds who could not understand" and who exposed their flock to the rapacity of "dogs" and "beasts of the field," that are "greedy and know not when they have enough[7]"; "shepherds who fed themselves and not their sheep[8]." This stray-

1 Cf. Ps. xcv. 7; Ezek. xxxiv. 31.
2 Ps. lxxvii. 21. 3 Ps. lxxviii. 52. 4 xvii. 16.
5 Is. liii. 6. 6 Jer. xxiii. 2. 7 Is. lvi. 11.
8 Ezek. xxxiv.

ing from the paths of safety led them into vicissitudes of all kinds. And Israel's most poignant sufferings, due not always to the error of their own ways, but caused by an adherence to their faith and by the cruelty of their oppressors, are pictured under the image of the flock ready to be slain[1], "of sheep being led to the slaughter[2]"; "nay, but for Thy sake we are killed all the day; we are accounted as sheep for the slaughter[3]."

The ultimate deliverance of Israel is likewise symbolised by pastoral imagery: the numbering and the ingathering of the flock[4]; the appointment of shepherds according to God's heart who shall "feed them with knowledge and understanding[5]" and "in the strength of the Lord[6]"; above all, the resumption by God Himself of the rôle of Shepherd of Israel, guiding and tending them with kindliness and consideration. Jeremiah devotes a whole chapter[7] to a description under pastoral simile of this divine care and attention; and less detailed references to God's ingathering of His flock are contained in other Prophetical books[8].

But apart from these connected and more or less complete scenes used in describing God's relations to His people, there are many other allusions to shepherd life scattered in the pages of the Bible.

We have similes taken from the nomad shepherds' life in such passages as "My habitation is plucked up and carried away from me as a shepherd's tent[9]." "Thine eyes shall see Jerusalem as a peaceful habita-

[1] Zech. xi. 4. [2] Is. xliii. 7. [3] Ps. xlix. 15.
[4] Jer. xxiii. 3; l. 19; Zech. x. 3; Mic. ii. 12. [5] Jer. iii. 15.
[6] Mic. v. 3. [7] Ch. xxxiv. [8] *Vide* Mic. ii. 12; Is. xl. 11.
[9] Is. xxxviii. 12.

tion, a tent that shall not be removed, the stakes whereof shall never be plucked up, neither shall any of the cords thereof be broken[1]."

We find images drawn from the assemblies of shepherds and their co-operative activities for the purpose of warding off a common danger to the flocks under their charge. "Like as the lion, or the young lion, growling over his prey, though a multitude of shepherds be called forth against him, he will not be dismayed at their voice, nor abase himself for the noise of them[2]."

We have further figures of comparison taken from the habits of the he-goats walking in front of the flocks[3] as well as from the colour of the sheep's wool[4].

Mid-rashic figures.

In the literature of the Midrash the religious purport of the pastoral figures of speech is similar to that of the Bible, and the images themselves are very much akin to those which are used by the Biblical writers. In fact many of the Rabbinic parables are based upon an amplification of Bible texts.

There are, however, many new touches of pastoral scenery and life in the Midrashic passages as the following examples will show:

The Tent similes of the Bible are thus developed in Rabbinic literature.

Like the tents of Kedar.

Commenting upon the text "I am black but comely, O ye daughters of Jerusalem, as the tents of Kedar, as the curtains of Solomon[5]," the Rabbi-preachers discoursed as follows: How is it with the tents of Kedar? Although they seem black and ugly and ragged from without, yet within they are full of

[1] Is. xxxiii. 20. [2] Is. xxxi. 4. [3] Is. i. 8.
[4] Is. i. 18. [5] Cant. i. 5.

precious stones and pearls; even so is it with the scholars; although outwardly ungainly in this world, yet are they filled with the knowledge of Torah (*Mikra*, *Mishnah* and *Midrash*, *Halachoth*, *Toseftoth* and *Aggadoth*). Lest you should think that just as the tents of Kedar remain unwashed [for washing is useless in their case], even so does Israel remain uncleansed: Therefore Scripture adds "as the curtains of Solomon," for just as a garment, if it become stained, is washed, and when stained again is washed once more, even so is it with Israel; although they may be stained with sin all the days of the year, yet the Day of Atonement comes and cleanses them, as it is said[1], "For on this day atonement shall be made for you, to cleanse you; that ye may be clean from all your sins before the Lord," and as it is further said[2], "Though your sins be as scarlet, they shall be as white as snow." Should you think that just as the tents of Kedar are moved about from place to place, so will it be with Israel, it is written "as the curtains of '*Shlomoh*' the God of Peace[3]"—they are like the curtains provided by God Whose bidding brought the world into existence, and which, once stretched tent-like, did not move from their place.

R. Eliezer ben Jacob (1st and 2nd c.) adduced a text from Isaiah to explain the above: "A tent that shall not be taken down[4]," *i.e.* it shall neither be disturbed nor moved away. Just as the tents of Kedar suffer not the yoke of any creature[5], even so will

1 Lev. xvi. 30. 2 Is. i. 18.

3 The Hebrew שלמה (Solomon) is explained etymologically to mean שהשלום שלו, "he to whom belongs peace."

4 Is. xxxiii. 20.

5 A reference to the freedom of the Bedouins.

Israel in the future be free from every human yoke. R. Ḥiyya (3rd and 4th c.) [in support of this view] quoted the verse[1]: "And I have broken the bands of your yoke and made you go upright[2]."

As the tents of the desert dwellers.

Expounding the simile which Balaam used in his description of Israel—"As the trees of aloes which the Lord hath planted[3]"—the Rabbis, with a play upon words[4], said: He (Balaam) wanted to compare Israel to the tents of the desert dwellers[5], which are torn up and moved from place to place, whereupon the Holy One, blessed be He, said unto him, "It shall not be as thou thinkest, but they will be set firm like those tents which are fixed solidly," *viz.* like the heaven and the earth, of which Scripture says[6]: "And he spreadeth them out as a tent to dwell in[7]."

The tent cords—the Sages of the Sanhedrin.

The Rabbis of the Midrash likewise assign a symbolic meaning to the tent-cords.

"(My tent is spoiled and) all my cords are broken[8]" is the dirge of Judah at the time of the destruction. The tent-cords, says the Midrash, signify the Sanhedrin, who were to the world what the cords are to the tent. For just as the tent cannot stand except with the aid of cords, so the world could not exist, even for a single hour, were it not for the aged men seated in the Great Sanhedrin, fixing the festivals, intercalating the years and the months, giving decisions as to what is permitted or forbidden, and arranging evenly the concerns of men[9].

1 Lev. xxvi. 13.

2 *Cant. R.* to i. 5; and in slightly varied form in *Exod. R.* 23, 10.

3 Num. xxiv. 6.

4 For the Hebrew אֲהָלִים, "aloes," used in the text recalls אֹהָלִים, which has the meaning of "tents."

5 כאהלים של סרקין.

6 Is. xl. 22.

7 *Yalkut Num.* § 771.

8 Jer. x. 20.

9 *Pesikta R.* xxviii, 134 *b*.

A similar typical significance attaches to the tent-pegs, which in Midrashic imagery symbolise the Patriarchs, the world's moral supports. On the text "And he [i.e. Abraham] gave him [i.e. Melchizedek, king of Salem] tithes from everything[1]," R. Judah bar Simon (4th c.) said: By virtue of that gift the three pegs of the world, Abraham, Isaac and Jacob, received full blessings. In the case of Abraham, Scripture says, "And the Lord blessed Abraham in all things[2]"; of Isaac it is written, "And I have enjoyed of all[3]"; and of Jacob it says[4], "God hath dealt graciously with me, and I have all things[5]."

The tent-pegs—the Patriarchs.

There is a natural association of ideas between the tent as a place of privacy and the modest woman of whom the Psalmist, according to the Rabbis, speaks as "the royal daughter whose glory is within" [the home][6].

The two tents—Ruth and Naomi.

In Midrashic poetry the tent is made to typify a worthy woman. "And Lot also, which went with Abram, had flocks and herds and tents[7]." R. Tobiah bar Isaac said: This refers metaphorically to the "two tents," *viz.* Ruth the Moabite and Naomi the Ammonite [descendants of Lot's daughters][8].

But the shepherd's hut is a more natural image for the Sanctuary, which is called in the Bible "the tent of assembly."

The shepherd's hut—the Sanctuary.

1 Gen. xiv. 20. 2 בכל *ibid.* xxiv. 1. 3 מכל *ibid.* xxvii. 33.

4 כל *ibid.* xxxiii. 11.

5 *Gen. R.* 43, 8; Bacher, *Pal. Am.* III, 180; cf. ref. to these blessings in Prayer Book, "Grace after Meals," Singer, p. 284, where a benediction is invoked upon the members of one's family and the guests who have participated in the meal: "As our fathers Abraham, Isaac and Jacob were blessed each with his own comprehensive blessing" (בכל מכל כל).

6 *Vide Yalkut* to Ps. xlv. 14. 7 Gen. xiii. 5.

8 *Gen. R.* 41, 4.

The Holy One, blessed be He, said unto Israel: Ye are My flock and I am the Shepherd; even as it is written[1]: "And ye My flock, the flock of My pasture, are men," and as it is further said[2]: "Give ear, O Shepherd of Israel." Make ye a hut for the Shepherd that He may come and provide for you. Wherefore was the command given[3]: "And let them make Me a Sanctuary, that I may dwell among them[4]."

Following the spirit of the Bible, the Shepherd in Rabbinic poetry denotes God; and His flock typify in turn the Patriarchs and Israel, over whom He watches and guards. He protects them against the attacks of ravenous wolves—rapacious foes—supervises their grazing, and keeps them from going astray.

The flock walking before the shepherd.

The third Patriarch exclaimed on his deathbed[5]: "God, before Whom my fathers Abraham and Isaac did walk." To this R. Joḥanan (3rd c.) said: Unto what might this figure of the Patriarchs walking before the Holy One, blessed be He, be compared? Unto a flock marching forward with the Shepherd following behind it[6].

Marking the sheep for slaughter.

"And when he sees the blood...the Lord will pass over the door[7]." This is the way of the world. Just as the slaughterer, when bringing in his flock, marks with a red sign the sheep or lamb he desires to slay, and in this wise distinguishes which is to be slain

[1] Ezek. xxxiv. 31. [2] Ps. lxxx. 2. [3] Ex. xxv. 8.

[4] *Exod. R.* 34, 3—quoted in Schechter's *Aspects of Rabbinic Theology*, p. 49.

[5] Gen. xlviii. 15.

[6] *Tanḥuma Lech Lecha*, 26; Bacher, *Pal. Am.* I, 299 Men say: One lamb follows another; like the conduct of the mother so is the doing of the daughter. (*Kethuboth*, 63 *a.*)

[7] Ex. xii. 23.

and which is not to be slain, even so it is said, "when he shall see the blood." God, as it were[1], took His stand at the door and thrust aside the destroyer that he plague not Israel[2].

The lamb among the wolves.

Israel's hazardous position in the world is safeguarded through the extreme watchfulness of the Divine Shepherd, Who wards off the attacks of hostile nations. The Emperor Hadrian (117–138) said unto Rabbi Joshua ben Ḥananiah: Great is the lamb that can endure amidst seventy wolves; and he replied: Great is the Shepherd Who rescues the lamb and destroys the wolves. Hence Scripture says[3]: "No weapon that is formed against thee shall prosper.... This is the heritage of the servants of the Lord and their righteousness which is of Me, saith the Lord[4]."

Another variant is the following: David said, A lamb among seventy wolves, what can it do? And Israel in the midst of seventy persecuting nations, what could he do, didst Thou not stand by him at every hour? As it is said[5]: "He delivereth the poor from him that is too strong for him[6]."

For nations are too ready to join hands in oppressing Israel.

The herd, the watch-dogs and the wolf.

"Avenge the children of Israel of the Midianites[7]." The Rabbis comment as follows: But had not the Moabites been first in this matter, even as it is said[8],

[1] כביכול, the Hebrew word used to introduce an anthropomorphism.

[2] *Exod. R.* 18, 7 (? R. Levi).

[3] Is. liv. 17.

[4] *Esther R.* to x. 11; in *Yalkut Kohel.* § 989, the reading is as follows: Wherein lies the power of that sheep (Israel) that it feed among seventy bears (nations)? and he said, Strong is the Watchman (חציף האי נטורא) that guards it against them all.

[5] Ps. xxxv. 10.

[6] *Pesikta R.* ch. IX, p. 32 *a*; Bacher, *Pal. Am.* III, 496, *s.v.* R. Tanḥuma.

[7] Num. xxxi. 2.

[8] *Ibid.* xxii. 7.

"And the elders of Moab and the elders of Midian departed with the rewards of divination in their hand; and they came unto Balaam and spoke unto him the words of Balak"? But throughout their existence these two had never been at peace with each other, only when they came to fight with Israel did they make peace with each other and contended against them.

Unto what might this be likened? To two dogs who were in a flock barking, and provoking each other. A wolf came to snatch a lamb from the flock, and one of the dogs engaged with him. Then thought the companion dog, if I do not go to help him now, the wolf will kill him and then proceed to cause my death. They therefore made peace with each other and together fought against the wolf. Even so had Moab and Midian never been at peace with each other, as it is said[1], "who smote Midian in the field of Moab," but when they came to contend against Israel, they made peace with each other, and fought against them[2].

The shepherd guarding his flock.

In reference to the pursuit of Pharaoh immediately after the Exodus and the divine deliverance of Israel at the Red Sea, R. Ḥama bar Ḥanina (3rd c.) gave the following exposition in the name of his father: This might be compared to a shepherd leading his sheep across a river. When a wolf came up to attack them, what did the skilful shepherd do? He selected a large he-goat and surrendered it to the wolf. Let him engage with this one, he thought, until we have crossed the river, and then I shall bring it back. Even so when Israel went out of Egypt the angel Sammael stood up to make charges against them.

[1] Gen. xxxvi. 35. [2] *Sifré* to Num. xxxi. 2, § 157.

"Master of the Universe," said he, "till now these have been worshippers of idols and yet Thou dividest the sea for them." What did the Holy One, blessed be He? He handed unto him Job, who was of the counsellors of Pharaoh, and of whom it is said[1] "a man perfect and upright." "He is thine," said God, thinking to Himself "whilst he [Sammael] occupies himself with Job, Israel will go down to the sea, emerge from it, and then I shall rescue Job[2]."

The lamb, the wolf and the shepherd.

Israel's complaint against Moses and Aaron, whose visit had resulted in aggravating the servitude, "Ye have made our savour to be abhorred in the eyes of Pharaoh, and in the eyes of his servants, to put a sword in their hand to slay us[3]," the Rabbis explained by means of a parable.

R. Judah Halevi, the son of R. Shalom (4th c.), said: Thus did the children of Israel say unto Moses: Unto what are we like? Unto a lamb whom the wolf came to carry away. The shepherd set himself in pursuit in order to rescue it from the mouth of the wolf. Between the shepherd and the wolf the lamb was torn. Even so, [said the Israelites], O, Moses! between thee and Pharaoh we shall surely die[4].

The solicitous shepherd.

Israel's exodus from Egypt and their travels through the wilderness are all adorned by pastoral simile. Israel is the flock and Moses the shepherd leading them under the guidance of the Divine Shepherd Himself.

"So Moses brought Israel from the Red Sea[5]." This corresponds to the text "He made His people

[1] Job i. 1.
[2] *Exod. R.* 21, 7; Bacher, *Pal. Am.* I, 25.
[3] Ex. v. 21.
[4] *Exod. R.* 5, 21; Bacher, *Pal. Am.* III, 439.
[5] Ex. xv. 22.

go forth like sheep[1]." Like which sheep? Like the sheep of Jethro. For just as the sheep of Jethro went forth from a populated land into the wilderness, even so did Israel go forth from Egypt into the wilderness, as it is said, "And he guided them into the wilderness like a flock[2]."

Keeping his flock in the open.

Just as the sheep are not led into the shadow cast by a beam [a periphrasis for being kept under the roof], even so did the Holy One, blessed be He, lead Israel into the wilderness for forty years[3].

Continually changing their pastures.

Just as no fodder is provided for the sheep[4] because they graze [in new pastures] every day, even so was no fixed provision made for Israel in the wilderness, as it is said[5], "And the people shall go out and gather a certain rate every day."

The sheep spoiling the trees.

Just as the sheep are not blamed by their owners when they spoil the trees[6], even so is it with Israel; although they sin, the Holy One, blessed be He, regards them guiltless like sheep[7].

The care for a solitary sheep.

As another explanation of the text "He made his people go forth like sheep[8]," R. Berechiah (4th c.) said, Come and see how beloved are the children of

[1] Ps. lxxviii. 52. [2] *Ibid. vide Exod. R.* 24, 3.

[3] In *Num. R.* 23, 2, "even so throughout their forty years in the wilderness Israel did not enter into the shade of the beam."

[4] *Exod. R.* 24, 3. There are varied versions of this passage. Jastrow suggests as the correct reading מה הצאן אין מתקינין לה איפוסין [איבום=?] אלא רועה בכל יום כך ישראל לא התקינו להם אפותיקאות במדבר: אפותיקין=ἀποθήκη=provision, fodder. In *Num. R.* 23, 2 the reading is מה הצאן אין כונסין לה אוצרות כך ישראל ניזונו בלא אצרות. [5] Ex. xvi. 4.

[6] מחבלים את האילנות; other readings given in the Notes in *Tanḥuma Beshallaḥ*, Ex. xv. 22 are משברת את האילנות, "breaking the trees"; מקרסמין, "nibbling at.'

[7] *Tanḥuma* here adds a saying of R. Joḥanan (3rd c.), "God regards them as sheep for punishment and as men for reward," צאן לעונשים ואדם למתן שכר. [8] Ps. lxxviii. 52.

Israel before the Holy One, blessed be He. He called them "sheep," as it is said[1], "Israel is a scattered sheep." Now he who has a single sheep gives it to eat and to drink in due time, because it is his sole charge. But whoso has a multitude of sheep cannot tend them all properly, for he is overmuch busied with them[2]. But come and see the love wherewith the Holy One, blessed be He, loved Israel. He called them "sheep," and yet He says[3], "I will increase them with men like a flock."

The guardian shepherd.

Yet one further explanation: Why like the sheep? Just as the shepherd tends his sheep during the day because of the heat, and by night on account of the wolves, even so did the Holy One, blessed be He, guard Israel, as it is said[4], "And there shall be a booth for a shadow in the daytime from the heat"; and again it is written[5], "He took not away the pillar of the cloud by day, nor the pillar of the fire by night from before the people"; and further it is said[6], "Thou leddest Thy people like a flock." What is the meaning of the expression: "Thou leddest"? It is a mnemonic (a *Notarikon*)[7] and is explained in a variety of ways which all imply protection[8].

1 Jer. iii. 17. 2 .אלא מתייגע עמהן הרבה 3 Ezek. xxxvi. 37.

4 Is. iv. 6. 5 Ex. xiii. 22. 6 Ps. lxxvii. 21.

7 *Notarikon* of נחית, "Thou leddest," according to varied opinions:

(*a*) נוראות הראית במצרים
חרונך שפכת עליהם
ימינך בלעה אותם
תהום כסית עליהם

(*b*) ר׳ יהושע אומר
נפלאות עשית לנו
חרות נתת לנו
ים בקעת לנו
תורה נתת לנו

(*c*) ר׳ אלעזר המודעי אומר
נסים עשית לנו
חיים נתת לנו
ידך הראית לנו
תלוי ראש נתת בנו

(*d*) וחכמים אומרים
נביאים העמדת לנו
חסידים העמדת ממנו
ישרים תמימים העמדת ממנו

8 *Tanḥuma Beshallaḥ*, § 15.

The faithful sheep.

Just as the sheep follow whithersoever the shepherd leads them, even so did Israel follow Moses whithersoever he led them, as it is written[1], "Draw me, we will run after thee"; therefore Scripture says[2], "And Moses made Israel to journey from the Red Sea[3]."

Gathering in the flock.

This last text is made clear by the following[4]: "He made his people go forth like sheep." And why like the sheep? Just as the sheep spread themselves about at random and the shepherd gathers them in, even so did the Israelites in the wilderness abandon themselves each one to his own inclination, striving and weeping and contending every hour; as it is said[5], "How oft did they provoke him in the wilderness and grieved him in the desert?" And yet the Holy One, blessed be He, did not withdraw Himself from them, but led them on like a flock[6].

The exposed flock.

Unto what was Moses our teacher like? Unto a faithful shepherd. A fence fell down towards nightfall. He restored the fence on three sides. But there remained yet a gap which he had no time to close up. He thereupon placed himself in the open breach: When a lion came he stood against him, and when a wolf came he did likewise. "But ye[7] did not stand in the breach like unto Moses[8]."

The raided flock counted.

Whenever they [*sc.* Israel] fell [in the plague], their numbers were afterwards taken. This might

[1] Cant. i. 4. [2] Ex. xv. 22. [3] *Exod. R.* 24, 3.

[4] Ps. lxxviii. 52. [5] *Ibid.* v. 40. [6] *Tanḥuma Beshallaḥ*, § 15.

[7] *I.e.* "the vile Prophets" in Israel who in the words of Ezekiel (xiii. 3–4) "follow their own spirit" and have become "like foxes in ruins"—a simile which the Rabbis explain to mean "like the foxes roaming about the ruins looking about for a place of safety to which to flee in case they should espy a human being."

[8] *Ruth R.* Introduction v; probably referring to the plea of Moses at the incident of the golden calf and the reference to it in Ps. cvi. 23.

be compared to a wolf who attacked a flock of sheep. Whereupon the owner of the sheep said unto the shepherd, "Reckon up and see how many are missing[1]."

The shepherd and the captured flock.

The plea of Moses to enter the Land of Promise and the divine refusal were clothed by the Rabbis in the form of a pastoral parable.

The Holy One, blessed be He, said unto Moses: How canst thou desire to enter the land? This might be likened unto a shepherd going out to tend the royal sheep. The sheep were taken captive. When the shepherd thereafter sought to gain admittance to the royal palace the king said unto him, "If thou enter now will not the people [seeing thee unconcerned] say that thou art to blame for the capture of the sheep?" Even so was it here. The Holy One, blessed be He, said unto Moses: It is to thy praise that thou broughtest out 600,000 of them, but now that thou didst bury them in the wilderness and art bringing in another generation it will be said that the generation of the wilderness has no portion in the world to come [hence thou didst leave them behind]. Remain therefore at their side and enter with them, as it is written[2], "There a portion [*i.e.* a grave] was reserved for the Lawgiver that he might come with the heads of the people. He executed the justice of the Lord." Hence Scripture says[3], "Ye shall not bring *this* congregation into the land," but the congregation [*sc.* resurrected] that came out with thee from Egypt[4].

1 *Num. R.* 20, 25, similarly in 21, 7.
2 Deut. xxxiii. 21.
3 Num. xx. 12. "Ye" referring to Moses and Aaron.
4 *Num. R.* 19, 13 *et cet. loc.*

The kids and the wethers.

Pastoral imagery is used by the Rabbis also in the sphere of Jewish Education.

"Yea, mine own familiar friend, in whom I trusted, which did eat of my bread, has lifted up his heel against me[1]," exclaimed the Psalmist. Metaphorically, say the Rabbis, this constitutes an exclamation of satisfaction and pride. Even my disciples in the end lifted their heel against me. In which manner? When entering the House of Study they enter into my presence like gentle kids, but as soon as they depart from me they become like unto wethers [*i.e.* engaging in deep dialectics] goring with their horns. The expression "bread" in the text signifies "the Torah," even as it is said[2], "Come, eat of my bread[3]."

"And it came to pass in the days of Ahaz[4]." What trouble was there[5]? The Syrians were in front [*i.e.* in the East] and the Philistines behind [*i.e.* in the West][6]. This might be compared unto a royal son whom the tutor conspired to kill. "If I kill him now," thought the tutor, "I shall be liable to death at the hands of the king; I shall withdraw his nurse and he will die of himself." Even so said Ahaz. "If there be no kids there will be no wethers; no wethers, no flock; no flock, no shepherd; and without a shepherd there will be no world." What he intended to convey was the following: If there be no children there will be no young students; no students, no

Destroying the kids.

[1] Ps. xli. 10. [2] Prov. ix. 5.

[3] *Shoḥer Tob*, 41, 7. [4] Is. vii. 1.

[5] The opening word ויהי, "it came to pass," is explained as a component of וַי יְהִי, "there was a cry of distress," and denotes an expression of sorrow. For the tradition that Biblical narratives beginning with ויהי or ויהי בימי contain an element of distress, and for instances to substantiate it, *vide Megillah*, 10 *b*.

[6] Is. ix. 11.

scholars; no scholars, no sages; no sages, no Prophets; and when there are no Prophets, the Holy One, blessed be He, will not cause His divine presence to rest upon the people. Hence it is written[1], "Bind up the testimony, seal the Law among my disciples[2]."

A similar use of the term is found in the following historical incident: When R. Ḥananiah the nephew of R. Joshua went to Babylon he used to intercalate the years and fix the new moons outside the Holy Land. They sent two disciples of the wise to him, R. José b. Kippar and the grandson of Zechariah b. Kabutal. R. Ḥananiah at first welcomed them cordially and spread their fame. But when these disciples began to question his decision he sought to nullify the reputation he had established for them. When they questioned his right to arrange the calendar outside Judæa, he replied, "Did not Akiba b. Joseph act similarly in Babylon" [*sc.* Nahardea]? Then said they to him, "Keep R. Akiba out of it, because [when he went to Babylon] he left not his equal in the land of Israel," and when he said to them, "I also have not left my equal in the land of Israel," they replied, "The kids which thou didst leave behind have grown into goats with horns, and they have sent us to thee[3]."

The lambs and the goats.

R. Simeon b. Ḥalafta, R. Ḥaggai in the name of R. Samuel b. Naḥman, expounded the following text: "The lambs are for thy covering and the goats are the price for a field[4]." The text says "lambs."

[1] Is. viii. 16.

[2] *Gen. R.* 42, 3. In *Esther R.* Introduction, § 11, the reading is "To a king who handed out his child to a tutor."

[3] *Berachoth*, 63 *a*; also *Jer. Synhedrin*, I, 19 *a*, top; *Jer. Nedarim*, 6, 40 *a*, mid.

[4] Prov. xxvii. 26.

What does it mean? As long as "the pupils" are small, cover up for them the words of the Torah[1]; but when they are grown up and have become [strong] like rams, then lay open to them the secrets of the Law, [like a field].

This is paralleled by the following exposition of R. Simeon b. Joḥai (2nd c.): "And these are the judgments which thou shalt set before them[2]." Just as a treasure[3] is not laid bare to every human being, even so may you not dive into the depths of the Law except in the presence of those who are fit and proper[4].

The ram and the he-goat.

Rabbi Tarphon (2nd c.) said[5]: [It is written] "I saw the ram pushing westward and northward and southward; so that the beasts might not stand before him, neither was there any that could deliver out of his hands; but he did according to his will and became great[6]." This typifies R. Akiba. "And I was considering, and behold, a he-goat came from the west on the face of the earth and touched not the ground; and the goat had a notable horn between his eyes. And he came to the ram that had two horns, which

[1] A play upon the word כבשים, which is explained to mean כְּבוֹשׁ לפניהן דברי תורה.

[2] Ex. xxi. 1.

[3] סימא which is suggested by the expression תשים.

[4] *Jer. Abodah Zarah*, 2, 41*c*; cf. *Ḥagigah*, 13*a*; R. Abbahu said: This regulation, *i.e.* not to instruct in the mysteries of the divine chariot לגמור במעשה מרכבה (that is mystic studies), may be derived from the following text: "The lambs are for thy covering." Things esoteric shall be kept concealed under thy garment דברים שהם כבשונו של עולם יהיו תחת לבושך. See *Dikduké Soferim*, *ad loc.* כבשים ללבושך א"ת כבשים אלא כבושים, and cf. *Yalkut* to Prov. § 961.

[5] This has reference to a heated controversy on a ritual question between R. José the Galilean and R. Akiba, in which R. Tarphon sided with the former. At a subsequent assembly of 32 elders held at Lydda, R. Akiba was voted to be in the right, *vide Tosefta Mikvaoth*, end.

[6] Dan. viii. 4.

I have seen standing before the river, and ran unto him in the fury of his power. And I saw him come close unto the ram, and was moved with choler against him, and smote the ram, and brake his two horns. And there was no power in the ram to stand before him, but he cast him down to the ground, and stamped upon him[1]." This symbolises R. José the Galilean. "And there was none that could deliver the ram out of his hand[2]." These denote the 32 scholars[3].

The lamb under examination.

Moral errors, say the Rabbis, may sometimes be overlooked in the case of ordinary people, but not so among the selected ones; the deeds of distinguished persons are more strictly scrutinised. This was taught in the following pastoral metaphor:

R. Simeon b. Joḥai (2nd c.) said: We do not say, "Examine ye the camel" or "Examine ye the swine" [to see if it has a blemish], but we say, "Examine ye the lamb." What does the latter symbolise? A scholar who has deserted the study of the Torah. R. Judah b. Lakish said: Any student-scholar who has abandoned the study of the Law to him applies the text[4], "As a bird that wandereth from her nest, so is a man that wandereth from his place[5]."

The loathsome goats.

Israel's defects and qualities are referred to by the Rabbis under a pastoral simile.

"Thy hair is as a flock of goats that trail down from Gilead," says the Song of Songs[6]. The Rabbis, who explain this whole book as an idyll of Israel, comment

[1] Dan. viii. 5–7. [2] *Ibid.* end of *v.* 7.

[3] *Sifré* to Num. xix. 9 and *Tosefta Mikvaoth, fin.*; Bacher, *Ag. Tan.* I, 356–7. These scholars זקנים (according to some 39) represent an assembly held at Jamnia (or at Lydda) at which a ritual question was discussed and in which the Rabbis here referred to participated.

[4] Prov. xxvii. 8. [5] *Ḥagigah*, 9 *b.* [6] Cant. vi. 5.

as follows: Just as the goat is loathsome[1], so were the Israelites made despicable at Shittim (through debauchery)[2].

The decency of sheep.

And on the text "Thy teeth are as a flock of sheep[3]" they say: Just as the sheep has an appearance of decency[4], so were the Israelites chaste and noble in their conduct during the war with Midian[5].

The beaten sheep.

The solidarity of Israel and their interdependence is emphasised by the Rabbis also through pastoral imagery.

"Israel is a scattered sheep," says the Prophet[6]. To which they add: How is it with the sheep? When it is beaten upon the head or upon one of its limbs all the other parts of its body also feel the blow[7]; even so it is with Israel; when one of them sins all are made to feel the effects[8].

The habits of harts.

The lethargy of their leaders is likewise reproved under a pastoral figure.

R. Ḥanina (3rd c.) said: Jerusalem was destroyed only because the people rebuked not one another. This is implied in the text[9] "Her princes are become like harts." Even as [*i.e.* in the flock] one ram keeps his head against the tail of the other [and follows him blindly], so did the Israelites in that generation

[1] Because it has no long covering.

[2] *Cant. R. ad loc.*; Bacher, *Pal. Am.* I, 16 and 179.

[3] Cant. vi. 6. [4] It is well covered. [5] *Cant. R. ad loc.*

[6] Jer. iii. 17.

[7] W. Einhorn in his commentary, *ad loc.*, remarks that this physiological characteristic is more apparent in the case of the lamb than in other animals. Friedmann in the *Mechilta* adduces the reading of the *Yalkut* to Jer. וכלן מרגישין, suggesting that when one lamb is beaten all the other lambs in the flock feel the blow. He is however inclined to accept the reading of *Lev. R.* in the first sense.

[8] Ḥizkiah, Ḥiyya's son (2nd and 3rd c.); *Lev. R.* 4, 6, reading וכל אבריו מרגישין; Bacher, *Pal. Am.* I, 53. [9] Lam. i. 6.

bend their faces down towards the ground and reproved not one another[1].

R. Simon said in the name of R. Simeon b. Abba and R. Simeon b. Lakish in the name of R. Joshua (b. Levi, 3rd c.): Just as the harts in time of the dry heat [helplessly] turn their faces towards one another, even so were the great ones of Israel; when they saw a sinful act they did not face it but turned their gaze away from it[2].

A similar Talmudic allusion to the helplessness of the flock under bad leadership is embodied in the following proverbs:

When the shepherd is angry with his sheep he sets a blind ram to lead them [*i.e.* when God is angry with His people He puts them under a bad leader][3].

When the shepherd strays the sheep stray after him[4].

The lame shepherd.

There is another pastoral figure in the form of a proverb which may here be mentioned: For three transgressions women die at the hour of childbirth.... And wherefore just at the hour of childbirth?... Mar Ukba (4th c.) said: When the shepherd is lame it is then that the sheep run away [*i.e.* when man is most helpless his sins come home to him]. At the gate of the fold there are words [bargaining], but in the stalls [where the sheep are delivered] there is strict account [*i.e.* in the critical moments a woman's sins are visited][5].

The cattle locked in the shed: the sand-girt sea.

And there is further an original application of a pastoral image to describe a natural phenomenon connected with the sea. "Thou hast set a bound that

[1] *Shabbath*, 119 *b*. [2] *Lament. R.* 1, 33. [3] *B. K.* 52 *a*.
[4] *Pirke di R. Eliezer*, 9. [5] *Shabbath*, 32 *a*.

they may not pass over[1]." In the same manner as some one, after bringing his cattle into the shed, locks the enclosure before them to prevent them going forth and grazing in the corn, even so did the Holy One, blessed be He, secure the sea with sand, adjuring it that it should not pass beyond the bounds; as it is said[2], "Who have placed the sand for the bound of the sea...that it cannot pass it[3]."

A beautiful parable illustrates a kindly Rabbinic view of the genuine proselyte:

A stag brought up in the wilderness came of his own free will and mixed with the flock. The shepherd gave him to eat and to drink and bestowed on him greater affection than on his sheep. Whereupon people said unto him, "Wilt thou tend this stag more affectionately than thy sheep?" And he replied, "How wearily have I toiled in rearing my flock, leading them out in the morning and bringing them in at nightfall? But this stag, although brought up in the wilderness and forests, joined my sheep of his own free will—shall I not show him special affection[4]?"

[1] Ps. civ. 9. [2] Jer. v. 22. [3] *Exod. R.* 15, 22.
[4] *Num. R.* 8, 2; *Shoḥer Tob* to Ps. cxlvi. 9.

SUMMARY

(1) THE POETIC POINT OF VIEW

In the Introduction attention has been drawn to the fact that the metaphors, similes and parables of the Midrash are to a large extent a reflection of the poetic instincts of the Rabbis, their power of observation of the phenomena of Nature and the movements of the world around them. The material presented in the body of the work which deals with agricultural and pastoral life affords some illustration of this characteristic of the Rabbis of the Midrash.

Their poetic inclination manifested itself in a variety of ways. It showed itself in their attraction to the poetic elements of the Bible, and the imagination with which they treated the poetic figures of speech used by the Biblical writers. It was further evidenced by the number of original Nature-touches which they introduced in the course of their explanation of the Scriptures.

Rabbi-agriculturists.

The Rabbis, many of whom were themselves owners of lands and vineyards, seem to have observed the process of field cultivation in all its aspects. They saw the preparation of the soil. They watched the grain from the moment it was sown till it was ripe for harvesting. They beheld the produce of the land being gathered into the threshing floor and the storehouses, and ultimately conveyed to the mills and the bakehouses. The same applied to the garden and orchard. The nature and growth, the peculiarities and characteristics of the different kinds of trees and plants, more especially of the cedar, the apple tree, the vine, the fig tree, the olive tree, the palm, the bush and the lily, are touched upon with an accuracy of detail and a poetic charm which mark the lover and observer of Nature. And similarly is this the case in the sphere of pastoral imagery, where they describe the grazing and tending of the flocks and herds, and note the life of the shepherd and herdsman.

Pastoral imagery.

Thus among the Tannaim of the 1st century we have R. Joshua ben Ḥananiah, by trade a blacksmith and a maker of needles[1], who yet observes and plays upon the agricultural use of the thorn-hedge and briers as fences to protect the open fields and orchards. There is also R. Eleazar ben Azariah, who refers to the familiar ploughing scene, where the cow is directed by the driving goad into its furrows. That he drew his simile from actual observation of Nature is almost certain, for we know from Talmudic sources[2] that R. Eleazar was a large cattle-owner giving an annual tithe of 1,200 calves, and therefore probably acquainted with these aspects of agricultural life. In the description of pastoral scenery we also find the names of R. Tarphon and R. Eliezer b. Jacob.

Agricultural processes.

Among the Tannaim of a later generation we meet with R. Meïr, who though a scribe by profession[3] speaks of intensive and extensive field culture, describing the sowing and springing up of the wheat-grain and referring proverbially to the properties of the wheaten bread. We note R. José ben Ḥalafta of Sepphoris, a tanner by trade[4], alluding to the agricultural process

[1] *Vide Berachoth*, 28 *a*, and *Jer. Berachoth*, 4, 1, p. 7 *c*.

[2] *Shabbath*, 54 *b*.

[3] *Erubin*, 13 *a*, and *Jer. Sotah*, 2, 4, p. 18 *a*.

[4] *Shabbath*, 49 *a*, *b*.

of beating the flax in order to improve it. We find R. Simeon ben Joḥai giving a detailed description of the process of sifting, which in some aspects is described even more minutely by R. Eleazar his son. We have R. Joshua referring to the familiar incident of a straying lamb being attacked by a pack of wolves, and R. José b. Kippar alluding to the growing up of the young kids into wethers.

And among the Tannaim of the last generation there is R. Judah Hanasi, a rich landowner[1], speaking apparently from actual observation of the work in the orchard and vineyard.

Arboreal and other similes.

Coming to the Palestinian Amoraim in the 3rd century we have among those of the first generation (219–279 C.E.) R. Joshua ben Levi who speaks of the trimming of the nut tree in order to make the shoots grow afresh, but who dwells more especially upon the ever-green olive tree which, unlike other trees, long retains its leaves which are affected neither by drought nor rain. There is R. Joḥanan of Tiberias, according to well-known Midrashic sources the owner of fields and vineyards[2]. He makes use of the agricultural phenomena of the thorn-hedge and briers as field-fences. He further describes with apparently inṭimate knowledge some features of field improvement such as the levelling of the ground for purposes of cultivation. He speaks of the shape of the fig tree and the constant discovery of new fruit in it. He refers to the process of pounding the olives for the production of oil. We find also R. Simeon ben Lakish, a very prominent Palestinian Aggadist, resident at Tiberias, who employs many

[1] *Jer. Shebiith*, 5, 1, end, p. 36 *c*.

[2] *Vide Cant. R.* 8, 7.

agricultural figures in the course of his addresses. He presents vivid pictures of the measuring of the grain at sowing time, of the winnowing of the grain, the transfer of the corn to the storehouse, and the measuring out again of the produce. He speaks generally of the tending of the orchard by increasing or reducing its plants, and in greater detail of the vine in its growth and development, and refers familiarly to the smoothness of the nut tree and the dangers involved in climbing it. He likewise alludes to the habits of the harts, characteristics noted also by R. Ḥanina. We have R. Ḥama ben Ḥanina who uses the figure of the vegetable field faded and run to seed, speaks of the special characteristics of the apple tree in which the fruit begins to develop before the leaves, and refers to the shepherd guarding his flocks against the attacks of the wolf. Also R. Samuel ben Naḥman whose son Naḥman, a very rich man possessing landed property[1], shows familiarity with the bush and thickets of reeds, as well as with the ways of the lamb and the goat. And R. Joshua speaks of the flocks marching before the shepherd.

Field and orchard.

Among the Amoraim of the second generation (279–320) there is R. Eleazar ben Pedath who speaks of the sown field, where a *Seah* of seed produces a *Khor* of grain, draws his simile from the yoke, and describes the storing of straw and the plucking of the lily from among the thorns. We meet with R. Isaac Nappaḥa who takes his simile from the measuring-out of the grain at sowing and harvest times, uses the figure of the winnowing fork or shovel and speaks of

[1] *Jer. Baba Bathra*, 17 *a*. According to the Responsum of the Ramban adduced in the Commentary מראה הפנים *ad loc.*

the beautifully situated sweet and shady fruit trees calling forth the weary traveller's blessing. And we have R. Levi who indulges in a considerable number of agricultural images especially concerning the orchard. He describes what must have been a frequent occurrence in the life of the people, the turning of the field into a vineyard. He refers with evident knowledge to the peculiar properties of the olive plants when grafted, and to the special characteristics of the palm tree which has its sap cells in the stem only but not in the branches. He contrasts the mode of planting the nut tree with the method employed in general tree planting. He describes with a delicate Nature-touch the myrtle and the rose bushes growing side by side, at first so much alike as to be hardly distinguished one from another, but each showing its own characteristics as its growth proceeds.

Among the less frequently mentioned Amoraim we have R. Judah ben Simon who describes the formation of the nut and depicts the Patriarchs under the image of tent-pegs; R. Judan who uses the vineyard simile of the leaves covering and protecting the grapes; R. Berechiah who besides speaking, like R. Judah ben Simon and others, of the structure of the nut, uses the image of the resin oozing out of the trees; R. Tanḥuma ben Abba, who also employs the vine simile of transplanting the vine for improvement and of making it trail over the dead branches of the trees; R. Judah bar Shalom who adduces the figure of the defenceless lamb, the ravenous wolf and the brave shepherd; and Mar Ukba who in terse imagery presents the picture of the lame shepherd and the helpless sheep.

Anonymous similes.

But a large number of the descriptive touches which show most intimate acquaintance with the world of Nature on the part of the Rabbis is recorded in Midrashic literature anonymously[1].

The special familiarity with the phenomena of Nature possessed by most of the Rabbis and the frequent use made of them in all discourses led to these figures becoming a kind of general stock-in-trade for all Rabbi-preachers, and the authors were not easily ascertainable. This is the case especially with the images drawn from the cultivation of the vine, the olive, the fig and the palm trees, objects of Nature which, as we know, were familiar in the times of the Palestinian Rabbis.

Thus we have a full and intimate anonymous description of the process of viticulture, the special tending of the ground, the clearing of rugged slabs and breaking of the clods under them, the planting and transplanting of the shoots, their arrangement in regular rows during the early period of their culture, and their training and trailing along steps and terraces in the later stages of their development.

We have an accurate portrayal, handed down

[1] There must have been from the very earliest times collections of Aggadic interpretation, not bearing the name of any individual author, but handed down through a certain school; and with the progress of time, when they became rooted in the life of the people, continued to be handed down altogether anonymously.

This is supported, *e.g.*, by such passages as *Jer. Shekalim*, 5, 1, where the authorship of certain collections of Aggadah and Halachah is ascribed by R. Jonah to R. Akiba and by others to a much earlier period, *viz.* the era of the Great Synagogue. Again, already of R. Joḥanan b. Zakkai, a pupil of Hillel, it is recorded that his studies included, among other subjects, the study of Aggadoth, a further proof that already in his time this was a recognised subject of study. This agrees with the view that Aggadic study goes back to the period of the Soferim.

anonymously, of the fig tree, how its roots penetrate through the layers of earth, its branches and foliage spread out luxuriantly, its mellow fruit ripens at different periods and is plucked little by little at various seasons. We find, without mention of the author's name, a detailed delineation of the picking of the olive tree, the gathering of the fruit, and the production of the oil. "The olive, while yet on the tree, is marked out for the press, afterwards it is taken down and beaten; after which it is transferred into the vat, put into the mill and ground. A net is then put around and stones are placed thereon; only then the olives produce their oil."

We have an example of minute observation of the character of the palm tree (and of the cedar). It has neither cavities nor excrescences, it is tasteless and odourless, it produces dates of different kinds as well as prickles; it is useful in all its parts, its bast being applied to the making of ropes, its leaves used in the manufacture of dyes, its planed trunks for the ceilings of houses. And in the pastoral sphere we have touches relating to tent-life and sheep-pasture, descriptions of the dangers to which the flocks were exposed and instances of the guardianship of the shepherds.

Poetic images.

Now the use which the Aggadists made of the different objects of Nature and the varied phenomena associated with their development is a further indication of the poetic instincts of these Rabbi-preachers. For the Nature studies conveyed to them a message and a significance which none but a poetic soul could discern and appreciate. Thus the natural image of the seed being put into the earth, decaying and then appearing in beautiful garb as a delight to the eye and an aliment of life, suggested to the poetic mind of R. Meïr the symbol of human death and resurrection.

R. Akiba, R. Simeon ben Ḥalafta in the first and second centuries and R. Abbahu in a later age, tell of the owner of the fig tree gathering the fruit at a seemingly inopportune moment, but with the calculated purpose of preventing threatening degeneration: in this they perceive a symbol of the divine removal of mortal man from this earth at a time which might appear to the human mind inopportune, but which in reality is the due season according to the all-seeing eye of the Creator.

R. Joḥanan of Tiberias and others reveal to us the process of extracting through pressure the best of the oil, and visualise in it the divine mode of drawing out what is noblest in man under the stress of affliction and pain.

R. Joshua of Sichnin, in the name of R. Levi, dwells upon the contrast between the rustling noises of the empty trees and the silent grandeur of the fruit-laden trees as a natural suggestion of the aggressive hustle of the ignorant boor and the calm composure of the man of learning.

R. Ḥanina ben Abba (3rd c.) charmingly points to the wind-tossed lily, bending and waving hither and thither at the blast of the rustling wind, yet holding its petal ever directed upwards, as symbolic of the rightful attitude of the faithful soul ever gazing heavenwards amidst the fury and storm of life.

R. Phineas (4th c.) heard the rattling sound produced when the cedar is cut down, and to him it seemed to typify the echo of the soul being torn away from the body at death.

And Rab Huna ben Joshua (4th c.) beheld in the life-sustaining ear of corn surrounded by the seemingly superfluous awn which imparted to the grain a sense of dignity and semblance of pride, a picture of the scholar replete with life-giving knowledge gaining in dignity and inspiring respect by a legitimate modicum of outward pride.

Typical examples.

The fatal effect of the noxious insect worming its way right to the core of the luscious fruit, causing inner rottenness and ruin often without the slightest outward indication of the havoc wrought within, kindled the imagination of the Nature-loving Rabbis who used it as an emblem of the pernicious effects of faithlessness stealthily creeping into the innermost parts of a blissful home.

The Rabbis draw attention to the lowly and drooping posture of the very heavily-laden bunches of grapes as symbolic of the attitude of humility which characterises the fully-equipped disciples of the wise. They allude to the agricultural custom of storing the best of the wines in the plainest of earthenware vessels, and again to the nourishing kernel of the nut enclosed in an outwardly soiled shell, in order to conjure up the image of the noble soul oft-time enshrined in a plain and even ungainly exterior.

They refer to the hardness and consequent fragility of the cedar and contrast it with the softness and flexibility of the reed, and by means of this touch of Nature seek to convey the moral exhortation to be ever yielding as a reed and not unbending as the cedar.

Some of these poetic ideas (as already indicated) became in a sense fixed figures of speech and formed part of the imagery—the poetic stock-in-trade—of Rabbinic literature, used for purposes of illustration by Rabbi-preachers of different periods.

Rabbinic symbolists. Thus, *e.g.*, the imagery from the vineyard and the wine was used by Rabbis of the 1st and 2nd centuries: R. Joshua ben Ḥananiah, R. Eliezer b. Hyrcanus, R. Eliezer of Modiim; by sages in the 2nd century: R. Judah b. Ilai, contemp. of R. Neḥemiah, R. Issi b. Judah b. Ilai and R. Eleazar b. Simeon b. Joḥai; by Rabbis in the 3rd century: R. Hoshayah, R. Joḥanan b. Nappaḥa, R. Simeon b. Lakish, R. Joshua of Sichnin and Rabbi Levi; by R. Abba and Mar Ukba, Rabbi Isaac bar Z'era and especially R. Tanḥuma b. Abba and R. Huna in the 4th century.

The fig-tree imagery was used by R. Akiba, R. Neḥemiah and R. José b. Durmaskith in the 2nd century; by R. Joḥanan b. Nappaḥa in the 3rd century; by R. Ḥiyya bar Abba, R. Ḥanina b. Papa and R. Abbahu in the 3rd and 4th centuries, and by R. Judan and R. Berechiah in the 4th century.

Figures from field cultivation and field products were employed by R. José the Galilean, R. Jonathan and R. Meïr in the 2nd century; by R. Ḥanina, R. Simeon b. Lakish and R. Samuel b. Naḥman in the 3rd century; by R. Isaac, R. Ḥanina b. Pazzi and R. Abba b. Kahana in the 3rd and 4th centuries; by R. Iddi, R. Huna b. Joshua and R. Aḥa in the 4th century.

In some cases we have the same object and the same aspect of it used by Rabbis of different periods for the purpose of illustrating an idea. We may assume that there was a great deal of borrowing and imitation, both conscious and unconscious, in the employment of illustrative material from the sphere of Nature. But, speaking generally, one may assert with justification that their observation of the phenomena of Nature, and the thoughts which these phenomena suggested to them, are a sufficient indication of the poetic instincts which characterised the sages of the Midrash.

(2) SOCIAL AND ECONOMIC SIDELIGHTS

From the material under consideration some light is thrown upon the social relations between Israel and the other peoples, the economic condition of the various classes of Palestinian Jewry and their attitude towards one another in the period under review.

Israel and the nations.

The repeatedly emphasised differentiation between Israel and the other peoples—between the "wheat" and the "chaff" as a Midrashic parable puts it—kept alive the spirit of exclusiveness among the Jewish people and affected their social relationship to the gentiles around them. And this tendency, religious in its origin, was considerably strengthened among the Jews of Palestine by political and economic causes, such as the innumerable burdens imposed upon them by the governors of the people, under whose sway they lived. The ruling Roman power—the "Kingdom of Esau" as the Rabbis figuratively called it—resembled in the poetic language of simile the entangling thorn-bush, constantly holding the subject people in its firm grip and collecting without any respite the *annonæ*, the poll-taxes and the levies to maintain the military legions. The feeling of exclusiveness on the part of the Jewish people was further accentuated by the spirit of hostility and oppression displayed towards them by their gentile neighbours. "They that were round about Jacob were his adversaries." For in Palestine Israel was like the rose, set among the thorns. The relationship between the non-Jewish towns of Ḥallamish, Jericho, Susitha, Castra and Lydda, and the closely neighbouring Jewish ones of Naveh, Naaran, Tiberias, Ḥaifa and Oni, says a 4th century Rabbi, was strained to the point of hostility. And we have instances recorded by Rab of similar local conditions prevailing in Babylon.

Internal social conditions.

But more vivid are the rays cast upon the internal social conditions of Palestinian Jewry itself. In the sphere of agriculture we note the existence of the following three main classes: (1) The Landowners or Landlords; (2) the various kinds of Contractors or Tenant-Farmers; and (3) the Labourers. Among the landlords we distinguish the smaller holders from the larger and more affluent ones, some owning one estate only and others possessing many properties, situated either close to one another in a single locality, or scattered over different parts of the country.

Landlord and tenant.

For the purpose of cultivation, these estates, gardens, fields and orchards were generally let out by their owners to tenant-farmers. Some of the latter held their tenure on the system of fixed rental, as *Ḥoker* or *Kablan*, paying the landlord in money or in kind. But the more frequent form of tenancy was that of "share-tenancy," the *Aris* (tenant-farmer) taking over the cultivation of the field (with the cattle, etc.) at his own expense and paying the owner a certain agreed share (one-half or one-third or one-quarter) of the year's produce in lieu of rent.

From the parables adduced in the foregoing chapters it would seem that the *Aris* was regarded as being inferior to the landlord in social position. "It is no shame for the rich to speak to the *Aris*," urge the Rabbis; "for did not God Himself speak to Adam, the first tenant-farmer on His earth?"

But the relationship between the two seems to have depended very largely upon circumstances, and more especially upon the nature and disposition of the parties concerned; personal relations were often friendly—sometimes quite intimate.

We see the landlord (the *Ba'al Habbayith,* as he is often termed) walking about in the field fraternising with his *Aris* and trying to dispel all notions of patronage, all feelings of inequality. We behold him treating his *Aris* kindly and liberally on settlement day, when, at harvest or vintage time, he called to settle accounts with the owner of the estate. But on the other hand we also find a rich landlord treating the *Aris* somewhat abruptly and arbitrarily when the latter pays a deferential visit for the purpose of handing over his dues.

The treatment of the tenant-farmer by the landlord appears to have depended also upon the impression which the latter was able to produce. A "clever" *Aris,* so one of our parables relates, always managed to secure a monetary accommodation in order to help him out of a difficult position into which he had fallen while carrying out his field contract.

Steward

In addition to the landowner and the *Aris,* we

and labourer.

meet also with the steward (*Ben Bayith*), a kind of manager or supervisor of the estate[1]. This steward stood in close personal relationship to the owner. We see them in our parables, consulting together about the prospects of the field. We find the owner ready to leave all matters affecting its cultivation to the sense of responsibility of his *Ben Bayith*.

We next have the actual labourers, *Poalim*, occupying themselves with various agricultural work as tillers of the ground, watchmen, carters or carriers. Among them are men engaged by the day and the hour as well as those employed for longer periods and who have an accumulating account with their masters. We have the trustworthy and conscientious workers who labour to the full extent of their power, and, side by side with them, the indolent and slothful who shirk their duties. Both receive their wages, but our parables reflect a tangible appreciation and encouragement on the part of the rich landlord for the conscientious and intensive worker. Jewish labour was likewise employed in the disposal of agricultural products, more especially in the sale of wine. We have a vivid parable depicting a Jewish carman purveying wine among the shopkeepers. Dogs as well as asses were used as beasts of burden.

Wisdom and ignorance.

A further division recognised among the Jewish population of Palestine in the period under review is that between the *Talmidé-Ḥachamim*, the students and devotees of the Law, and the *Ammé-Haaretz*, the boorish and ignorant. In the poetic imagery of the Rabbis these two classes are symbolised respectively

[1] Like the Roman Villicus; the relations of Horace and his steward afford a good parallel.

by the fruit-bearing and the fruitless trees. In the class of *Talmidé-Ḥachamim* the scholars of Palestine are described as gentle and pleasant in contradistinction to their colleagues in Babylon, who have the reputation of being somewhat harsher and more austere. Among the learned, we note again different categories, specialists in their particular department. Some are styled *Ba'alé Mikra*, men versed in the Scriptures, others again are known respectively as *Ba'alé Mishnah*, *Halachah* or *Aggadah*—specialists in the various branches of oral tradition.

That there was a kind of class-distinction maintained between the learned and the ignorant is certain. It would even appear that the untutored were in a measure looked down upon by the *Talmidé-Ḥachamim*. But due recognition was given at all periods to the utility of the *Ammé-Haaretz* and the importance of their position in the sphere of social economy.

"The fruitless trees no less than the fruit-bearing ones have their uses." "The leaves of the vine protect the grapes." "The shells of the nuts protect the inner kernel." These are some of the Nature similes employed by the Rabbis in regard to this subject. And they are adduced for the purpose of impressing the timely lesson that just as in the case of these plants the apparently superfluous parts supply the necessary protection against unfavourable conditions, even so do the *Ammé-Haaretz* provide the material support for the maintenance and preservation of the schools of learning.

Rich and poor.

That there were rich and poor in Palestine during the period under consideration (as indeed there have been throughout all periods of Jewish and general history) is almost axiomatic. "For the poor shall never cease out of the land" (Deut. xv. 11). This fact is sufficiently evidenced by the numerous enactments and practical institutions with which Rabbinic literature abounds in reference to the treatment of the poor. In the early centuries of the current era, the general economic conditions of the bulk of the Jewish population in Palestine were very precarious.

Dr Büchler in his essay on the Economic Conditions of Judæa after the destruction of the Second Temple[1] has brought out this point in most vivid and masterly fashion. The present material helps us but little to illustrate this state of things. We have, it is true, many parables taken from the apparently rampant evil of field-spoliation. Again and again we meet with bands making raids upon fields, vineyards and wine-cellars. These incidents give us sidelights upon the distressing social and economic state of the population who were driven to these acts of depredation. But these raiders were not Jews. They were bands of Bedouins from among the neighbouring tribes. There is, however, an indication of the urgent need of charitable help which must have existed among the Jewish population and which in itself points to a state of poverty.

We find R. Levi, the great Preacher, in a popular Nature simile, inveighing against the hard-hearted who will yield to no entreaty but open their hands only under the pressure of physical illness; encouraging the more charitable ones, who are amenable to persuasion, and publicly praising the generous-hearted,

[1] Jews' College Publications, No. 4, London, 1912.

who, like the soft-shelled eatable nut, open out of themselves in their charitable and benevolent impulse.

(3) THE COMPARATIVE POINT OF VIEW

In the Introduction and subsequent chapters some points of similarity or contrast between the figures of speech in Rabbinic writings and those contained in kindred literature, both Biblical and post-Biblical, have already been noted.

In this section it is proposed to summarise and enlarge upon these general aspects of comparison with a view to stimulating further consideration and more intensive study.

First as to the comparison of the Rabbinic similes with those found in the Bible.

Prophets and Rabbis.

It will have become sufficiently clear that in spirit and in purpose the two sets of Hebrew similes are in a large measure alike. The object in each case is obviously didactic. Both the Prophets and the Rabbis (as Aggadists) were mainly teachers of religion, ethics and morality, and the metaphorical imagery they employed was intended, as has already been stated, to illustrate and to emphasise more effectively leading religious ideas. Even in the few Biblical instances where the poetic and artistic sides of the figures are elaborated, this feature is of secondary import. The primary purpose is unmistakably religious. The same holds good of the Rabbinic similes. Every part of our collection fully supports this assertion, and the fact will be made more patent in the next section, where a summary is given of the religious ideas conveyed by the similes and parables.

Inner purpose and outward form.

But while in both cases there is absolute likeness in the spirit and purpose underlying the similes, there is a marked difference in regard to form. The Biblical comparisons are bolder and more majestic in conception, and indicate a fresher and more vigorous imagination. There is about their figures of speech, as about the form of their teaching, the ring of intense inspiration. Their images are more concise, "pure, direct and perspicuous." Many of them are compressed metaphors without comparison or middle term. And even the similes are short.

It is true that there are also in the Bible a few more or less fully elaborated figures. The tree simile in Psalm i. 3; the agricultural parable in Is. xxviii. 23–9; the dirge in Ezek. xix. 10 ff. are notable examples. But, speaking generally, the points of comparison even in this class of Biblical similes are only just tersely marked, whilst details which would indicate the nature of the similarity are as a rule dispensed with.

In Rabbinic literature, on the other hand, there is less sublimity and creative energy. Simile and parable preponderate over metaphor; and the similes themselves are elaborate and explicit. There is, it is true, a considerable number of pure metaphors also in

Rabbinic metaphors

Rabbinic literature, as may be seen from the following examples:

"God is the space of the universe[1]."

"Truth is the seal of the Holy One, blessed be He[2]."

[1] *Gen. R.* 68, 9; *Pesikta R.* ch. XXI, p. 104 *b et cet. loc.* *Vide* Schechter's *Aspects of Rabbinic Theology*, p. 27.

[2] *Shabbath*, 55.

"God entwineth man with a thread of Grace[1]."

"The angels weave man's prayers into garlands round the Godhead[2]."

"The Patriarchs [models of righteousness] are the chariot [or throne] of God[3]."

"The righteous man is the splendour of a city[4]."

"The school-teachers are the guardians of the town[5]."

"The soul is a guest in the human body[6]."

"I shall lose my jewel in a stained soil[7]."

"The heavenly angels and the earthly saints seized hold of the Holy Ark [*i.e.* the soul of Judah Hanasi]; the angels prevailed over the saints and the Ark was captured[8]."

"The heart and the eyes are the two agents [brokers] of sin[9]."

"Torah and Benevolence are Israel's advocates[10]."

"The place where heaven and earth kiss each other" [*i.e.* the horizon][11].

"The mountain [*sc.* the head] is snow white, the surroundings [*sc.* the cheeks and chin] are full of hoar frost, the dogs [*sc.* throat and tongue] bark no longer, the millstones [*i e.* molar teeth] grind no more[12]." (Description of old age.)

But the majority of such figurative expressions are symbolical, euphemistic and allegorical, types which occur rarely in the Bible.

[1] *Ḥag.* 12 *b.* [2] *Exod. R.* 21, 4.

[3] *Gen. R.* 47, 6; *vide* Schechter, *Aspects of Rabbinic Theology*, p. 30.

[4] *Gen. R.* 68, 6. [5] *Lam. R.* Introd. 2. [6] *Lev. R.* 34, 3.

[7] *Jer. Kilaim*, IX, *ad fin.*, 32 *c* below (*i.e.* I shall die outside the Holy Land), "jewel" denotes the "soul."

[8] *Ket.* 104 *a.* [9] *Jer. Ber.* 1, 4, p. 3 *c*, top. [10] *Exod. R.* 31, 2.

[11] *B. B.* 74 *a.* [12] *Sabb.* 152 *a*; cf. Eccl. xii.

Strings of similes.

Again, in the Midrash as in the Bible, there is frequently an accumulation of comparative imagery to illustrate the same thought and express the same truth. But here also the difference in form between the two is clearly marked. In the Bible we have, for the purpose of intensifying a central idea, the stringing together of a number of pregnant similes or metaphors, comparable to the bold and effective touches on the canvas of an artistic genius.

The Song of Songs affords ample illustration of this characteristic. Take the following example:

My beloved is white and ruddy,
Pre-eminent above ten thousand.
His head is as the most fine gold,
His locks are curled,
And black as a raven.
His eyes are like doves
Beside the water brooks;
Washed with milk,
And fitly set.
His cheeks are as a bed of spices,
As banks of sweet herbs.
His lips are as lilies,
Dropping with flowing myrrh.
His hands are as rods of gold
Set with beryl;
His body is as polished ivory
Overlaid with sapphires.
His legs are as pillars of marble[1].

There are further instances in other books of the Bible. Two or three examples will suffice:

Now my days are swifter than a runner;
They flee away, they see no good.
They are passed away as the swift ships;
As the vulture that swoopeth on the prey[2].

[1] Cant. v. 10 *ff.* [2] Job ix. 25–6.

Therefore they shall be as the morning cloud,
And as the dew that early passeth away.
As the chaff that is driven with the wind
Out of the threshing floor,
And as the smoke out of the window[1].

His raiment was as white snow,
And the hair of his head like pure wool;
His throne was fiery flames,
And the wheels thereof burning fire[2].

The Mashal.

In the Midrash we have the slower, although in many cases no less effective, process of the painstaking master—a sequence of parables, elaborately worked-out in order to produce a similar effect. For the Rabbis laid great store by the *Mashal.* Here is a passage on its value as a vehicle of elucidation.

On the text "And besides that Koheleth was wise, he also taught the people knowledge; yea, he pondered and sought out, and set in order many proverbs[3]" the Midrash proceeds: This might be compared unto a large palace which had many doors and whoever entered therein began to lose himself. What did a certain wise man do? He took a coil of rope and tied one end of it to the entrance; he went in along the unwound rope and came out alongside of it. Whereupon all others went in and came out by way of the clue. Even so did Solomon by his *Mashal* aid in unravelling the tangle of the Torah.

Again it was like a thicket of reeds, into which no one could enter, for whosoever penetrated began to stray. What did a wise man do? He took the scythe, kept cutting down the reeds and forcing his way in. He entered by way of the cut path and

[1] Hos. xiii. 3. [2] Dan. vii. 9. [3] Eccl. xii. 9.

emerged by the same road. Whereupon all went in and came out by way of the cut path. Even thus did King Solomon.

Furthermore, it was like unto a basket which was filled with fruit, but had no handles and therefore could not be carried. A wise man came along, supplied the handles, and by means of them the basket became moveable. Even so did Solomon render the words of the Torah more serviceable.

Or it was like unto a cauldron full of boiling water which had no handle. A man came and supplied the handle so that it could thereby be moved.

Again it was like unto a deep well full of cold, sweet and refreshing water, but no one could drink of it. A man came, tied cord to cord, rope to rope, drew water from the well and drank. Whereupon all began to draw and quench their thirst. Even so by stringing together proverb to proverb King Solomon drew out the secrets of the Torah.

Let not the *Mashal* be light in thine eyes. For by means thereof one can comprehend the words of the Torah. It may be likened unto a king in whose house was lost a golden coin or precious pearl—does he not find it with the aid of a lighted wick worth a paltry *As*? Even so let not the *Mashal* be of small account in thine eyes, for with the aid thereof one may discover the meaning of the Torah[1].

Inspiration and instruction

These dissimilarities of form are due to the difference in calibre and conception on the part of their respective authors and the varying conditions under which they lived. The one taught under the impulse of inspiration, the other expounded as an ordinary

[1] *Cant. R.* 1, 8.

instructor. The imagination of the Prophet and Psalmist was fired by the very grandeur of his subject: to cry out against the sinful city, to envisage deliverance even when engaged in bitter denunciation, to conjure up the vision of the ultimate triumph of right; all this gave impulse and momentum to the Prophet's powers of imagery.

The Rabbis, on the other hand, were teachers of the school-house; they had to give definite exposition on fixed subjects, their fancy was exercised to point a moral and adorn a tale. Their style of illustration was more detailed and more diffuse.

Objects in simile.

As regards the objects which supply the materials for the metaphorical imagery there is likewise both similarity and contrast between the Bible and the Rabbinic writings.

As in the Bible, so also in the Midrash, the figures are taken invariably from common and familiar objects; subjective imagery from sensation and thought is extremely rare. But whereas in the former the majority of similes are taken from the open country life and very rarely from the sights and avocations of city life, in the latter the balance is in the other direction. It is true that a considerable number of the comparisons in the Aggadah are drawn from rural and pastoral life, but by far the larger number reflect the pursuits of town life and deal with aspects of trade, commerce and industry.

New Testament parables and Rabbinic.

In comparing the parables and similes of the Rabbinic writings with those in the New Testament, one or two considerations must be constantly borne in mind. As far as the similes, including allegories, and metaphors are concerned, it will no doubt have been observed that even in regard to mere form the Rabbinic figures of speech bear favourable comparison with those in the kindred literature.

And as to parables pure and simple, when emphasis is laid upon the peculiar grace of style and polish of form which characterise the parables of the New Testament, as contrasted with those in Midrashic literature, it must be remembered that the New Testament parables, as is generally admitted by Christian scholars, have in the course of transmission, and especially when clothed in a Greek garb or translated into other versions, been subjected to editorial embellishments, whilst the parables of the Midrash "have remained from first to last jewels; successive generations of artists have not provided increasingly becoming settings to enhance their splendour[1]."

In considering the subject-matter and moral teachings of the similes and parables, N.T. and Rabbinic, we must repeat what has already been stated in an earlier part of this work, that Rabbinic literature in its mass of roughly preserved material presents a rich treasury of the noblest thoughts and highest conceptions.

It is perhaps but natural that the personality of the founder of Christianity and the position of the New Testament as a guide of religious life for the believing Christian should invest the N.T. parables for him with a peculiar sanctity and grandeur. But equally so do the personalities of a Hillel, an Akiba, a R. Meïr and a R. Levi invest their figures of expression with a peculiar beauty of holiness for

[1] I. Abrahams, *Studies in Pharisaism and the Gospels* (1st series), ch. XII on the "Parables," p. 97.

the Jew, and the spirit of their elevated teachings touches a readily responsive chord in the soul of their Jewish audiences.

One further point. The considerable, though far from exhaustive, collection of metaphorical imagery in this volume will, it is hoped, be sufficient to modify the views of critics like Fiebig and others as to the aspects of life upon which the Talmudic Sages drew for the inculcation of their moral teachings.

They will come to realise that although the Rabbis, in addressing themselves to people living in cities and engaged in trades and handicrafts, dealt very largely with town life, they yet took no little account of the processes of Nature—"sowing and harvest, growing, flowering and fruitage"—and that they drew many effective comparisons from Nature under cultivation. The Jewish Sages, like all great teachers of religion and morality, did not hesitate to use God's Nature to turn mankind to Nature's God.

(4) RELIGIOUS TEACHINGS

We have already stated that metaphors, similes and parables constituted a popular medium of expression which the Rabbis of the Midrash employed for the purpose of impressing upon their audiences religious truths and ethical conceptions.

Here we shall gather up some of the threads of the religious teachings, which are woven into the mass of agricultural and pastoral images presented in the foregoing chapters, although these strands by no means complete the texture of religious ideas embodied in Midrashic figures of speech.

First and foremost is the conception of the relationship between God and Israel, the latter's selection from among the nations and his position in the world.

Israel and his position in the world.

The supreme importance of Israel is repeatedly emphasised under a variety of figures. He has attributed to him a higher worth than belongs to other nations of antiquity. He is, as it were, the "grain of the world," life-giving and sustaining. But he is not the ordinary grain; he is the first and choicest of the grain, religiously lifted up from the rest, and set aside for more sacred use. He is the "*Terumah*," the heave-offering, of the nations, consecrated for divine service. The same conception of a privileged position being assigned to Israel in the economy of the universe, where he is able to render certain, though oft unrecognised, benefits to mankind, is conveyed also in a somewhat different manner. Himself firmly fixed by the hand of God, like the heavenly tents, Israel forms a fence round the world, guarding and protecting it against dissolution and ruin. He is frequently the saviour of the Universe, averting from it the wrath of the Creator, even as "the single lily often saves the whole garden from destruction." Having been thus selected by Providence for the special purpose of benefiting mankind, Israel naturally became a special object of divine care and attention. This divine regard for him has manifested itself from the earliest moment of his national history; his removal from Egypt, his wanderings through the wilderness, "tended like the sheep by a kindly shepherd," and his settlement in the land of Canaan, cleared of all impeding obstacles, were carried out with the greatest care. The many incidents in his march of progress from slavery to freedom, such as his frequent numberings during his journeyings, "like the raided flock counted by the solicitous shepherd," and the protection vouchsafed to "the solitary lamb among seventy wolves," bear testimony to a divine affection for the people specially selected to be the human instrument for the uplifting of mankind.

The religious basis.

For this divine selection of Israel, this recognition of his superiority, which in its origin rests partly upon the principle of *Zechuth Aboth*, "the merits of the Fathers," has a religious basis. It is due to the fact that Israel had readily and willingly assumed duties and responsibilities which no other nation had consented to take upon itself. In this respect Israel resembled his ancestors who always walked before God like flocks before the shepherd, and who constituted themselves the "tent-pegs"—the moral supports of the universe. The Rabbis lovingly dwell upon the fact that at the supreme moment in history, when the most precious spiritual treasures of law and morality were about to be revealed to mankind, it was the people of Israel alone who chose to dwell in the glow of Divine Revelation, and who in a spirit ot simple and implicit faith, promised obedience to the Law before they knew the details of its contents. "We will obey" they exclaimed with all the impetuosity of religious enthusiasm, and then, as a kind of afterthought, they added: "We will hearken."

Israel's distinctiveness.

By thus accepting the tenets of the Torah Israel has become distinctive and distinguishable. The House of Israel is so ingrained with natural characteristics and signs of religious observance that no member of it is able easily to hide his identity. In the language of the poetic Aggadists: "Because of the fragrance of divine precepts with which he is imbued, he cannot be ignored or passed by."

It is true that from time to time Israel proved a source of disappointment—as the Rabbinic Similes expressed it, "the crops in the divinely selected *Pardes* often failed to fructify"; "the straying sheep frequently abandoned themselves to their evil inclinations"—but the disappointment was only temporary and transient. Soon Israel roused himself to a sense of duty. He became purified and assumed a normal condition through the power of atonement, thereby making himself again worthy of the divine love.

The repository of spiritual gifts.

This divine preference for Israel showed itself not alone in the supply of his physical needs, the "constant change of his pasture" and the "provision of suitable shelter," but also in the bestowal upon him of precious spiritual gifts, including, as one of the greatest and most cherished, the ideal of Justice and Righteousness, which is specially singled out as the peculiar possession of Israel.

A religious national aristocracy.

It has been part of the divine plan to preserve the religious aristocracy of Israel as a nation. With this object in view He gave them the Torah and surrounded them with its "fences," in the shape of distinctive laws and special observances, so that by the help of these protective measures God's people might retain their national identity and not become absorbed and assimilated among other nations.

A magnetic moral force.

But, while Israel was thus kept distinct as a nation, it was further the divine intention that he should also become a world-wide influence, and a light to all the families of mankind. And so, under the protection of these "fences" God scattered Israel as a kind of magnetic moral force among the nations, thereby bringing into his camp the righteous ones from outside and grafting proselytes on to his stock.

Israel's death-lessness and exalted destiny.

Israel's historic career has been most chequered. But his wanderings and vicissitudes have only emphasised his stability and deathlessness as a messenger nation of divine truth, as the embodiment and teacher of the ideals of the Torah. He survived even the catastrophe of the destruction of the Temple, and will, so the Rabbis in the spirit of the Prophets repeatedly assure us, emerge unscathed from all future calamities. His low estate is but temporary; his exaltation will come in the end and endure for all eternity. Moreover, to compensate for his state of lowliness in this world, he will attain greatness in the world to come, and his final redemption will synchronise with the day of perfect rest.

His moral support.

And what was the moral support and mainstay which helped to preserve Israel, and make him impregnable through the centuries? The answer which the Rabbinic figures of speech so forcibly supply is unmistakable. The elements that preserve the Jewish people are the Torah and the Merits of the Fathers. Under these benign influences, the bitterness of Israel's sufferings was mitigated, and the burden of his oppression considerably lightened; the "yoke of the nations was broken" by the study of the Torah. Amidst all trials and tribulations these higher forces stimulated Israel to maintain an undivided heart—a heart directed towards his Father in Heaven. He suffered in silence and yielded his

Maintaining an undivided heart.

best under the trial of affliction. For the encouraging hope was ever held up to him that he should surely survive his sorrows, whilst his enemies should in the end receive retribution, for in oppressing God's people they sin against God: "When my people are afflicted, says the Almighty, it is I Who need to be comforted, even I the Owner."

The principle of equality.

Side by side with the theory of this national aristocracy of Israel the principle of the equality of all members within the House of Israel is repeatedly emphasised. And this principle is based upon the idea of equality of all in the eyes of God. Again and again stress is laid upon the fact that the different grades constituting the people of Israel are interlinked and interdependent, each having his assigned sphere of usefulness in the world.

Interdependence of all Israelites.

Even the seemingly worthless have their place, the Rabbis teach in parable, "just as the barren trees in the garden, no less than the fruitful ones, perform a useful function." God's praise rises, not alone from the mouths of the righteous, but also from the lips of the wicked. And this interaction amongst men of all classes shows itself most clearly in the varied ways in which members of society affect and influence one another. Punishment is often brought into this world by the wicked, yet it falls, and sometimes even falls first, upon the righteous. For the righteous are carried away with the wicked, "the burning thorns set fire to the stacks of corn" and "when one lamb is beaten all the flock feel the blow," even as, contrariwise, the worthy person is sometimes the salvation of multitudes, "a single lily saving a garden from destruction." Punishment is often averted by the Merit of the Fathers. The death of the righteous follows upon the sins of their generation. The good men among us, say the Rabbis, applying again the simile of the fence in the garden or field, act as a safeguard and protection. Moreover the terms "righteous" and "good" are relative ones. They are determined by the standard of conduct which obtains among the men of that particular generation—a further suggestion of the inter-connec tion between the individual and his surroundings.

Importance of Torah and the disciple of the Law.

The next conception, emerging clearly from our collection, and emphasised by the Aggadists of the Midrash, is the importance of the Torah. The eulogy of the Law is the companion idea to the eulogy of Israel, and together they form the two elements of the Cabbalistically conceived trilogy—"Israel, the Torah and the Holy One, blessed be He, are one." The Torah imparts an added zest to life and life's work; it constitutes the salt, pepper and spice of the world. The Schools and Houses of Study are Israel's nurseries, and the enemies of Israel have always aimed at closing the schools in order to destroy the religious vitality of the nation. The existence of the school must, therefore, be secured. The Torah must be studied regularly and persistently; put metaphorically—"The sound of the grinding must never cease." Knowledge should be added to knowledge (always bearing in mind the needful gradation of knowledge to be imparted to the student, beginning with the revealed and following with the more hidden portions of the Law), for the more one meditates in the Torah, the more palatable it becomes. The Law, moreover, should, according to some (referring to the easier economic conditions prevailing in Babylon), be studied by a man when he is married, and therefore has his mind clear from the temptations and frivolities of life, although others (having in mind the harder economic conditions of Palestine in the 3rd century) think that the responsibilities of married life are in themselves a hindrance to devoted study.

The true mark of the scholar

As a corollary to the importance of the Torah is the position of the disciples of the Law, and Midrashic poetry in its popular illustrative style has much to say about the requisite qualifications of the *Talmid-Ḥacham.* The words of the Torah abide with those who are of a humble disposition, and the greater the scholar, the deeper is his sense of humility, even as the fuller clusters of grapes droop lower than the less heavily laden. It is the boor, the ignorant, who makes the greatest noise, just as in the realms of Nature it is the fruitless tree that rustles the loudest. Yet even the disciple of the wise must possess a modicum of pride in order to help him to retain his independence and self-respect.

The learned and the ignorant.

The cultivation of the distinctive qualities thus imposed upon the scholar may, it is true, lead to the formation of an exclusive circle, and an aristocracy of learning. But according to the Rabbis, the maintenance of such an aristocracy of the learned class is neither unimportant, nor even undesirable. And they emphasise this desirability all the more strongly in the case of marriage, where the union of like with like—"the grapes of the vine" with "the grapes of the vine"—is particularly praised and encouraged. But as a safeguard against the abuse of such a position of privilege it is urged that the scholar should recognise the place and worth of even the ignorant in the plan of creation. "Let the learned pray for the illiterate even as the bunches of grapes are concerned in the preservation of leaves," for often the *Ammé-Haaretz* protect the *Talmidé-Ḥachamim*.

The jar and its contents.

Although the scholar should deport himself with a dignity inspiring respect—for the Torah imprints its stamp upon its devotee—yet a warning was sounded by the Rabbis against the tendency to regard the outward appearance of the scholar as the criterion of his inner worth: "Black yet comely like the tents of Kedar"; "Look not at the jar, but at its contents." But this guiding principle in no way exonerated the scholar from paying heed to his mode of life and general demeanour.

The duties and responsibilities of the man of learning.

The high standard of his conduct, say the Rabbis, must be made patent to all. The transgression of the scholar, they insist, is more culpable than the sin of the ignorant. "Search for the blemish in the lamb," says the proverb, because it is selected as a gift for the sacred altar. Even mere frivolity in the learned is culpable, seeing that it impedes the free flow of the Torah. The scholar's deeds should exceed his wisdom, for in the language of metaphor "The worth of a tree depends upon its fruits." The student of the Law must not be self-centred or companionless. He must seek to teach as well as to learn, as otherwise he may fail to wield the wider influence expected of him, and become merely "like the myrtle in the wilderness." He should present his teachings in popular form, remembering that the text of the Torah is made palatable and pleasant by acceptable exposition.

The quest for knowledge. But if it is the duty of the scholar to teach, it is equally the duty of everyone to seek instruction. This instruction should in preference be sought from those ripe in years, for knowledge improves with the scholar's age, even as wine becomes better with years. According to some, it should be sought from one teacher in order to maintain continuity, and according to others, from many teachers, so as to ensure variety of presentation.

The encouragement of study. In view of the supreme importance of the Torah and its study, those who engage in its perpetuation are deserving of every means of encouragement. "Shear yourself of your possessions and give to the scholar," is an emphatic demand of the Rabbis. It is certainly, they insist, a most advantageous investment.

The creation of the world. The creation of the world, and man's conduct in it, are subjects which always occupy the attention of theologians of the Rabbinic age, and enter also into the imagery of the foregoing chapters. In regard to the Creation one meets with the interesting idea—evidently intended to allay the perplexities of the people in the face of the current philosophical theories as to the world's beginnings, as well as to explain seeming difficulties in the book of Genesis—that all the elements which came into visible existence on the different days of the week had been created at one and the same moment, remaining *in potentia* until the divine command bade each in turn make its appearance.

Man's need of caution and But whilst propounding certain theories and possible explanations, the Rabbis counselled extreme caution in the handling of these problems. The conception of the Creation is according to them no easy matter for human comprehension. It is impossible for mortal man to gauge the order of the Universe, and he is enjoined to exercise the utmost circumspection when entering into the *Pardes* of metaphysical speculation. Not that a ban is placed upon honest enquiry. It is more a question of the enquirer's mental attitude, the amount of reverence which pervades the searcher after truth. It is the wise man's duty to remove the errors from the fields of philosophy and speculation. In the metaphor of the Sages, "While the sandal is on thy foot cut down the thorns," for scepticism is a grievous and most insidious sin.

reverence in the realms of metaphysics.

As in the Bible so also in the Midrash, the principle is laid down that the world thus created by the divine Designer was intended for the benefit of man, especially for the good of the righteous and of Israel. Man may freely enjoy the fruits of this earth, but, add the Rabbis, he must not make use of the mundane benefits before he has performed the religious "act of redemption." This act of redemption is the pronouncement of a benediction for the things he enjoys, as a thanksgiving to the divine Provider of all earthly blessings.

The world for man's use.

In regard to human conduct the injunctions are definite and clear. It is not for man to weigh the divine precepts and decide upon the worth of each one in relation to the reward attached to its performance; for the whole work needs to be done, and each man must do that part of it which lies nearest to him. Moreover no one can estimate the exact value of a particular act; thus the same promised reward of long life attaches to one of the greatest of the divine

His duties to the world.

injunctions, *viz.* the honouring of parents, as to the apparently smallest of precepts, *viz.* the duty of sending away the mother-bird when taking the young from the nest. The entire field of religious activity must be cultivated; no single portion must be neglected. It is for man to do his duty, leaving it to the Master to do that which seemeth right in His eyes.

The attitude towards the sinner.

The teaching of the Rabbis on the attitude which men should adopt towards the sinner is varied. Whilst some Rabbis (*e.g.* R. Levi and R. Eleazar bar Simon) propound the somewhat harsh theory that the wicked are as thorns in the divine garden, and God is thankful to man for removing them from the Universe, another Sage (R. Joshua b. Korḥah) urges with greater clemency that it is not for us to clear away the thorns. Let the Owner of the vineyard Himself remove them if He so choose.

The effects of comradeship and association.

But, whilst some hold that it is not man's province to interfere with the evil-doer, all are agreed in their insistence that man should be circumspect in the choice of his companions, for far-reaching are the good and evil effects of comradeship and association. Nay, more, one's companions, the Rabbis declare, are an index to character; like meets like. This idea of kinship and association is in some respects raised by the Rabbis to a higher and a more mystic plane, when they assert that the righteous have a longing for God, and their hearts are always directed heavenwards.

Some requisite ethical qualities.

As regards the requisite ethical qualities in man our Midrashic similes supply useful rules. Obstinacy is discouraged. Pliancy (like that of a reed) and not hardness (as of the cedar) must be man's motto in conduct. Purity equally in thought as in action is enjoined, and especially in conjugal relations. Like the Wisdom Teachers of the Bible, the Rabbis, too, fixed upon the earliest period of the child's training as the most useful for commencing the moulding of character. For the bent of one's nature, one's tendencies and desires, begins to show itself in early youth. As they metaphorically expressed it: "Immediately the rose and the thorn spring up, the one emits a sweet odour, the other displays its prickles."

Man his own friend or foe.

But if it is a man's duty to guard against evil companions in general, it is equally his obligation to protect himself against the greatest of his seducers, namely his own self. For man's own actions bring about his salvation or destruction; the tree provides the handle for the axe wherewith it is felled.

The problem of suffering: "chastisements of love."

The ever-perplexing mystery of the suffering of the righteous and the prosperity of the wicked, which occupies so large a place in the theodicy of the Bible, is naturally a subject dealt with in Midrashic simile, as indeed in all Rabbinic literature. As a consolation for man's sufferings the doctrine is propounded of "the chastisements of love"; of afflictions as the dissembled favours of a kindly Providence. And in like manner an attempt is made to explain and reconcile the apparent injustice of the prosperous position of the wicked in this world and the sufferings of the righteous. God afflicts the righteous, say our Sages, in order to exhibit to the world the heights of resignation to which the pious and the faithful are able to rise; even as it is the *sound* flax that is beaten, and the *strong* cow that is made to bear the yoke.

Suffering—A danger signal.

On the other hand, suffering is oft the danger signal in the path of human life pointing to the urgent need of betterment. Sometimes ennoblement comes to man solely through affliction. Sorrow lends wings to the soul in its struggling flight towards the source of purity whence it was taken, even as earthly fortune loads it with a heavy weight which drags it downwards. God chastises the righteous in this world in order that they may inherit the world to come. The wicked are laden with earthly belongings in order that they may be brought down to the lowest depths in the future life. Man, therefore, urged the Rabbis, should bless God for apparent evil even as he does for the good that befalls him.

Readjustments in a future life.

For there is a complement to earthly human existence in a future life, where inequalities will be adjusted and the long-deferred reward will be duly meted out to the righteous. As to the form in which reward and punishment will be apportioned, the Rabbis generally maintain that since the body and the soul are jointly responsible in man's stewardship on earth the two will be linked for judgment in the world to come.

Resurrection and immortality.

In God's good time there will be a Resurrection of the dead when, as the Aggadists taught in parable, the souls will rise fully clothed in their earthly garb. The death of the righteous, they continue, is far-reaching in its effects, for they cannot easily be replaced. And yet even in death the righteous enjoy an earthly, no less than a heavenly immortality, for the repetition of their wise teachings by disciples and followers makes them live again. In the bold figurative Rabbinic application of a Bible verse this repetition causes "the lips of those who sleep [in death] to move" in the grave.

Death in due season.

Midrashic poetry describes how loth is the soul ever to leave its mortal shell; its cry at severance from the body resounds through the ends of the earth, although the pain of parting is less acute in the case of those who die aged and full of years. But the Rabbis have a comforting thought concerning the departure from this life of those who, according to mere human judgment, have not yet completed the full number of their years. God knows best, say the Rabbis, when the hour for the removal of the righteous has come, and He takes them hence, "even as the owner of the fig tree is the best judge as to the right season for plucking the figs."

There remain two other conceptions which should here be mentioned. The one relates to the position of Palestine; the other concerns the efficacy of Prayer.

The Holy Land.

As regards the Holy Land, the cradle of the Jewish race and the home of its national development, the Rabbis of the Midrash in the spirit of the Bible continue to emphasise its unrivalled importance and the supremacy of its religious position in the divine scheme of world-administration. God's favour towards it was made sufficiently manifest when this "granary of the world," the "larder of the nations," became the Chosen Land of His Chosen People. But this divine love will become all the more apparent and recognised in time to come when Palestine is restored to its rightful place of honour as the religious centre of the Universe. The Holy Land will then, figuratively speaking, broaden out on all sides and extend in every direction, wielding a world-wide influence both amongst Israel and the nations.

The efficacy of prayer.

As to Prayer, the Rabbis certainly recognised and taught its subjective, no less than its objective, purpose. Our collection of similes supplies one striking figure of speech which clearly emphasises the latter aspect. Prayer, say the Sages, is like a fork or shovel, and even as these implements of the field turn the grain from one side to the other, so does the instrument of the human heart transform the divine wrath into mercy and compassion.

INDEX I

RABBINICAL AUTHORITIES CITED

[Except where B.A. = Babylonian Amora is added, the Rabbis are Palestinians]

INDEX II

SCRIPTURAL PASSAGES QUOTED

A. HEBREW BIBLE

B. APOCRYPHAL

C. NEW TESTAMENT

INDEX III

RABBINIC PASSAGES QUOTED

A. TALMUDIC

[In the Jerusalem Talmud the page references are to the Krotoshin edition; sometimes the chapter (*Perek*) and *Halachah* are added.]

B. MIDRASHIC

[The references are to the following editions: *Midrash Rabbah*, Vilna folio; *Tanḥuma, Lekaḥ Tob, Pesikta, Shoḥer Tob, Midrash Samuel*, Buber; *Mechilta, Sifré, Pesikta Rabbati*, Friedmann; *Mechilta di R. Simeon b. Joḥai*, Hoffmann; *Yalkut*, Warsaw folio.]

INDEX IV

GENERAL

For EU product safety concerns, contact us at Calle de José Abascal, 56–1°, 28003 Madrid, Spain or eugpsr@cambridge.org.

www.ingramcontent.com/pod-product-compliance
Ingram Content Group UK Ltd.
Pitfield, Milton Keynes, MK11 3LW, UK
UKHW010348140625
459647UK00010B/913